COLIN BAXTER ISLAND GUIDES

Shetland

Acknowledgements

I am grateful to so many people - Shetlanders, specialists, family and friends - without whose advice, information, patience, help and support this book could never have been written. The following names are not exclusive and I apologise for any which do not appear on the list, which could have filled a small book of their own: Neil Anderson, Julian Arculus, Ina Bairnson, Andrew Blackadder, Rhoda Bulter, John and Cissie Copland, Ronnie Eunson, Allen Fraser, Lollie Graham, Edith Grey, Jimmy Grey, Alistair Hamilton, Andrew Harmsworth, Paul Harvey, Janet Henderson, Derek Herning, Rhoda Hughson, Mary Isbister, Maggie Laurenson, Kevin Learmonth, Agnes Leask, Jane Mack, Vina Malcolmson, Jim Nicolson, Mary Ellen Odie, Dave Okill, Mike Pennington, George P.S. Peterson, Mary Peterson, Derek Rushton, Jean Sandison, June Sandison, John and Eileen Scott, Walter Scott, Margaret Slee, Brian Smith, Janis and Edward Smith, Mary Smith, Stella Sutherland, Jonathan Swale, Christian Tait, Ian Tait, Bobby Tulloch, Val Turner and Tammy Watt.

Archive photographs on pages 84 and 85 reproduced courtesy of The Shetland Museum, Lerwick.

Poem extracts, reproduced with permission:
Page 9:   From 'Bide A Start Wi Me' by Rhoda Bulter. In *A Nev Foo A Coarn*,
            Thuleprint Ltd, 1977. © Rhoda Bulter 1977.
Page 15:   From 'On a Raised Beach (to James H Whyte)' by Hugh MacDiarmid. In *Hugh MacDiarmid Selected Poetry*,
            edited by Alan Riach and Michael Grieve, Carcanet Press Ltd, 1992. © Hugh MacDiarmid 1992.
Page 58:   From 'Löd A Langer' by Rhoda Bulter. In *Snyivveries. Shetland Poems*, The Shetland Times Ltd, 1986.
            © Rhoda Bulter 1986.
Page 61:   From 'Burgawater' by Vagaland (TA Robertson). In *The Collected Poems of Vagaland*,
            The Shetland Times Ltd, 1975. © Vagaland 1975.
Page 96:   From 'Shetlandic' by Rhoda Bulter. In *Link Stanes*, The Shetland Times Ltd, 1980. © Rhoda Bulter 1980.
Page 165:   From 'Sunset Trowe Da Gaada Stack: A Response to a Photographic Image by Colin Baxter',
            by Christine De Luca. In *Plain Song*, The Shetland Library, 2002. © Christine De Luca 2002.
Page 169:   From 'Macarism' by Rhoda Bulter. In *Snyivveries. Shetland Poems*,
            The Shetland Times Ltd, 1986. © Rhoda Bulter 1986.
Page 207:   From 'The Clift Hills' by Christian Tait. In *Spindrift*, C.S. Tait, 1989. © Christian Tait, 1989.

First published in Great Britain in 2003 by
Colin Baxter Photography Ltd
Grantown-on-Spey, PH26 3NA Scotland

www.colinbaxter.co.uk

Text © Jill Slee Blackadder 2003
Colour Photographs © Colin Baxter 2003
Drawings © Iain Sarjeant 2003
Geology Map © Allen Fraser 2003
Maps © Wendy Price 2003 Cartographic Services, Inverness, Scotland IV1 3XQ
Information used in the creation of the maps on pages 8, 12, 13, 98, 114, 124, 130, 146, 161, 164, 168, 200, 206 and 228 came from the Royal Commission on the Ancient and Historic Monuments of Scotland, The Macaulay Institute, Shetland Islands Council and Shetland Islands Tourism.

ISBN 1-84107-125-0

Front Cover Photograph: The Kame and North Bank, Foula.
Back Cover Photograph: Atlantic Puffin ('Tammie Norie').
Page 1: Dragon head on the prow of replica Viking Longship or Galley, Up Helly Aa festival.
Page 3: Fair Isle North Lighthouse.

Printed in China

COLIN BAXTER ISLAND GUIDES

Shetland

Jill Slee Blackadder

Colin Baxter Photography, Grantown-on-Spey, Scotland

Wall of croft building, Papa Stour.

Contents

KEY FOR MAPS

- � Nature reserve
- 🏛 Museum/visitor centre
- 🏛 Other ancient monument
- 🏰 Castle
- ◉ Broch
- 🗼 Lighthouse
- Cliffs
- Sandy beach
- Viewpoint
- ⛳ Golf course
- † Religious building
- ☆ Other place of interest
- ⃛ Swimming pool/leisure centre

Preface

Islands are worlds in miniature. They have a wholeness, a completeness that wraps their inhabitants about with a deep sense of belonging. Shetland's islands are a cluster of over a hundred of these small worlds, each unique, each filled with a rich heritage of nature and history which is linked to its neighbours, yet entirely different from them. The shoreline defines the boundaries and marks the limit of land, tracing the profiles and character of each isle. The sea is an ever-changing presence, bringing, in quick succession, scenes of breathtaking wildness and calm, spellbinding beauty which have inspired poets, lured adventurers and provided a living for those who stayed.

Birds may have drawn people to Shetland first. No rock above sea level escapes the eye of a bird and Shetland has been home to hundreds of thousands of them for countless centuries. Whether to native seabirds, passing migrants or summer or winter visitors, Shetland affords shelter from the storm. The first human settlers, in all probability, were well aware of the birds' movements and also of the reasons for their journeys. After all, man was once – and in many lands still is – a migrating species. Birds were a source of food in themselves and their eggs were collected in large numbers until relatively recent times. But like Noah's dove, they were also reliable indicators of land, where restless tribes might settle. Seabirds might lead to food sources such as fish. It would have made great sense for early mariners to follow the feathered pilots as they headed north, or west, to see what rich pickings might be had over the horizon's mysterious curve.

No two people see Shetland in exactly the same way and my own experiences and perspective inevitably colour my reflection of the islands in the text. During the writing of this book I have been conscious of the debt that I owe all those to whom I have turned for information or advice, including the wealth of authors and experts whose knowledge and skill has furnished the islands with a rich store of literature of all kinds. Shetland is far bigger than many people at first realise and is crammed with history and an endless diversity of wildlife. It has proved impossible to do much more than touch briefly on the many facets of the islands. I apologise for any omissions, inaccuracies or faults, which are all my own.

Sunset behind Muckle Roe and across Olna Firth to the north of Mainland Shetland.

Shetland

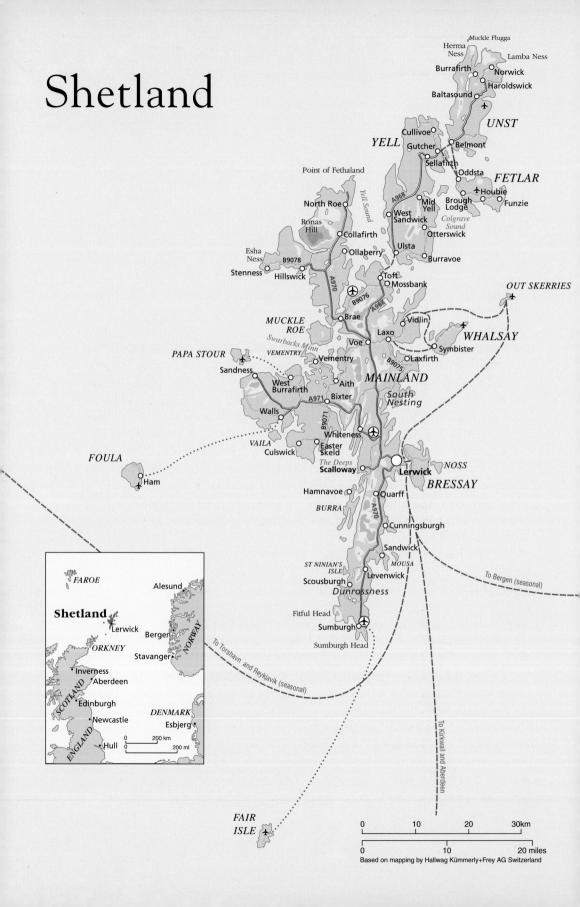

Muckle Flugga
Herma
Ness
Lamba Ness
Burrafirth
Norwick
Haroldswick
Baltasound
UNST

Cullivoe
YELL
Gutcher
Belmont
Sellafirth
Oddsta
FETLAR
Point of Fethaland
Houbie
Brough
Lodge
Funzie
Mid
West
Yell
Sandwick
Colgrave
Sound
North Roe
Ronas
Otterswick
Hill
Collafirth
Ulsta
Esha
Ollaberry
Burravoe
Ness
B9078
Stenness
Hillswick
OUT SKERRIES
Toft
Mossbank
Vidlin
MUCKLE
Brae
WHALSAY
ROE
Laxo
Swarbacks Minn
Voe
Symbister
PAPA STOUR
VEMENTRY
Laxfirth
B9075
Vementry
MAINLAND
Sandness
West
Aith
South
Burrafirth
Nesting
A971
Bixter
Walls
B9071
Whiteness
NOSS
VAILA
Easter
FOULA
Culswick
Skeld
The Deeps
Scalloway
Lerwick
Ham
BRESSAY
Hamnavoe
Quarff
BURRA
Cunningsburgh
Sandwick
ST NINIAN'S
MOUSA
ISLE
Levenwick
Scousburgh
Dunrossness
Fitful Head
To Bergen (seasonal)
Sumburgh
Sumburgh Head
To Torshavn and Reykjavik (seasonal)
To Kirkwall and Aberdeen
FAIR
ISLE

FAROE
Alesund
Shetland
Lerwick
Bergen
ORKNEY
NORWAY
Stavanger
SCOTLAND
Inverness
Aberdeen
DENMARK
Edinburgh
Esbjerg
Newcastle
ENGLAND
Hull
0   200 km
0   200 ml

0   10   20   30km

0   10   20 miles
Based on mapping by Hallwag Kümmerly+Frey AG Switzerland

Introduction

Come, draa dee shair up ta da fire an bide a start wi me,
While I tell dee o da Hameland – da isles across da sea;
Whaar dir birds ta watch an fysh ta catch an heddir hills ta clim,
An times whin darkness niver faas idda laand o da Simmer Dim.

From *Bide A Start Wi Me* by Rhoda Bulter.

Shetland is a cluster of windswept islands which lie at the most northerly point of the British Isles. But that is only the beginning of the story. Far from being remote or peripheral, Shetland is at the hub of a great north Atlantic seaway. The Shetland Islands lie almost exactly at the centre of a triangle, with Norway approximately 200 miles to the east, Scotland slightly closer to the south and Faroe a similar distance away to the north-west. Shetland extends from latitude 59° 51' north to 61° north and from longitude 0° 45' west to 1° 45' west. The north of Unst lies, along with Anchorage in Alaska, Bergen in Norway and Leningrad in Russia, at about 61° north, the same latitude as Helsinki in Finland, and the southern tip of Greenland. Lerwick is in fact closer to the Arctic Circle than to London!

There has been much debate over the precise meaning and origins of the name 'Shetland'. References to the islands have been written more than twenty different ways in documents and on maps through the centuries. Experts may never agree on a single explanation. A selection of the variations found on records include: Syettelandia, Thule, Zetland, Hjaltland, Yeitlande, Hidland, Hiadtlandh, Hetlandt, Schytland and Hiatland. One possible derivation, 'land of the Cat tribe' has been suggested, relations perhaps of the tribe which may have given Caithness its name. Others include 'land of the story tellers', 'land of the sheltering or halting place', 'island of the sword hilt'. You can muse on all these and more; no one will ever know for certain.

Shetland is over 100 miles long from the Out Stack in the north to Fair Isle in the south. Yet despite its key location, its size and the number of islands, national maps and atlases often relegate Shetland to a corner of sea on a page showing Scotland several hundred miles further to the south. Shetlanders complain about these map-designers' distortions, yet often when making their own maps, commit the same crime by leaving Foula and Fair Isle inset into boxes many miles away from their true positions!

The distinctive silhouette of Foula seen from the north-east.

The Shetland archipelago consists of over 100 islands, seventeen of them inhabited at the turn of the new millennium, though a century ago it would have been twice that number. Its complex of islands, heavily indented by the sea, makes it difficult for visitors to orientate themselves.

The islands have been a historic centre for seafarers for thousands of years, an invaluable stepping stone between far-flung destinations. Sailors of many nationalities came and went, exchanging goods for fresh food and water. Here through the centuries, generations of islanders lived, fished and worked the land. Through the influences of new settlers, wars and increasing trade, language, culture and traditions of both Norse and Scots peoples have blended. Enriched through time with Dutch and German, Russian and Spanish, Shetland now has a community and culture of remarkable richness and diversity which is still evolving. Chinese, Thai, Indian, Filipino and Pakistani children mingle with Shetland Scots, English and other nationalities in island classrooms. With each fresh chapter in the histories of fishing, oil exploration and wildlife watching, new human migrants arrive and many stay and raise families. Some residents came first as visitors on holiday, so beware, you may fall under Shetland's spell yourself!

The first, distant glimpse of Shetland from the sea would have appeared little different all those years ago from that of sailors and passengers arriving here today. Fair Isle and the great bulk of Fitful Head stand proud of the sea for miles

Shapes from the land and sea of Northmavine.

if you reach Shetland from the south. Vikings from the east would have seen a different profile, with the impassive crest of Noss dominating the horizon long before the low-lying Out Skerries come into sight. Fishermen returning from the fishing grounds to the west would have seen Foula's great cliffs, second only in height to those of St Kilda. Early Arctic whaling ships on their way home would have seen the steep twin headlands of Hermaness and Saxavord in north Unst. But from whatever direction the first settlers came, the islands would have spelt rest, refreshment and shelter, for man and bird alike.

Despite, and maybe because of, its remoteness, the challenge of travelling to Shetland brings immense rewards. In today's modern and ever-changing world, Shetland can give a breathing space, a chance to connect with the past and reach out to the future with a refreshed spirit and renewed excitement.

This Guide falls into three main parts. It begins with a general account of the history of Shetland, starting with the rocks themselves and continuing with a simplified account of the evolving story of Shetland's wildlife and the human life which followed it, through to the present day. The second section covers the islands themselves, north to south, village by village. Lastly there are specific notes and checklists for visitors and those with special interests. Whether islander, incomer, visitor or browser, the book is intended to draw the reader to Shetland, its dramatic scenery, its fabulous wildlife, its spectacular archaeology, its history and people.

Shetland

UNST
Muckle Flugga
Herma Ness
Lamba Ness
The Nev
Norwick
Burrafirth
B9086
B9087
Haroldswick
Baltasound
Balta
Uyea
Belmont
Gloup Ness
Gloup
Cullivoe
Gutcher
B9082
Sellafirth
A968
Burra Ness
Hascosay
Camb
Oddsta
Brough Lodge
FETLAR
Funzie
B9088
Houbie

YELL
Nev of Stuis
Point of Bugarth
B9081
Mid Yell
Otterswick
Ness of Gossabrough
Gossabrough
Burravoe
Ramna Stacks
Gruney
Point of Fethaland
Ulsta
Samphrey
Linga
Lunna Ness
Lunna

Uyea
Fugla Ness
Isbister
West Sandwick
Lamba
Mio Ness
Uynarey
Bigga
Mossbank
Collafirth
WHALSAY
Grif
Skaw
Brough
Vidlin
Laxo
B9071
Tagon

North Roe
Skelberry
NORTH ROE
Romas Hill
Heylor
Collafirth
A970
Ollaberry
Bardlister
Sullom Voe Oil Terminal
Sullom
Scatsta
Toft
A968
A969
Busta
Brae
A970

Muckle Ossa
The Faither
Esha Ness
Hamnavoe
B9078
Tangwick
Stenness
Isle of Stenness
Urafirth
A970
Hillswick
Nibon
Egilsay
Strom Ness
MUCKLE ROE
Gillarona

Housay
Bruray
Out Skerries

Ve Skerries

0   5   5   10 km
0   5   10 miles

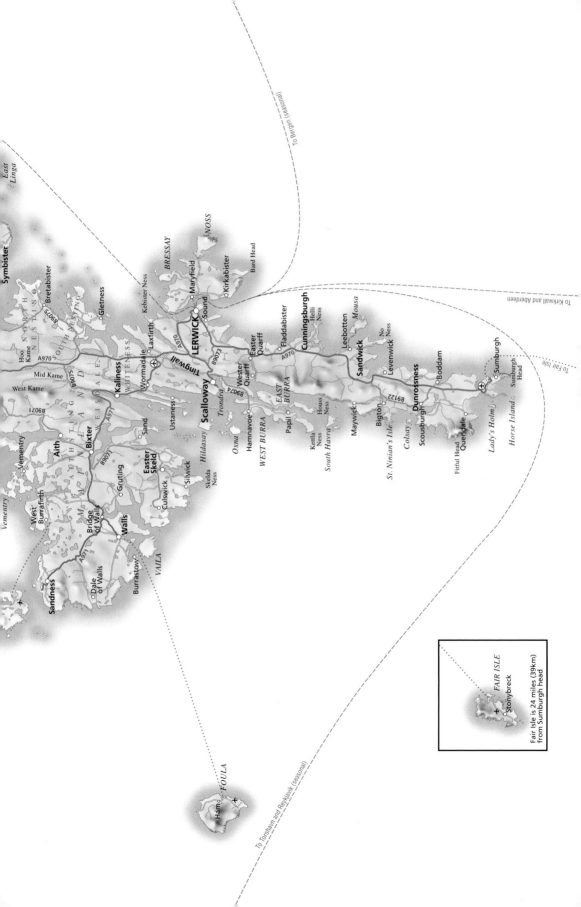

The Landscape

These bare stones bring me straight back to reality.
I grasp one of them and I have in my grip
The beginning and the end of the world,

From *On A Raised Beach* by Hugh MacDiarmid.

Shetland owes its very existence to an extraordinarily rich underlying geology. Upon the ice and sea-worn, wind-battered rocks, soils of varying quality and chemistry have built up to support a unique community of plants and animals. This section of the Guide follows a sequence of topics through the evolving land- and seascapes of Shetland.

So how did Shetland come to be here at all? The islands have rocks of such remarkable variety, age and rarity, that a whole library could be filled with existing publications on the subject. But a simplified account is needed to set the stage for the subsequent human history of the islands. Without the 'auld rock', as Shetlanders affectionately call the islands, there would have been no story to tell. If the rocks could speak, what stories would they tell of the peoples who came first to the islands' shores and the fortunes of those who followed them?

GEOLOGY

For many people, it is enough simply to know where the most attractive beaches and the most spectacular cliffs can be found; Shetland's beaches alone are reason enough to make the journey here. There is a list of the best at the end of the book. As well as the miles of peaceful deserted sandy ones there are also endlessly engrossing pebble beaches where you can find sea-worn treasures for the pocket or the mantelpiece, not just indigenous pebbles either. Ballast in the form of stones from all over the world has been left on Shetland's beaches for centuries. But for those who would like to know more, a simplified account of Shetland's geology may help to explain how the islands came to be where and how they are today.

Rock is assumed to be solid, but to understand Shetland's geology, it must be thought of as a flexible, mobile material, constantly changing as a result of tension or stress of some kind, but mostly on a vast and slow timescale. You only have to glance at a geological map to see the enormous variety of rock types in Shetland and how far, through faulting, they have moved. So colourful and

Eshaness, Northmavine.

The north-east cliffs and stacks of Foula from Soberlie Hill.

decorative are the contrasting coloured bands and patterns of the rock alignments that some people buy one of these maps just to frame and hang on their walls. It is also useful to remember the three key words used by geologists: igneous (molten in origin), sedimentary (eroded and laid down in layers on sea beds by water action) and metamorphic (disturbed, altered by heat and pressure into rock of a very different appearance).

The rocks of which these islands are constructed are the surviving stumps of mountains formed about 420 million years ago during what is called the Caledonian Mountain building period. They were thrust up at the point where two great continental plates on the Earth's surface were gradually colliding. The new mountain ranges were built up over far older rocks, of which traces still remain. At Uyea in the north-west Mainland, and the Ve Skerries, north-west of Papa Stour, there are rocks from the Pre-Cambrian period. These are thought to be contemporary with the Lewisian gneisses, believed to have been formed at least 2000 million years ago.

The Caledonian Mountains would have been worn down, or eroded, by climatic conditions too violent and interminable to imagine. The land surface then was without life, so no roots held soil to protect the open land from the relentless assaults of water, wind and frost. Thunderstorms, thought to have lasted for countless years, rainstorms and ferocious winds eroded the lifeless landscape and washed the resulting vast quantities of rocks, pebbles, gravel, sand and mud down ancient river beds into ancient seas. Sea cliff erosion has exposed sections of river beds and alluvial fans to the north of Lerwick. So much rock was worn away that, through time, it buried all but the remaining higher hilltops. Erosion products from the mountains built up deep layers, forming what are now called the Old Red Sandstone, examples of which are found in the South Mainland and on Bressay and Noss.The sandstones can be found along much of Shetland's southern and eastern shores, where the strata are seen in the cliff faces. Here, in ledges carved by today's weather out of the varying bands of fine and coarse rock, Shetland's famous seabird colonies nest in spring. In Noss, Bressay and Sumburgh kittiwakes and guillemots, razorbills and fulmars jostle in the tiny pockets for shelter from the rain, wind and sea spray.

Although there is little geological evidence for life on the land surfaces of the earth, species of simple plants, invertebrates and primitive fish did live in the inland seas. Fossil traces can be found in rocks in Foula, Bressay and Sumburgh. Noss sandstones have signs of minute animal tracks, made perhaps by primitive worms or crustaceans. At Exnaboe, Walls and Sandness traces of Devonian fossil fish lie among finely banded shales. Seas supported life for millions of years, successive generations of creatures dying, their bones and shells building up to great depths.The calcium-rich sediments on these ancient seabeds, buried and altered in later times, may have formed the crystalline limestones which played such a key role in Shetland's human landscape and settlement patterns by giving rise to bands of fertile soils such as those of Whiteness and Tingwall.

Older sediments, under intense pressure beneath the roots of the Caledonian Mountains, had been so altered by heat that their quartz and felspar had partly dissolved and recrystallised, giving the ancient layers their fretworks of brightly coloured veins. What was once a sandstone can be 'cooked' into a coarse gneiss, with just the faint traces of banding left as witness to former sedimentary layers. Finer schists may have originated as silts, the finest of all becoming silvery phyllites, like the pebbles at St Ninian's Isle. Shetland is composed of vast masses of these metamorphic schists and the shining pebbles and glittering rock faces are very much a part of the landscape throughout Shetland, especially in Yell.

During periods of volcanic activity, the sediments would have collected particles of ash and eroded lavas then in the atmosphere, altering the chemistry of the sand and mudstones and producing, after millions of years of alteration, schists with quite different composition. Screes can be fused into breccias, pebble beds into conglomerates like those near Lerwick at Rova Head. In Fetlar, ancient pebble deposits have in turn been buried and reheated, altered, squashed out of shape and now form parts of new cliffs and shorelines. Eshaness in Northmavine and Papa Stour have cliffs cut through sections of volcanic rocks. Red granites of Muckle Roe and Ronas Hill are all fine examples of Shetland's igneous rocks.

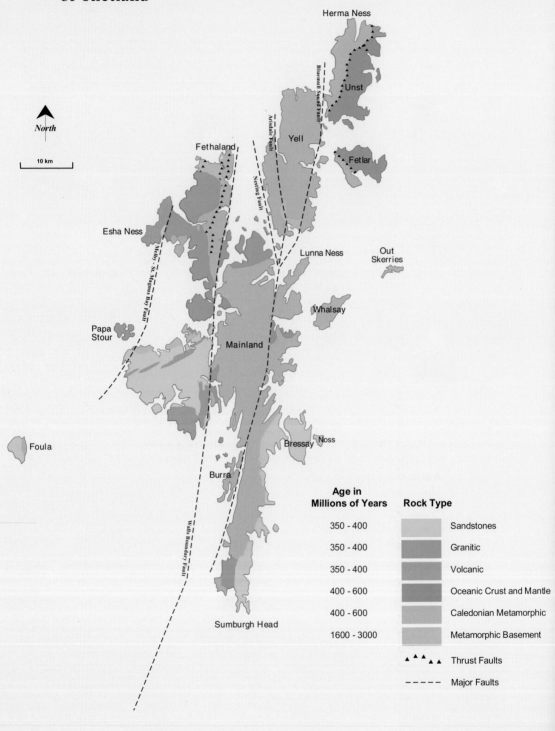

Geological Sketch Map
of Shetland

North

10 km

Herma Ness

Bluemull Sound Fault

Unst

Yell

Fetlar

Arisdale Fault

Fethaland

Nesting Fault

Esha Ness

Lunna Ness

Out
Skerries

Melby - St. Magnus Bay Fault

Whalsay

Papa
Stour

Mainland

Foula

Bressay

Noss

Burra

Walls Boundary Fault

Sumburgh Head

Fair Isle

Age in Millions of Years	Rock Type	
350 - 400		Sandstones
350 - 400		Granitic
350 - 400		Volcanic
400 - 600		Oceanic Crust and Mantle
400 - 600		Caledonian Metamorphic
1600 - 3000		Metamorphic Basement
▲ ▲ ▲ ▲ ▲		Thrust Faults
– – – – –		Major Faults

Red granite cliffs on the west of Muckle Roe, seen beyond Vementry.

Tensions in the Earth's crust which from time to time released themselves in massive splits and faults, created in Shetland some of the finest fault features found anywhere in Britain. One of the most important fault lines in Shetland, called the Walls Boundary Fault, is almost certainly the northernmost section of the Great Glen Fault which lies across northern Scotland from the Firth of Lorn to Inverness. It runs almost due north-south from Reawick to Brae and into Yell Sound. Just north of Ollaberry, a short section of tear fault is exposed in a remarkable and dramatic sheer face slicing out in an impressive wedge across a quiet sandy bay. Another long fault line, the Nesting Fault, runs parallel with it, to the east up Clift Sound and through north Central Mainland, along Yell's south-western shoreline. There are many other smaller fault lines.

Unst, too, displays some major faults and is famous for its serpentines and gabbros, giving rise to wonderful pebble beaches. Serpentines, rare exposures of ocean crust formed when the Iapetus Ocean closed, have moved from the deep seabed to Unst where they now form hills, exposed to the elements. This faulting has caused many very different rock types, formed far apart, to be brought close together, giving the islands' rocks a strongly defined north-south trend, with remarkably narrow bands of a whole variety of rocks lying alongside each other. The island is a geologist's dream. Talc, steatite and chromite have been quarried in the past and minute traces of gold and platinum have been detected.

'The Drongs', sea stacks near Hillswick, Eshaness.

During periods of climatic deterioration, ice caps and glaciers formed over the land surface of this part of Europe, ice advancing and retreating many times over thousands of years, each advance wiping out traces of earlier movements. Glaciers tore rocks from their beds and carried them great distances before they were dropped. Sometimes geologists can trace such 'erratic' boulders back to the rock they once came from. Most glacial erratics in Shetland are rocks of local origin. A single exception is the Dalsetter erratic, built into a South Mainland wall, which has been traced to Tonsberg in Norway. There is thought to have been a small, local ice cap near Voe which may have formed part of the last and most recent chapter of the Ice Age. Masses of large boulders can still be seen around the Loch of Voe, lying where they were dropped. The ice retreated from Shetland, leaving in its wake bare, scraped hills and valleys with, here and there, pockets of debris; clay, glacial till, boulder clay and erratic blocks. The Stanes of Stofast on Lunna Ness form one of the most spectacular clusters of erratics but there are thousands of smaller ones, often with their own local names and even legends attached.

Ice Ages came in waves and it is difficult to determine how each one affected Shetland. Sometimes clues can be found, however. At Fugla Ness in north-west Shetland, ancient peat layers have been exposed, buried beneath boulder clay from later ice movements. Traces of plants were preserved such as oak, Scots pine and Mediterranean heathers, indicating a much warmer climate at the time when they were growing, roughly 40,000 years ago. The last ice cover is believed to have retreated from Shetland about 10,000 years ago.

More recent peat deposits have formed since Shetland was first settled. Its acid depths, preserved remains of small trees, bark, hazel nuts, roots and branches have been and are often found when 'casting', or digging for peats. Peat levels can also preserve archaeological remains and even traces of volcanic ash and dust, datable evidence of eruptions in Iceland. Peat is still freely available but the number of households still casting and using peat for home use is steadily falling. This was the energy which was said traditionally to warm you three times; once when you cast (cut it from the peat banks and stacked it to dry), once when you raised it (lifted it and built it into stacks for drying) and once when you burned it.

Rivers can run under glaciers, sometimes forced through very restricted channels, wearing away the solid rocks of their beds. In Shetland short stretches of steep-sided ravines and gorges are thought to have been formed by these meltwater channels, notably the Daal of Lumbister in Yell, Valayre north of Brae, Fladdabister, Sundibanks and Tactigill on the Mainland. These gorges have been crucial in the preservation of Shetland's native wild trees, providing precious havens of protection from sheep. Only the hardest rock types, the strongest formations, resisted the ravages of ice and sea and these form the higher features of the present-day landscape. The 'Quarff Gap', visible as a deep notch in the hills from far out to sea from both east and west, prompts some geologists to argue that a massive river system once flowed east through the Gap, subsequent earth crust faulting leaving just this short section visible today.

Such depths of ice built up over Europe that the weight depressed much of the centre of the continent, allowing the fringes to rise up where ice and sea met. Now, the great ice masses which once weighed down the continent are melting and the landmass is rising. The edges, formerly forced up by downward pressure at the centre, are settling gently back down again. The rate of sinking is fairly slow, but in terms of the appearance of the islands today, it is significant. In a number of places, peat deposits, complete with fragments of ancient tree stumps, can be seen below low-tide mark; former moorland and scrub woodland has sunk and become shallow seabed habitat instead.

Shetland's geology is still evolving. Erosion wears away the higher outcrops and sea cliffs, and the sea washes the fragments along the coast and slowly down into deeper water. Because of the gradual sinking of the islands, a number of special features are found around Shetland. Bay head bars, ayres or shingle bars often form across the heads of the voes. Some become sealed off from the sea, allowing small salty or brackish lochs to fill up behind them. Saltmarshes can be found in a few shallow voe heads. Offshore islands are sometimes connected to the land by sand or shingle causeways or tombolos, such as the marvellous one at St Ninian's Isle near Bigton.

Sediments continue to settle ever deeper, like their ancient counterparts in the Old Red Sandstones. Minor earth tremors still occur, and are a serious factor taken into account by those responsible for designing safe oil extraction and pipe-laying along the seabed. Modern development erodes inland sites even more quickly than natural weathering and, as tourism increases, public awareness and concern are growing factors where plans for new housing, industry and other

Flett, near Voe, Central Mainland.

developments are discussed. This will be an interesting area to watch in the coming years as employment patterns change and entrepreneurs cast greedy eyes at Shetland's wild spaces and seemingly limitless resources of aggregate-rich hills and cliffs.

A variety of different climatic elements controls the weathering of the Shetland island mass and a brief look at Shetland's weather may help set the scene for life on the land.

WEATHER AND CLIMATE

Throughout Shetland's history, climate change has directly affected human settlement, with swings from warmer to colder periods and back again.

As long as you are out of doors among the superb scenery, Shetland can be beautiful whatever the weather, but on a still, midsummer day it is exquisite. Winter days are short and dark, but in a roaring gale, with the sea crashing in towering clouds of spray against the streaming cliffs, it is magnificent. The sea to a large degree controls Shetland's weather. Warm it up in July and after a day or two of almost Mediterranean scenery and heat, fog descends. Cooled down, spring seas glitter under steady blue skies and you can see for 50 miles. The sun is above the horizon for almost 19 hours in midsummer and at night its light never leaves the sky. Lochs form their own mist patches and there is no stranger and

Gruney and Ramna Stacks from near West Sandwick, Yell.

more haunting sight than that of a deserted valley, filled with small lochs, from whose mirror surfaces, in the half light, mist rises in swirls into a deep blue-green sky. The 'Simmer Dim', as this time is called, is a natural spectacle not to be missed. Reflections in still voes at night are so perfect that a photograph could be inverted without detection.

A poor start is often followed by a rapid improvement and vice versa. Shetlanders adapt constantly to the changing weather conditions. A head teacher might allow a slightly longer playtime than usual on a hot sunny day and, contrastingly, wedding plans have bad weather fall-backs for photograph venues (though modern studios now have special effects technology which enables a couple to appear to be on a tropical beach, even if it is blowing a gale outside!). It is always advisable to go well prepared, however auspiciously a day may start. But should you be unlucky with a day of really bad weather, Shetland is small and diverse enough for there always to be places which will be calm and sheltered. If the wind is from the west, try to locate an east-facing bay and vice versa. The Best Beach Guide at the end of the book lists wind directions from which the beach may be best sheltered. Weather statistics can give an idea of typical conditions, but they can only give a general indication of what you might actually experience.

The Lerwick Observatory, which is perched on the top of a hill overlooking the town, experiences colder, windier, mistier conditions than those felt in the town, just a mile away. Wind speeds, chill factors and temperatures vary dramatically between sea level and hill tops. The changeability sometimes means that national radio weather forecasts, dependent on local reports, can be wrong, sometimes describing heavy rain or strong winds in Shetland, when it is actually dry and warm! Complaints are sometimes made about this, as these forecasts can obviously have an effect on prospective visitors. Radio Shetland broadcasts the best forecast from Monday to Friday at 5.30 pm. *Shetland in Statistics*, first published in March 1972 and each year since, gives detailed records of the weather as well as island distances, economic data and a wealth of other useful facts and figures.

One delightful advantage of the changeability of Shetland's weather is the rainbows. When it does rain, there is usually some sun about too, so frequent, vivid rainbows are something of a speciality. Hazy summer skies towards evening sometimes produce special effects such as 'gaas' – sun dogs, or false suns. Haloes, or 'brochs', around the moon as well as the sun are seen often enough to have their own dialect names. But the most magical of all the sky effects have to be the Merrie Dancers, or the northern lights (aurora borealis), seen in northern skies in autumn and winter. When Shetland's weather is hot and sunny, landscapes rival the Greek islands for sheer loveliness, and are greener by far. People come out and make the best of every glorious day, never taking the next day's sunshine for granted.

But on the few occasions in the year when a real blaster of a tempest erupts over the islands, it is a very different matter. Ferocious gusts of wind can knock a grown man off his feet and houses creak and groan, the glass in their windows bowing and bending under the pressure. Thunderstorms are relatively rare, as are true heatwaves. Snow falls, but seldom for long enough to lie long and a good, snowy, sledging winter is every bairn's dream.

Some Shetland dialect words express the weather far better than their English equivalents. A 'day atween wadders' is a glorious day sandwiched between stormy periods. A 'blind moorie' is the name for blinding, gale-driven snow, a particularly dangerous winter feature. 'Flans' are vicious gusts of the kind that could easily overwhelm a small boat out at sea. People find the weather an endless source of interest and conversation and over the years, certain phrases and comments have become classics. Here are a few just for fun: 'If you don't like Shetland's weather, hang around for a few minutes!' 'In Shetland it rains between showers!' 'Shetland has four seasons in one day.' After a particularly fine day, you may be asked, tongue in cheek, 'did you enjoy the summer?' But for all the humour and cynicism, there is a pride in the hardiness and toughness of the island people who stay and make the best of every fine period, never wasting a moment's sun and calm. I will never forget the day I walked, head bent against a stiff, rain-filled breeze, and saw an old man striding towards me. 'Fine day!' he said and walked cheerfully by.

INLAND LANDSCAPE

The inland landscape may at first sight appear bare and treeless. Exposure to glaciation and the ravages of some of the worst seas around the British coastline have certainly taken their toll. But the ice also helped to shape superb valleys, freshwater lochs and magnificent gorges where foaming waterfalls cascade into pool after pool before reaching the sea. Miles of burns flow through the hills, trickling peacefully in summer, but foaming yellow and brown in winter spate.

Crofting still dominates the landscape, with sheep grazing most of the hills, moors and pastures of the islands, even the uninhabited ones. You can see herds of cattle in the richer pastures and wide fields of 'tatties' (potatoes) and 'neeps' (turnips) in the South Mainland. Here and there the odd pocket-handkerchief-size patch of silver-green Shetland oats, or dark green 'kale', or Shetland cabbage, is still grown for fodder. Many crofters augment their incomes, if they can, with part- and even full-time work in a different area of employment. Hill dykes can still be seen as great sweeping curves above the townships, but modern fencing methods have put an end to the well-maintained stone and turf barricades of their heyday. Much hill land has been taken out of the common grazing and straight lines cut starkly through the shifting shades of brown, leaving improved grazing, glaring green, in their wake, where as long as the application of the lime and seed mixtures continues, the heather is killed off.

A few corners of the islands remain much as they would have been 50 years ago, but most are increasingly overlain by the tracery of modern, technological life; fast roads, power lines, new housing estates, factories and business units. The old strip fields or 'rigs' of arable land once framed every township in Shetland, but sadly almost all small-scale cultivation has ceased. The area of land suitable for cultivation is roughly 871,000 acres (352,000 hectares), but much of this has returned to grass; the faint parallel lines of old shared cultivation strips showing clearly through the green. It has been estimated that 90 per cent of cultivated ground has been lost to the Shetland landscape in the last 50 years.

Hills and moorland rise dark and brooding over vivid lower pasture and grassland, broken here and there by magnificent wild inland cliffs with their rare flora and ferns. Blanket bog, one of Britain's rarest habitats, has built up in many places. Everywhere there are lochs, their surfaces glass still, reflecting the hills and skies; dark, or rippled, or wild with trailing streamers of spray, depending on the state of the wind. High ground in Shetland is a relative term. The highest hill, Ronas Hill, is only 1486 feet (453m) high at the summit, but because of the Shetland climate, conditions there are known to be equivalent to those at 3000 ft (915m) over on the mainland. Other hills dominate the skyline in the west, north and south of the island mass. To the far west, the sea cliffs of Foula are the second highest in the whole of Britain, St Kilda's cliffs beating them by only a few feet.

SHORE- AND SEASCAPES

The sea, reaching up where glaciers once flowed down, cuts deep into the land, creating superb scenery everywhere you go. The long, narrow inlets, called voes, have afforded splendid shelter for boats through the centuries. Most are relatively shallow, but Ronas Voe is exceptionally deep and long, more like a Norwegian

North and South Benelip, and Filla from Out Skerries with Bressay and Noss in the distance.

fjord, allowing two whaling stations to be established there at one time. There are miles upon miles of low, rocky shore, of fine, deserted sandy beaches where seals, otters and shoals of tiny fish enjoy the relatively warm shallows.

Seventeen islands were still inhabited at the start of the twenty-first century, the majority of the population living on the largest island, Mainland, with sizeable numbers of people living in Unst and Yell, Whalsay, two islands in the Out Skerries group, Bressay, Muckle Roe, Trondra and East and West Burra, with smaller numbers in Fair Isle, Fetlar, Papa Stour, Foula, Vaila and (by bird wardens in summer only) Noss. Many of the other islands were inhabited within living memory. Houses and outbuildings in some of them are still kept up by the descendants of those who once lived there and are used for short periods for seasonal work with sheep, and occasionally for holidays.

Smaller islands often have ruins and other remains, traces of early settlement, going back several thousand years. Vementry, Papa Little, Hascosay, Uyea, Mousa, Hildasay, Oxna, Papa, South Havra and Linga are all deserted, but a few former inhabitants are still living and keep the memories and stories alive. Balta, Huney, Haaf Gruney, Urie Linga, Brother Isle, Samphrey, Cheynies, North Havra, Colsay, Little Roe, Lamba, Egilsay, Nibon, Uynarey plus another half dozen Lingas are still home, if not to folk, at least to the seabirds and otters. The names of these now uninhabited islands read like a

Moo Stack and the cliffs of Eshaness in a storm.

line of ancient poetry and a summer's day spent in any of them is one of the most wonderful experiences to be had in Shetland.

Where the sea batters against higher ground, dramatic cliffs result, producing spectacular scenery, often providing marvellous seabird breeding habitats. Wild seas have torn at the coast, creating magnificent sea stacks and caves, natural arches and sea-carved tunnels. These are featured in many geography text books as classic examples of their kind. Each headland, or ness, jutting out into deeper water and every innermost beach differs subtly from every other. A wealth of Norse place names describes these differences with fascinating words: *houb*, *ayre*, *wick* and *geo* occur time and time again as part of coastal place names. In places the coast looks as if it has been slashed by a giant axe. These deep cuts, typical Shetland features, are called *geos* ('geo' is pronounced like 'go', with a small 'i' in the middle). They are havens for wild cliff flora and nesting seabirds. Winter seas drive air and water into the geos, often creating sea caves and blow holes. Such is the sea's force that the rock above occasionally weakens and collapses, creating great holes in the ground. The Holes of Scraada at Eshaness, Kirsten's Hole in Papa Stour and the Kirn of Cumlewick are fine examples of collapsed sea caves.

The sea is an endless source of interest in Shetland. Today's seascapes are filled with activity of all kinds. Fishing boats, with their high-tech catching gear and safety features, convenient and comfortable crew facilities and bright colours are a far cry from their open, six-oared ancestors. A few older, smaller boats still work for shellfish, but the big fleets can venture hundreds of miles and spend weeks at sea. Lerwick Harbour is busy with ships of every kind from tiny rowing boats, or 'punts' as they are called, to monster cruise ships, oil service boats, geo-survey ships and fisheries protection vessels, and flotillas of visiting yachts contrast with the occasional appearances of old sailing ships. The *Dim Riv*, a replica of a Viking longship, makes short trips round the harbour in Lerwick, and a restored 'zulu' fishing boat, the *Swan*, takes people on trips round the islands, and to Norway or St Kilda. Island seascapes often feature mussel rafts with rows of floats like enormous necklaces; salmon cages like giant floating hoops and salmon boats ferrying feed between them. But apart from modern shipping, there are more traditional things to look for.

THE SEA

The sea is the place to watch for incoming weather. Distant squalls approach in a white blur over far-flung islands, allowing enough time to bring the washing in before they sweep in over the whole scene. Glance at the sea in the morning and the colour, patterns and movement of the waves will tell you how much wind there is and from which airt, or direction, it is blowing. When winter gales reach a critical strength, the wave crests tear, sending white water flying ahead of them in smoking trails of spindrift. But on a calm summer night, you can see not only the sky, but reflected stars as well in the still surface. Sunrise over the eastern sea is a breathtaking blaze and sunsets can often transform the end of an otherwise dark day when the sun appears briefly out of the heavy cloud layer over the horizon, emerging in a glory of reddening waves and blinding light before sinking into the sea.

If you could venture down below the waves and explore the hidden panorama deep beyond the shoreline, you would discover Shetland's true nature, that of a small fragment of eroded hill system stretching out towards the deep Atlantic and reaching back towards the rest of Europe. Shetland is situated at a key point in the fishing atlas, where the North Sea and Atlantic meet. The North Atlantic Drift swings away from the Gulf Stream and washes our shores all year round. Arriving from the south, the warm currents from the Gulf Stream sweep past Shetland, meeting the colder Arctic currents, and veer away to the west, along the shores of Iceland. Here, the Irminger Current, as it is now called, swings south again as it approaches Greenland and is deflected eastwards, where it rejoins the North Atlantic Drift and the circular flow begins again.

The seabed around the islands is as full of varied habitats as the land. All submarine habitats have their unique range of wildlife and just as land masses have prevailing winds, so seabed territory has prevailing currents, which shift, seasonally, in much the same way as air currents in the world above the waves.

The currents carry with them the constant stream of plankton on which all sea life depends. As well as moving with the current, great masses of plankton rise towards the surface at night and sink again as day breaks, a process known as vertical migration. Flat sandy and muddy areas support young fish and are the seed beds of the Shetland fishing industry. Large areas of rocky, uneven seabed lie between jagged tangles of outcrops and boulders which could tear fishing nets if they were set in the wrong place. Here and there submarine ridges run far out to sea from the shoreline, one reaching from Shetland all the way to Fair Isle and Orkney. There are steep-sided gullies, disconnected ridges and strings of small mountain peaks, the crests of which make up many uninhabited offshore islands, stacks and skerries. Some areas of the seabed are covered by 'stonefields', rough tracts of boulder-strewn sand and mud where huge sea spiders and various species of fish are found.

Currents affect surface water conditions too, but less strongly than the tides, whose influence can be altered greatly by the prevailing wind situation. Tides which run between islands create powerful and fast-changing tidal streams, which can present problems for boats unfamiliar with Shetland waters, especially when visibility is poor. For several thousand years mariners have negotiated Shetland's beautiful but dangerous coastline, each new generation learning from the previous one how to navigate safely around the islands. Thorough knowledge of local underwater rocks, tidal patterns and weather conditions saved many a life in days before radar and navigation charts. Today, newcomers must study for certificates before they can take charge of even a small fishing craft. A copy of the *North Coast of Scotland Pilot* will give the casual reader a completely different perspective of island life, with its current and weather charts, shelter havens, and descriptions of the islands seen from the open sea.

Standing stone at Skellister, South Nesting.

Natural History

Islanders and visitors find Shetland's wildlife rich and spectacular, despite the fact that scientists often describe it as 'impoverished'! As a general rule, the greater the land mass, the greater the number of wild species found, thus leaving small islands with a narrower range of species than comparable areas of land elsewhere. But the wildlife which inhabits islands has a tendency to evolve slightly different features from those found on the mainland. Shetland has its own range of unique species and subspecies of plants and animals which greatly add to the interest for specialist and casual visitors alike. This chapter looks first at the wildlife and then at the introduced domestic species.

Soils vary in quality and chemistry in Shetland. In general, sandstone and limestone areas produce the most fertile soils and the richest growth of wild plants and crops. Moorland with its peat, heather, mosses and coarse grasses is acid and less productive. Small areas of late glacial sediments exist where local clays and gravels are found. Wherever the few good rich brown soils are found, farms have been built and fields established. The levels of many rigs and small fields were raised over centuries of wearying effort, baskets, or 'kishies', full of earth from pockets found here and there, being carried and tipped out on the land. Manuring and the use of seaweed as fertilizer each year also built up soil fertility and the green places remain long after cultivation has ceased.

WILD FLORA

Traditional crofting systems encouraged the rich growth of wild flower species. Shetland is a wild flower haven for plant lovers despite many changes and degradations to its landscape in recent years, and there are delights for the amateur and professional botanist alike. The unique position in the north Atlantic, close both to Europe and the Arctic Circle, has enabled plants from very different regions to grow here. However, despite the enormous numbers of wild flowers in certain places in spring, under present legislation it is an offence to uproot any wild plant unless you have a licence. Certain rare species are listed and these may not be picked or destroyed at all. One of the best ways to remember the flowers is to take close-up photographs. A small folding screen can be used to deflect the wind which might shake them, causing blurring of pictures.

Despite its treeless reputation, Shetland has a considerable amount of native woodland, but it is only a few inches high! Dwarf species of native

Atlantic Puffin ('Tammie Norie').

willow are common across much of the
islands' clifftop pasture and some areas
of heath. Native species of rowan,
aspen, hazel, birch and even crab apple
all exist, though in desperately fragile,
tiny sites where sheep have not gained
access. These sites are being afforded
more protection and efforts at propagating
and restoring native tree populations are
beginning to bear fruit.

Edmonston's Chickweed.

Springtime conjures up images of flower masses;
golden valleys drenched with kingcups, primroses and
celandines; sea pinks carpeting the short coastal turf in June; meadows brimming
with orchids; higher hills transformed into seas of blue with squill flowers, and
roadside verges in Dunrossness flooded with bird's-foot trefoil and regal purple
swathes of tufted vetch. But to get the most out of Shetland's flora, you need to
look more carefully at the different habitats and the different soils which nurture
them to discover the rarities and specialities in the islands. The following
account of Shetland habitats begins at the highest places in the islands and
works its way down to sea level.

Shetland's highest hills do not reach a very great altitude, but they are
exposed to such severe weather conditions that the plant communities resemble
those growing at 3000 feet in mainland Scotland. Shetland's highest point is the
top of Ronas Hill, where the uppermost Shetland habitat is, literally speaking,
bare rock. On the surfaces of all exposed rocks in Shetland, lichens of many
kinds have become established, as they would have done after the ice retreated
for the last time, about 12,000 years ago. Lichens, a life form composed of a
remarkable combination of alga and fungus, are among the oldest of all
Shetland's plants, and are a well-known indicator of clean, unpolluted air, of
which Shetland has vast quantities. Natural dyes were extracted from lichens
long ago and there has been a revival of interest in this old craft. Algae,
liverworts, and club mosses can all be found within the environs of Ronas Hill.
Ferns grow in the deep cracks between rocks and in sheltered gullies.

Between the weathered rocks, fellfield habitat has formed on the granite
dome of Ronas Hill. Fellfield is an area of high, exposed, rocky ground where ice
action causes the stones to shift little by little every year. A range of low, tough
mountain plants grows here among the widespread woolly hair moss, including
trailing azalea, bearberry, alpine bearberry, alpine lady's mantle, alpine clubmoss
and juniper. Interesting grasses and sedges can be found here too, but so small
and reduced as to prove difficult to identify for those familiar with their
appearance in less harsh conditions. Fellfield has also formed on the serpentine
of the Keen of Hamar in Unst and here you can find arctic sandwort, northern

rock cress, fragrant orchid and the unique Edmondston's Chickweed, or Shetland mouse-ear, which has beautiful white starry flowers on short, furry stems.

Further down the lower slopes there is heath, where water drains freely through thin soils. Heather, crowberry and a range of grasses cover the ground, with here and there, bell heather and cross-leaved heath. Several tiny flowers, including tormentil, heath milkwort, eyebright and heath spotted orchids, all add splashes of colour.

Moorland differs from heath as it is formed over deep peat layers. Heather grows here too, as well as deer grass and cotton grass or bog cotton, which in Shetland rejoices in the wonderful name of *Luckaminnie's oo* (wool), Luckaminnie, or Luckie, being an old name of a legendary witch. Moorland is rich in moss species, especially sphagnums, as well as many fascinating sedges and rushes. Drainage gullies in the moorlands support different flora and you can find round-leaved sundew, lousewort, hard fern, butterwort and bog asphodel.

The term 'relict vegetation' refers to plant species that were common in Shetland long before humans and their grazing animals. Today, a few sites survive in places which are inaccessible to sheep. Gorges with steep sides where streams race through, inland cliff faces, outcrops of rocks, deep cracks in rock formations and small islands or holms in lochs all provide a safe foothold for some of Shetland's loveliest plants. Wild rose, honeysuckle, great woodrush, roseroot, meadowsweet, and even some small native trees can be found here, among a glorious display of other flowers. Look for (dwarf) golden rod, ferns, hawkweeds, sheep's bit and lady's bedstraw. The underlying rocks, whether schist, limestone or granite, sandstone or serpentine, all tend to support slightly different plant communities. One great rarity, common on mainland Scotland, is the harebell, or Scottish bluebell, which only survives in a few tiny sites in Shetland.

Fungi deserve a mention in their own right and a surprising variety are found in Shetland, many of them edible. 'Piddock stools', as they used to be called in Shetlandic, grow mainly in the autumn, especially on well-grazed coastal pasture. Field and horse mushrooms are common and a range of the wax caps, which come in scatters of shiny scarlet, yellow and orange, arrive slightly later. Shaggy ink caps occur in large numbers in certain years and puff-balls of several species can be found, including occasionally giant puff-balls of enormous size.

A number of fungi common on willow trees can be found growing apparently in grass, but on closer inspection can be seen to be growing on some of the tiny dwarf willows which flourish in many coastal areas. There are also many dwarf, delicate fungi, frequently found on sheep dung. Shetland naturalist Bobby Tulloch, famous for his bird photography, was also a keen observer of fungi and added many hundreds to Shetland's fungus record list in the 1980s.

Sea cliffs can produce superb displays of sea campion in white cascades, warm drifts of sea pinks, or thrift, the miniature hyacinth-blues of spring squill,

Thrift (Sea Pink).

and, early in the season, low pink cushions of the heavily scented moss campion. Stacks and skerries offshore are rich in vegetation and the steep-sided geos spill over gold with bird's-foot trefoil, rich glossy green Scottish lovage, purple thyme, eyebright and a wonderfully deep carmine, furry stemmed form of red campion, known affectionately as Shetland red campion.

Freshwater lochs and pools afford yet another habitat for wild plants. But here, even more than on land, the underlying rock chemistry dictates the nutrient richness and variety of the flora. There are four splendidly tongue-twisting names for the main types, in ascending order from poor to rich: dystrophic, oligotrophic, mesotrophic and eutrophic! In the nutrient-poor, peaty lochs with their deep-brown water, mosses, especially sphagnums, provide almost the only colour with a remarkable range of greens, yellows and maroons. A few may have colonies of 'carnivorous' bladderworts (they catch tiny water creatures inside underwater bladders) and perhaps bog bean. The latter deserves a more attractive name and if you do find it in flower, have a really good close-up look at the beautiful flowers with their intricate fringed petals. A few peaty lochs in the far west of Shetland have small populations of water lilies, with white, waxy petals enclosing dense clusters of yellow stamens.

By contrast, lochs over granite have exceptionally clear water. Also poor in nutrients, they support rather more species, of which water lobelia is particularly attractive. A whole range of different pondweeds and rushes tend to do well in the third category of loch, such as Sand Water in the Lang Kames with its waving forest of bullrushes. But the most interesting are those in the last, and in Shetland the rarest, category, the eutrophic lochs. The rich plant life supports an abundance of minibeasts. Waterfowl visit regularly on migrations, to feed before resuming their flights. Some of the best birdwatching in Shetland can be enjoyed here. Loch of Hillwell and Loch of Spiggie in the South Mainland and Loch of Clickhimin in Lerwick are good examples. Look for water crowfoot, water forget-me-not, water speedwell and several different pondweeds, among many other species.

Burns (streams) and roadside ditches are great places for wild flowers, with an abundance of marsh-marigolds in the lower reaches in spring. But the flowers in fact grow mostly along the edges, rather than actually in the water. Marsh cinquefoil, water forget-me-not and lesser spearwort bloom in abundance and monkey flower or mimulus transforms ditches into dazzling golden trails in summer; it is a relatively recent incomer to the islands, but is certainly very successful. You may see the rich orange double version in a few places. In some peaty burns, a dark, almost black-green moss is found in shaggy cascades along the water edges. This is *fontinalis antipyretica*, a moss well known for having fire-resistant qualities, which was said to be packed in-between stones when building lums, or chimneys. Springs up in the hills often seep out across stony ground and are frequently surrounded by lush vegetation. Some interesting species can be found among these 'flushes', especially in more fertile areas, of which grass-of-Parnassus must be the finest.

Wetlands occur where water cannot freely escape. Marsh and bog plants grow here and yet again, the richness of diversity reflects the chemistry below. A sequence of rushes, mosses and sedges grows through the marshes from dryer conditions to wetter and then dryer again on the far side. Mosses, in particular, grow well and there are records of sphagnum being harvested during the First World War and dried for use as a medical aid in the war effort for both their absorbent and anti-fungal properties as well as for padding and protection. Blanket bogs occur in some areas of Shetland and are gradually becoming valued and protected as rare and special habitats in their own right. White drifts of bog cotton stand out brightly against the darker peat moors. But the richer swampy ground is a place in which to spend hours just revelling in the mass of different species and the sheer quantity of plants and colours: lady's smock and marsh bedstraw, marsh-marigold and yellow flag iris, northern marsh orchid, marsh lousewort and sneezewort, marsh cinquefoil and creeping forget-me-not, and the frilly carmine drifts of ragged robin, take the breath away.

There are several kinds of grassland in Shetland, almost all heavily affected by years of grazing or cultivating. Pastureland near the sea, rich in red fescue, creeping bent and Yorkshire fog (grass) is grazed nearly down to the roots and wild flowers tend to grow almost unrecognisably short and small. Cliff edges are mostly well fenced off and the contrast in size between a spring squill or a devil's-bit scabious flower on the cropped turf and one growing behind the protective fence is startling. In really exposed places, grass gives way entirely to sea pinks, scurvy grass, sea and buck's-horn plantain. Sea plantain leaves can be as little as half an inch in length here, whereas on a sheltered cliff face, or a small offshore island, the leaves can reach eight or nine inches and are wide and succulent. Where the sward approaches the sea it changes into saltmarsh and a whole new range of plants takes over.

On some ungrazed headlands and holms grass can grow almost knee high, threaded through here and there with narrow otter trails. Limestone grassland has a different range of flowers from granite and sandstone areas, and hay meadows are different again; rich in different species, they are a gradually diminishing sight, silage having become the preferred method of saving fodder for the winter, and there has been a consequent decline in many of the bird species which nested among the hay, notably the corncrake. There are many different grasses in Shetland but identifying them can be difficult. It is worth mentioning a few of the more striking and obvious ones for those who are interested.

Yellow Iris.

Look out for viviparous fescue with its very heavy heads made up entirely of small grass seedlings. These tiny plantlets have minute tufts of leaves and little tangled roots, all ready to start growing the moment they fall from the parent plant. Wavy hair grass grows much taller and the delicate flowering heads glitter in low sunlight as each gleaming awn is illuminated on its tiny crimped stem. The short, bluish-purple moor grass can tint whole areas of hill when almost in flower. A grass to look out for in moorlands is mat grass, a short, tufty grass with flowering heads rather like narrow hair combs. Press a finger onto one and as it bends, the 'teeth' of the comb open and you can see them clearly. Cocksfoot grass grows very tall and lush, particularly along new roadside verges. Bents, with their minute awns, when growing in profusion, give a misty effect to the ground. Great tall stands of reed canary grass grow in some damper pastures, prized in days gone by for its qualities as a thatching grass. Meadow grass is often picked by Shetland children who hold up the flowering head and say, 'Look, a tree in spring', then strip the awns clear and hold up the skeletal stem, crying 'and now it's winter!'

Beaches are a Shetland speciality, but each supports very different vegetation, depending on its type. Sand dunes are good places to find marram grass and lyme grass, both excellent for stabilising the dunes against wind erosion, and they grow so tall that smaller plants can often be found in the sheltered spaces between them. Sea rocket makes a splash of colour on the seaward fringes of the dunes and the upper shore of sandy beaches, and there may be patches of sea sandwort and orache. Autumn gentian can sometimes be found in the grass above the beach.

Shingle beaches and bars often have an interesting population of small plants, as well as a good summer display of the yellow sow thistle, red campion and sea mayweed, often depicted in local artists' paintings of boats and sea-shore scenes. Nettles and goose grass, or cleavers, may grow onto the edges of the shingle, but, sadly, you are unlikely to find one of Shetland's loveliest but rarest plants, the oyster-plant, which has been declining in recent years. Saltmarshes occur at the head of some voes, but they tend to be fairly small. However, they support a range of curious and resilient plants which are well worth investigating. Pink flowering orache, glasswort, tasselweed, greater sea spurrey and sea arrow grass may be unfamiliar names, but they have a long Shetland pedigree. This habitat is an excellent place for indicating the degree of marine pollution in Shetland waters and certain sites have been regularly monitored ever since the oil terminal was constructed at Sullom Voe.

Eel grass is the only flowering plant actually to grow in the sea below low watermark. This is the territory of the seaweeds, marine algae, of which Shetland boasts well over 300 species. They fall loosely into three categories: the greens, the browns and the reds. Rock pools are often filled with yellow-green strands of gut weed, and bright green blades of sea lettuce are often cast up by the waves. Tangled masses of coarser seaweeds are thrown up onto shores after heavy seas and in former times would have been safely gathered in and spread on the land as fertilizer. From the 1720s until the late 1800s these were gathered, burnt and the resulting residue sold and transported south for industrial use to augment local incomes. But the most attractive stranded seaweeds are the red species. You can pick up a pink frond here and a small purple bunch there and examine the differences between their filmy fonds, fringed blades and fern-like trails. The changing sequences of marine habitats continue out of sight, deeper and deeper into increasingly unknown territory.

Another wild plant treasure found on Shetland's beaches is the sea bean. Rounded, flattened and chocolate brown, the seeds of the tropical vine *Entadas gigas*, known as Molucca beans, occasionally wash up on Shetland shores, having drifted all the way from the Caribbean via the Gulf Stream. Several other species have been found here; some have even sprouted when planted indoors and kept at high temperatures, but none has survived for long.

GARDENS

Gardens are increasing in popularity and size to such an extent that Shetland now has several full-time garden nurseries and landscaping businesses. Shelter has to be the watchword for gardening in the islands and there is an amazing range of tricks and strategies for keeping the wind off plants, from hedges to fish boxes, upside-down sweetie jars to expensive windbreak fencing. Until recent years the flower park in Lerwick was the only garden open to the public. But the late John Copland, a crofter from Islesburgh in Northmavine, opened a garden with a plant-sale section in the 1980s. His book *Hardy Plants of the North* sold out immediately and since then there has been a rising tide of interest. Many primary schools have been establishing gardens since the 1980s and in the late 1990s a community gardens initiative began to catch on; there is a splendid one at the Old Haa, Burravoe, in Yell.

Greenhouses have been constructed in increasing numbers in recent years and here and there you will see a geodesic dome. Pioneering initiatives came from some individual Shetlanders, such as the late John Williamson from Ollaberry, who grew much-admired peaches, plums, apples and cherries in tiny, interconnecting greenhouses. Several businesses, responding to the growing interest in gardening, have begun marketing new outdoor cultivation equipment and hardware. Tingwall has an annual garden fair which is well worth visiting if your stay happens to coincide. The Planticrub, a plant nursery and shop, was set up in the late 1980s and for many years supplied Shetland with much of its tomato and cucumber requirements. Strawberry cultivation was introduced commercially in Yell and the Tingwall Valley Herbs business was set up, producing dried and fresh herbs and local pickles and chutneys.

Trees have been planted ever since the first of the 'big' houses began to establish their own gardens. Sycamores, first recorded in the early 1700s, grow very well, even managing to set seed. There are sizeable trees in walled gardens in Busta, Veensgarth, Tresta, Scalloway, Lerwick, Swinning, Voe, Kergord and in Baltasound at Halligarth, Britain's most northerly wood. As part of an agricultural experiment, substantial plantations were established in Shetland in 1913. In Weisdale, 'Kergord Forest' with its tall conifers, and the monkey puzzle pine in the garden of Kergord House, are on almost all tour-bus itineraries. There were several more shelter-belt plantation experiments in the 1920s, '50s and '60s.

The gardens of the big houses are an interesting facet of Shetland's garden history. Certain lairds and lesser gentry vied with each other to lay out magnificent gardens in so far as it was possible. A number still retain many features from early design stages, but most have changed completely, deteriorated over the years or even vanished altogether. Gardie House in Bressay and Sandlodge in Sandwick open their gardens occasionally in the summer for charitable purposes. The once-famous garden in Vaila fell into decay and all but vanished, but is being gradually restored.

Look out for old varieties of daffodils and narcissi, which in much of mainland Britain have long since disappeared. Hedges of flowering currant, daisy bush, Japanese rose and fuchsia abound. Old favourites – bachelor's buttons, lupins, roses, primulas, mimulus and michaelmas daisies – thrive in older gardens. Magellan ragwort, or Australian daisy, is a curiosity from the South Atlantic, said to have been brought back by whalers. A species of grass from the Falklands, known as tushie girse, or tussock grass, also grows in a few places.

Exotic species and hardy hybrids appear as gardeners get more adventurous. Spring bulb flowers do especially well and the council has started planting daffodils along selected roadside embankments. Fruit bushes, especially blackcurrant, grow well in Shetland provided that they have reasonable shelter too, though raspberries are less successful. Strawberries can produce remarkably good harvests. Among the most successful is rhubarb, which grows so well that some plants are left uncut, their flowering stems reaching six feet high at times. The best place to appreciate the full range of Shetland garden produce is at a county agricultural show when the cherished produce of many a local gardener is arranged and displayed, potatoes neatly cut in halves and both fruit and vegetables glowing with mouthwatering freshness.

FAUNA
INSECTS

Minibeast- and insect-watchers are becoming almost as keen as birdwatchers in Shetland and the recently established Shetland Entomological Group produces a regular report, listing migrant moths, butterflies and other insect groups, with contacts given for helping with identification of specific groups of insects.
The lists of recorded species are growing, both for passing insects blown across to Shetland from the continent and for native breeding species. Occasionally insects make it into the news when, for instance, massive invasions hit the headlines, like the millions of Silver Y moths which, along with hordes of other insects, swept over the islands one summer. As with wild flowers and some subspecies of animals, there are a number of Shetland variations of insect too. A sizeable number of moth species have significantly darker markings than in those found in other places, and were much sought after during the great Victorian insect-collecting boom.

The geographical isolation of the island group means that there are bound to be fewer native species of insect than in an area of equivalent size on the mainland, but loss of certain habitats and their wild plants may increase and speed up these losses. Native small blue butterflies are recorded as having once inhabited the dune pasture behind Quendale beach but they seem to have died out. A number of butterflies lay eggs which hatch and pupate, but are unlikely to be able to overwinter here. South-easterly winds in summer often bring in 'falls' of peacock butterflies, painted ladies, red admirals, small tortoiseshells and an occasional Camberwell beauty.

There are instances of strange imported insects arriving with timber, plants, vegetables or fruits, such as the banana stowaway moth. The only resident butterfly species now is the cabbage white, believed by many to have been introduced among cabbages imported during the Second World

Peacock Butterfly, migrant insect.

War, though several reports of white butterflies are recorded by visiting scientists from earlier times. Vine weevils are a most unpopular recent accidental import, as is the dreaded New Zealand flatworm, which, though not an insect, prowls slowly through a small but increasing number of Shetland gardens seeking earthworms.

Earthworms are plentiful in the islands on cultivated land. Unfortunately for gardeners, so too are slugs, of which several species are found. Large black slugs, golden brown ones and an occasional stripy one can sometimes be found quite high up in the hills. But those creating most havoc in the gardens are tiny, grey-brown slugs with a passion for newly planted vegetable seedlings, primuli and daffodil petals! Snails are less widespread, but they are locally quite common. Sand dunes are good places to find the yellow and black stripy ones.

Hawk-moths migrate south through Europe and occasionally during south-easterly gales, a few are blown west and land on Shetland. Convolvulus hawk-moths are the most frequently recorded, but privet, humming bird and death's head hawk moths have also turned up. Large burying beetles are found every year, often clinging to salmon cages, having apparently been blown across the sea to Shetland. Ladybirds too can appear in some numbers, and shield bugs occasionally descend on certain areas apparently out of nowhere. Some dialect insect names are clearly Scottish in origin, others less so. 'Forky tail' is well known as a name for earwigs, shiny, large black beetles hurrying along are referred to as 'clocks' and many people call bluebottles and house flies 'bees' as opposed to 'buzzy bees' for bumble or honey bees. Shetland is not an easy place for bee-keepers to succeed, but there have been as many as eight registered bee-keepers in the past at one and the same time.

Wasps are a recent and unpopular coloniser of Lerwick but they have not yet reached large numbers. Midges do live in Shetland, but they tend to come out now and again for short periods and are not the constant blight of summer days that they can be in the Highlands. Mosquitoes, if they feature at all, are a rarity. I have never seen or heard one in twenty years of living in Shetland. The Shetland white-tailed bumble bee, on the other hand, is a familiar sight in the islands and long may it remain so. Bumble bees are declining in far too many areas in the south. A number of island-wide surveys of wildlife species began when the Shetland Biological Records Office was established in 1999, including one on bumble bees in May 2000. More surveys will follow as the whole of Shetland's range of wildlife comes under the spotlight.

BIRDS

Shetland is world famous for its seabird colonies, its rare and less rare native species and endlessly varied migrants. So it was strange once to hear a newcomer to the islands confessing to a surprised Shetlander, how much she missed the birds! Many of the commoner garden birds familiar to visitors from Scotland as well as England and Wales are missing altogether from the Shetland scene; no

Arctic Tern ('Tirrick').

use hanging up nut baskets for blue tits here. Members of the tit family, thrushes and chaffinches are seen only very fleetingly on their migrations to more gentle climes. Shetland has its own wren, a slightly larger fellow than its mainland British counterpart. There is no dawn chorus of the deafening kind enjoyed by those living in tree- and hedge-rich countryside further south in mainland Britain. Instead, you must seek the sea cliffs and be deafened by the hordes of noisy nesting seabirds, not to mention being overwhelmed by the smell!

Shetland's special bird life owes its existence to certain habitats and geological features in the islands. Sea cliffs have formed in ancient rocks, some of which, notably those at Sumburgh and Noss, have weathered into horizontal ledges, ideal for seabirds to nest on. Combinations of geology and climate have created moorlands which are home to important colonies of breeding waders, as well as merlin, pipits and wheatears. Nearly all Britain's whimbrel breed in Shetland and the exquisite red-necked phalarope breeds in Fetlar, home to the snowy owl not many years ago.

As autumn approaches, millions of wild birds begin to leave their breeding grounds in northern Europe (including Shetland) and the Arctic. There are parent birds, immatures and newly fledged young ones. They head steadily south for warmer wintering lands, where food will be plentiful until the following spring. They fly day and night to Britain, southern Europe, and some go as far as Africa. Arctic terns, Shetland's 'Tirricks', fly halfway round the world to the Antarctic. In spring the same thing happens in reverse. This time, flocks are heading north for the breeding season and are in peak condition for their journey after the long winter feed. They arrive as their breeding lands burst into flower and insects hatch out in large numbers.

Should bad weather arrive, with strong winds from the south-east, large numbers of birds will be driven off course, and after fighting the turbulence, lose height and, as they are driven out to sea, look desperately for somewhere to land. Ships at sea often find exhausted migrants perching on rails or in rigging; many almost certainly drown, but hundreds and thousands every year make a temporary, emergency landfall in Shetland, where the birdwatchers are ready for them.

Serious birdwatchers frequently travel up by plane when a rarity appears, sometimes even chartering a special flight just to be able to see it and tick it off their special list. These enthusiasts, or 'twitchers' as they are termed, can often

Black Guillemot ('Tystie').

be seen in clusters, green-clad, telescopes and 'bins', or binoculars, to their eyes, scanning the neighbourhood for a glimpse of an unusual migrant, or hiding behind walls making sibilant noises in an attempt to flush out a weary rarity.

Many birds are still referred to in Shetland by their local names. The red-throated diver is called the 'raingoose'; seagulls in particular are known as 'maas', with 'scories' as the term for immature gulls. 'Swaabies' are the great black-backed gulls. All the other gulls have local names too, but their use is declining. Great skuas are called 'bonxies' and this name has become the common name for them even among birding circles. Tirricks are the seabird equivalent of the swallow, Shetland's harbinger of summer. There is a checklist of birds with their Shetland names at the back of the book.

In spring and summer, the sight of a bonxie sweeping past overhead scarcely raises a second glance, as these birds, one of the rarest species in the rest of Britain, are common in Shetland, with their numbers rising steadily. In the evening, the peaceful summer light seems to go on for ever and the rapid, sharp, quack-like flight call of the red-throated diver is a familiar sound. This lovely bird is another national rarity, yet in Shetland a pair or even several pairs grace many a loch during the nesting season. It is one of the most protected of all Shetland's breeding birds, listed as a Schedule 1 species, and an official permit has to be obtained before you can photograph it. If you walk among the hills and remote lochs on misty days listen out for their haunting cries as they call across blank spaces, the plaintive sounds mingling with the drumming of snipe and the sad, falling notes of golden plover.

Puffins, or 'tammie nories', perhaps the most photographed of all Shetland's bird species, throng to Shetland each spring for their nesting season, before resuming their wandering seafarer lives in early August. Their small size often amazes people, many of whom expect them to be much larger. There are cliff tops in Foula, Unst, Fair Isle and Sumburgh where they can potter up to within a few feet of you if you keep still for long enough. They peer up at you, head tilted first one way, then another; even stopping for a quick preen. One once nibbled curiously round the toe of my wellington boot as I sat motionless on the thrift-carpeted cliff top overlooking a geo in Fair Isle. Listen patiently near their burrows and you might hear the curious growling, grumbling 'puffin speak' as they talk to their chick. Magical moments with wild birds are a Shetland speciality, free for those who are willing to watch and wait.

Fair Isle is the Mecca for British birdwatchers, with its bird observatory and excellent study and accommodation facilities. You can use the library and also watch the bird warden and research staff catching and ringing, weighing and recording an amazing variety of birds. But there are superb bird cliffs everywhere in Shetland and for those coming between May and August, it would be a great mistake to miss seeing at least a few of them. Hermaness, Noss, Fetlar – these world-famous bird reserves act as magnets to the thousands of birdwatchers who visit Shetland each year. The Out Skerries are also excellent places to watch for newly arrived migrants. Individual sites are described later in more detail, in the regional and island descriptions.

A brief run through the Shetland bird year will help to set the birds in context.

January: the start of the year sees short, dark days and a wintry bird setting but plenty of colourful winter visitors. Great northern divers, whooper swans and sea ducks such as long-tailed ducks enliven the bird scene. Harbours attract seagulls and the observant watcher may spot glaucous or Iceland gulls foraging and wheeling among the more familiar herring and black-backed gulls.

February can see some of the leanest, meanest weather and the birds are hard-pressed. Herons stand knee-deep in the voes, motionless in icy shallows; curlews forage widely across grassland and open ground; ravens tumble and cavort in the skies, starlings battle for scraps with sparrows and blackbirds around the houses and crofts and the 'shalders', or oystercatchers, return.

Gradually, as March approaches, some birds will prepare themselves for the long haul to their summer breeding grounds. As they fly north, our winter visitors – long-tailed ducks, whooper swans and snow buntings – may well meet different species flying in the opposite direction. Among the migrants seen most frequently are waders, meadow pipits, skylarks, chaffinches, goldcrests, redwings, fieldfares and bramblings. There is always the possibility of seeing great rarities among these tiny birds, as now and again the odd individual arrives from America, or even the far east, having survived unbelievably long journeys. Ravens may still be displaying.

April brings to an end the winter residency of great northern divers and long-tailed ducks. Ravens begin to nest and so do lapwings and golden plover. The first skylark's song is a cause for celebration, signalling the ending of long, dark days. There is great competition in Shetland in late April and early May for the first recorded sighting of Arctic terns. Their sharp cries and dancing flight herald true spring at last.

Skylark ('Laverock').

The local radio and newspaper announce their arrival as well as that of other species, bonxie, or great skua, Arctic skua and red-throated divers. The courtship, pairing and mating of birds gets underway in earnest and frantic nest-building begins in the islands.

May is the best month for watching spring migrants and the main nest-building effort goes into top gear. These days, Arctic terns in particular are carefully monitored as their breeding success has been subject to violent fluctuation over recent years. There has been a problem with sand eel populations (at one time heavily fished) which form the bulk of the tern chicks' diet and a debate as to which of many possible causes is responsible has been fierce at times. Other rarities include whimbrel, now protected by additional reserves, and red-necked phalarope, helped by the improvement of some of their breeding grounds in Fetlar. Migrants can still turn up, including an occasional waxwing, flycatchers and various warblers. The latter tend to be small and brownish, earning themselves the nickname of 'LBJs', ('Little Brown Jobs') among the birdwatching fraternity.

June is the most spectacular time to visit the seabird colony reserves, when there is a frantic, tireless traffic of parent birds flying to and from nest sites, threading their way through a moving maze of other parent birds, always with half an eye cocked for trouble. Danger is everywhere; jealous neighbours, unpredictable weather, wind turbulence around the cliffs, but most of all, the vicious and scheming attentions of the pirate skuas. These and several species of gull depend on scavenged free meals, whether of fish brought for chicks, or the chicks themselves. Even the adult birds aren't safe. Visitors to the seabird colonies face gruesome sights of nature at its reddest, in beak and claw. Fully grown puffins and kittiwakes are knocked into the sea and drowned, then eaten by their bigger, cannier predators.

July is the last month for reasonable seabird watching. Young guillemots and other seabird chicks are fledging and the parent birds are frantically trying to feed them and guard them at the same time. There is one small bird though which attracts visitors every year to witness a unique spectacle. Storm petrels are at sea all year round, either flying or swimming, except for a brief visit to land for breeding. They are shy, secretive birds and nest in a very few sites in Shetland, only appearing after dark. There are few experiences in Shetland more worthwhile than the storm petrel boat trips to Mousa at night. After dark, if the weather is favourable, the boat takes you across from Leebitton and you walk along the shore and sit inside the ancient broch out of the wind and wait. The first parent bird returning to feed her chick may pass unnoticed, but after long minutes of still, silent darkness, the stones begin to reverberate with a churring, creaking sound. From deep inside the old broch walls the fledglings are singing to their parents. Soon after midnight, as if at a secret signal, the sky is alive with them; tiny, silent, black and white birds, they streak out of nowhere. Each adult miraculously homes in on the precise crevice between two stones where its own young are waiting.

By August the activity has wound down to next to nothing and most of the parent birds and their young will be out at sea. Whimbrel and red-necked phalaropes are unlikely to be seen by the middle of the month and September will find most of the summer breeding visitors leaving. A few puffins may still be seen, to delight late summer tourists, but the main spectacular bird event of the year is all but over and the great cliffs of Noss and Hermaness are virtually silent.

September brings thrills of a different kind, with the start of the autumn migration. As one group leaves, another appears. Depending on weather and wind direction, Shetland can seem to fill up overnight with a vast mixed flock of newcomers, all taking a rest on their long journey to warmer climes. Rather than brace the south-easterly gales for several days, these autumn visitors will land, exhausted, and feed and forage desperately to rebuild their depleted energy stocks.

Considerate birdwatchers will observe them carefully from a respectful distance, resisting the temptation to hound the weary strangers for a better view as they feed.

October too can still be a good month for the unexpected and the local newspaper keeps amateurs and fanatics alike abreast of each new arrival and departure. The *Braer* oil

Whimbrel ('Peerie whaap').

spill left at least one beneficial item behind in its wake, namely the Oiled Bird Unit in Tingwall. Here, under the watchful eye of the local SSPCA representative, weary or injured birds are often housed and tended while they recover. Their subsequent release is carefully planned and timetabled. Often a real rarity, such as an egret, osprey or hawk, is shipped or flown to a reserve further south.

November sees the return of the whooper swans and other wildfowl, geese and ducks migrating south from Iceland and further north. These winter visitors begin to coast in and seek out their favourite haunts. Fieldfares and redwings, snow buntings and twites are seen, often in large flocks. A flock of snow buntings can make a spectacular sight as they fly and then turn simultaneously, their wings all flashing silver at the same instant. Some roost for a night or two, then fly on. Others may stay a while longer, or even all winter. Gardens well endowed with trees and wet areas can attract water rails, moorhens, robins and some finches who may decide to stay right through until March or even early April.

December rolls down the daylight to a bare minimum, the sun barely skimming above the southern horizon as it glides through the short days. The bird year is complete.

Some wild breeding birds in Shetland, despite being locally quite common, are extremely rare on a worldwide scale. Their numbers are closely monitored, their breeding successes a matter of international importance; specific legislation has been introduced to help support their conservation. A number of laws exist specifically to ensure the upholding of international agreements designed to conserve and protect nature and wildlife. The following information is a summary of the main points.

The principal agreements are the 1979 Convention on the Conservation of European Wildlife and Natural Habitats (The Bern Convention); the 1979 European Community Directive on the Conservation of Wild Birds (The Birds Directive) and the 1992 European Community Directive on the Conservation of Natural Habitats and of Wild Fauna and Flora (The Habitats Directive). The 1981 Wildlife and Countryside Act offers various levels of protection to groups of listed species. In general, it is an offence to kill, injure, capture or keep *any* wild bird. It is also illegal to destroy or take birds' eggs, to sell or advertise for sale any wild bird or eggs. Destroying, taking away or damaging wild birds' nests while they are building or using them is also an offence.

In addition, a 'Schedule 1' list has been drawn up of rare species which it is an offence even to disturb while they are nest-building, sitting on eggs, or rearing young. The young birds are also protected until they are fully independent. Schedule 1 species in Shetland include red-throated diver, corncrake, long-tailed duck, peregrine falcon, scaup, merlin, whimbrel, whooper swan and red-necked phalarope. Scottish Natural Heritage in Lerwick (tel: 01595 693345) can provide advice on licences should you wish to photograph these birds.

Red-Throated Diver ('Raingoose').

WILD ANIMALS

Wild animals seen in Shetland today are thought to have been artificially introduced into the islands at one time or another during the past 6000 years. Even the otter, some people believe, is unlikely to have made the sea crossing unaided. Rabbits were introduced long ago and are plentiful, despite several serious attempts to reduce their numbers. What is certain is that there are now special Shetland subspecies of a number of wild, as well as domestic, animals which have evolved slight differences from others of the same species on the mainland. There are a number of distinct variations of Shetland mouse.

Field mice are widespread in Shetland. They have slightly redder fur than mainland mice and distinct island subspecies have been described from Yell, Foula and Fair Isle. Similarities with field mice in Norway suggest that Shetland field mice were inadvertently brought in by Viking settlers. Recent archaeological evidence, however, has shown that the house mouse was here far earlier, as remains have been found on an Iron Age site at Scatness. Both Shetland field mice and house mice have been found to be slightly larger than their equivalents in the rest of the UK and beyond. On a warm autumn evening mice are often seen in car headlights, racing across the road. They frequently nest in stone walls, as well as in byres and other buildings. In the days when hay and corn were grown, mice would gather in stacks and stooks, giving the sheepdogs cause for great excitement when the last of the store was removed.

Rats tend to live near the seashore, especially among the boulders arranged as sea defences, where they are sometimes seen, foraging and fighting. High tides and floods occasionally unseat these less well-loved animals and very rarely they may take up temporary residence in cellars, garages or outbuildings.

Shetland's wild otter population is said to be the highest of any county in the UK. The animals are often seen at close quarters and most easily at dawn and dusk. There are so many about that you might be lucky and catch a glimpse at almost any time of day. The most usual sight is that of a dark, streamlined shape in the sea, smaller than a seal and, unlike a seal, tending to disappear for a few minutes, reappearing a little further away. On still days a trail of bubbles in calm water immediately betrays the presence of an otter. If you sit still and wait you will almost certainly be rewarded with excellent views. The otter may surface unaware of your presence and, if not disturbed, may even come ashore and feed.

It is not so many years since otters were far more timid, as they were regularly hunted for their skins, which fetched good prices; many a poor family benefited from the income brought by selling them. Traps were sometimes built on the routes which otters were known to take between loch and sea. You can still find otter traps in varying states of collapse in Shetland today. The well-known Shetland saying, 'Lat be for lat be', originated from the story of a man checking his otter trap one day and finding a live otter in it,

Shetland is rich in Otters.

clubbing it and carrying it home over his shoulder. Shortly afterwards, the otter, which had only been stunned, came round and sank its teeth into the man's backside. Crying 'Lat be for lat be!', the man let the otter go and, presumably, headed for home as fast as he was able.

For those really intent on watching wild otters, Lunna Ness, East Yell, Nesting and South Whiteness are the places I have most frequently had success. Find a suitable time – early evening, or very early morning – and a suitable place, such as a deserted stretch of low, rocky shore, with a reasonably sheltered, comfortable corner to sit in, and wait. Otters, surprisingly, have rather poor sight, but they can detect movement rapidly, so avoid being silhouetted against the horizon. Sadly, a growing number of otters are being killed on Shetland's roads. Every year, a number of these dead otters are sent south for tests; much valuable data about Shetland otters has been built up by researchers at the Banchory Institute of Terrestrial Ecology over the years.

Having originally escaped or been released, 'pole-ferrets' (a polecat-ferret cross) have multiplied and are a menace to poultry and ground-nesting wild birds. A trapping system has been introduced and the stock of traps is almost permanently in use by crofters. A number of these animals are knocked down by cars on the roads and you may see one lying on a verge. They are attractive creatures, with bodies varying from dark cream, through chestnut, almost to black, with little white faces and paws. But despite their appealing looks, they are bad news for wildlife and many people would like to see them eradicated.

Rabbits are present in large numbers in the islands. Don't be surprised if you should see black, piebald, albino or even bright apricot-coloured rabbits in the hills. Shetland's wild rabbits have only man as a major predator and their natural colour range has been able to flourish without selective reduction as tends to happen in mainland Britain. First recorded the early 1600s they have spread fast and periodically reach such numbers that attempts are made to reduce their numbers. Myxomatosis was introduced on more than one occasion and had an effect for a while. The recent rabbit viral disease seemed to have an effect only on pet rabbits as wild populations appeared to continue unaffected.

Hares are said to have been introduced for sport. Two species were found in the islands, both brown and mountain hare. The blue, or mountain, hare, famous for its white (or almost all white) winter coat thrived best. Shetland is seldom snow-covered and the poor animal is so noticeable, white against the dark moorland, that the camouflage could not be less appropriate. The brown hare eventually died out.

Hedgehogs are a relatively recently introduced species and have adapted well to the Shetland environment; their numbers have rocketed. Second broods are sometimes managed within a year, but the later offspring seldom manage to hibernate successfully as they are too small and light to withstand the long winter hibernation. They have acquired some popularity in recent years and their numbers have certainly risen dramatically, judging by the growing number of road casualties. Hedgehogs can be found on most of the inhabited islands and are greatly beloved of gardeners as they help reduce the vast slug population. Seagulls, curiously, have begun to evolve ways of keeping down the hedgehog population too. Several have been seen gripping small hedgehogs and flying up with them, then dropping them onto roads, and after several 'drops', eating the creatures.

By the time frogs were introduced to Shetland, local interest in wildlife and conscious attempts to experiment were increasing. There are a number of documented introductions and probably many more unreported ones. Several buckets of frogspawn were brought up from Aberdeen at the request of a couple of Shetlanders from Scalloway. They were released into a number of lochs, streams and ditches, and have spread widely. In late summer there is sometimes a reported mass movement of frogs, seen hopping across roads in their hundreds. The increasing popularity of gardening and pond making has allowed their numbers to grow still faster.

I was told the story of one of the first recorded local sightings of an adult frog. It was a few years after the frogspawn had been released and happened one late summer during the 1920s, when hay was being cut. One elderly lady from Blydoit near Scalloway must have disturbed a frog while scything her way through the hay. A frog jumped away from her and, being utterly unfamiliar and weird, it gave her the scare of her life. She apparently shrieked and ran to a neighbour who was cutting his own hay not far away, crying, 'Wullie, Wullie, der a baist in da mudoo!' (Willie, Willie, there's a beast in the meadow!)

Toads have been introduced experimentally from time to time, but appear not to have survived beyond a few months or a year or two. No evidence of toads came to light in surveys in the 1990s.

Stoats are widespread in much of Shetland. John Brand in part of his 1703 *A New Description of Orkney, Shetland…etc*, recounts a story he was told, about stoats being originally introduced to Shetland by 'the king's falconer' as revenge for the refusal of Shetlanders to continue the practice of providing hens for food for the royal hawks. Known as 'whitrits' (white rats) in Shetlandic, stoats are on record as having occasionally taken up residence in attics, where they have been very content, and it has taken a lot of determination to shift them.

A mink fur farm was established in Shetland at one time and a number of mink escaped. This could have presented Shetland with a major problem for its ground-nesting birds. Fortunately the animals were recaptured. There are no mink farms in Shetland now and it is highly unlikely that permission would ever be granted to set one up in the future.

Wild foxes are not found in Shetland, but a few introduced foxes have been seen on occasions over the years. They never seem to thrive and have never been known to breed, possibly as a result of hostile climate, or, perhaps more likely, have been eradicated by quiet but determined crofters. A dead red fox was found beside the main road in the late 1990s and a dead Arctic fox found in similar circumstances near Voe. Both were suspected of having been killed and dumped.

Feral cats have established tiny colonies here and there in a number of places in the islands in recent years and measures are taken to eradicate them. Particular efforts were made in Noss to remove a feral cat colony because of the damage to ground-nesting wild birds in the reserve and there is concern too for the Manx shearwater colony in Fetlar, similarly at risk.

Weasels are not found in Shetland, neither are deer, badgers, squirrels, voles, shrews or newts.

DOMESTIC ANIMALS

A working sheepdog stands among the special Shetland breeds, which is believed to have evolved in the islands in the same way as native cattle, sheep and ponies. Like them, it too is smaller than its southern collie counterparts and comes in a wide range of colour combinations. Tough, courageous, intelligent and hardy, the 'sheltie', as dog breeders call them, is ideally suited to working in Shetland. In 1909 the Shetland collie, or *Toonie Dog*, was officially recognised as a separate breed by the Scottish Shetland Sheepdog Club and by the

The unique Shetland Pony.

Kennel Club in 1914. When tourism increased in the early 1900s, many visitors bought a sheltie to take home with them. The breed eventually, like the Shetland pony, became more numerous on the mainland than in the islands.

Ponies have been in Shetland for over 4000 years. Horse teeth were found on the site of a Neolithic house at Ness of Gruting during an archaeological excavation in the 1950s and fragments of bone were found at Stanydale. Horse teeth have been found on other Neolithic sites, suggesting that they may well have been part of the early Shetland farming scene, along with oxen and sheep. Shetland ponies are well suited to the climate and they may have been here almost as long as human beings. They shouldered much of the hard labour of farming in the islands for the best part of 50 centuries, from pulling carts to ferrying peats back from the hills.

A whole range of harnesses and equipment was used, much of which can be seen in the Shetland Crofthouse Museum. There are places where horses are used occasionally for agricultural work and Shetland still has a blacksmith, but ploughing matches are no longer on the agricultural show programme. In 1842 the introduction of the Mines Act by the British government put an end to the use of women and children to drag coal wagons down the mines and Shetland ponies began to be bred for the purpose instead. There were several pony enclosures, or 'punds', large, square, stone enclosures with characteristically heightened corners and roofed stalls inside. Noss has a restored pony pund with an interpretive display featuring the pony-breeding history of the Marquis of Londonderry's stud, which was established in the 1870s.

Today, thankfully, the ponies no longer slave below ground and on land too Shetland ponies are less often worked, but are bred, shown, ridden and exported to breeders all round the world and have become a much-loved symbol of the islands. The pony sales in October are well worth seeing, but most visitors enjoy the herds of ponies in May when the tiny newborn foals are at their most irresistible. Horse riding has become popular and many breeds of riding horses are kept in the islands. Recent interest in Icelandic horses led to an indoor riding centre being established in Mid Walls.

Cattle have been part of the Shetland scene for as long as ponies, and oxen have been used for centuries to pull carts and drag ploughs. Shetland cattle, or 'kye' as they are known, came originally, like Shetland sheep, ponies and poultry, in a variety of colours and patterns and were once universal in the islands. But they began to die out as larger, better milking breeds became available. Today a range of breeds of cattle are kept and Shetland is virtually self-sufficient in dairy produce. Recently, however, the Shetland kye began to make a comeback. It seems that overbreeding may have reduced the digestibility of beef flesh and fat, whereas Shetland cattle appear to have more digestible protein in their flesh and milk. As research continues into this subject, local herds are growing steadily in numbers. Today you are likely to see them only in black and white, as limited numbers of surviving Shetland bulls meant that the wide range of colours was no longer available for breeders.

Shetland sheep have their detractors but there are many who hold them in great regard. Their wool is exceptionally soft and the ewes are renowned for being wonderful mothers. Hardy and adaptable, able to steal a living from ill-fenced gardens as well as near-vertical cliff ledges, scavenging seaweed on beaches and ripping every blade of green from accessible acres and hills, they have largely created the treeless, barren slopes of the islands for thousands of years. Fencing and boundary walls have been essential through the centuries for anyone wishing to raise crops and the Shetland sheep has grown wily and inventive at finding ways through. They come in a bewildering variety and range of colours and patterns, most of which have ancient words to describe them: *moorit* for brown, *shaela* for grey are two well-known terms, but there are dozens more.

Shetland lamb meat, too, as with Shetland beef, has proved to have uniquely healthy qualities and may well soon be sold at a premium, unlike their fatter, whiter rivals, the Blackfaces, Suffolks and Cheviots which crowded into the islands after the Clearances. Famous long ago for their soft, fine wool, the fleeces are small and to increase the quantity, rams, or 'tups', of different, larger breeds were introduced. The *Shetland Flock Book* was established to try to preserve the pure breed. Shetland fleeces fetched poor prices for many years, but they deserve higher, rather than lower rates. New marketing initiatives began in the late 1990s with an international conference held in the islands. Perhaps this century will see greater rewards for Shetland sheep breeders.

'Shetland' pigs survived into the first decade of last century, but sadly, have become extinct. Thought to have derived from those brought in by the early Norse farmers, virtually every croft had its pig. During the summer the pigs ranged freely over the hills, feeding and sometimes breeding there. Later on they were brought in and kept in sties or even indoors during the winter. Sties had to be floored with stone or the pigs would tear their way out by tunnelling under the walls. Croft hill dykes had to be pig-proof too, as a pig could create havoc among crops.

Stories of these pigs still abound. They were said to be small, dark, hairy, full of character and voracious. There is one marvellous tale of two brothers visiting lady friends in a neighbouring district rather late at night. They waited until the old parents were seen to retire for the night before tapping on the window. The delighted lasses insisted that the men stayed the night, and woke them before daylight to allow them to return home before the old folk rose. To mingled horror and amusement, it was discovered that the house pig had shredded and eaten their clothing during the night.

A range of breeds of pig were kept in small numbers last century. Recent pig-rearing and butchering enterprises have been very popular and may prove successful.

A number of other animals have been introduced to Shetland over the years. Goats do well with care and extra shelter, as do angora rabbits and bees. Both earthworm- and snail-farming have been tried at various times. Resourceful Shetlanders and unwary newcomers are willing to try almost anything which seems to have a chance of success, so don't be surprised to find the unusual among the familiar wherever you go.

SEA LIFE AND FISH

Without fish, there would probably have been no permanent human settlement in Shetland. The earliest evidence of fishing – simple fish-catching tools, net sinkers and fish bones – comes from archaeological sites. In days gone by, a trained eye could detect a shoal of fish from the tell-tale patterning on the sea surface. A group of small feeding whales, their dorsal fins breaking the surface like small black sails, would make men head for their boats. You can watch for whales today too, or seals, otters and the ever-present seabirds. Initially, fish kept people alive, then as the centuries progressed, it became an increasingly vital element in the trade which fed the island economy. A particularly rich fishing area lay to the south-west, known as the Burra Haaf. Over 60 species have been recorded from recent landings in Shetland. The main commercial species are cod, haddock, mackerel and herring, ling, whiting, monkfish, halibut, plaice and sole.

Other fishing grounds include the Fetlar Firth, St Magnus Bay, and the Bressay and Bergen banks. It is believed that global warming may have increased the movement of some fish and other marine species from far to the south. Rarities occasionally end up in the nets of Shetland fishing boats, arousing much interest, whether unusual sharks, leatherback turtles, sunfish or even on one occasion a marbled electric ray. The protection of the spawning areas for cod, haddock and other species is of crucial importance. Each species of fish has its own specific life history of breeding areas, feeding and, in some cases, migrating patterns. More and more is being learned and discovered about the natural history of this hidden world and not before time, as fish stocks are desperately depleted.

Progress in fishing technology carries with it the seeds of its own destruction. Shellfish can be very sensitive to pollution and in places the techniques of one kind of fishery have created problems for another. As technology has advanced, the impact of increasingly efficient fish-location systems and catching-gear has resulted in fewer boats but greater numbers of fish caught by a single boat than ever before. This, and the growing number of foreign fleets fishing the same grounds, has had an increasing impact on fish stocks and one species after another has been fished to the brink. Efforts have been made to seek new species to catch, including deep-water fishing, which has brought new and strange fish to light. Boats these days are colossally expensive to equip and require massive investment. Once working, they and their crews cannot just be 'switched off' while stocks build up.

Conservation efforts are coming, but it is a controversial and complex business and far from resolved. Aquaculture is the main development area today. Salmon farming has brought in increasing income in recent years, but this industry too has its problems. Halibut- and cod-farming experiments are in progress and every possible new avenue is explored. Shetland is at the forefront of research into the ecology of commercial fish and shellfish species and the next few years may well see major changes in the ways in which traditional fishing methods are used. Meanwhile, the future employment for children of traditional fishing families, following in their parents' footsteps, grows steadily less certain.

Traditionally, young Shetlanders were introduced to fishing from the shore from an early age. A jam jar for catching sticklebacks was discarded for a length of string with a bent pin on one end as a simple fishing line by young bairns, graduating to their own first 'waand' (rod) later. Favourite places for fishing along a rocky shore, known as 'craigs', still attract islanders in their spare time. This method of adding food items to the general pot must be one of the oldest skills in the islands. Limpets, traditionally ground up for bait, are abundant. Small bowl-shaped depressions can sometimes be found carved into solid rock at the sea's rim. Here, for centuries, limpets were pounded to pulp, the resulting mass was chewed and then 'frooshed', or spat out, over the sea to attract fish which could be caught by rod or net as they surged in to feed on the floating morsels.

In addition to fishing, shellfish gathering was important for the larder, especially during periods of low tides. Shetland's seashores are great places for finding seashells. Winkles, or 'whelks' as Shetlanders call them, are gathered in large quantities and sold at certain times of year, making a relatively lucrative pastime for youngsters as well as more serious adult gatherers. Some families actually earn their summer holiday money this way. Depending on the nature of the nearby seabed, a range of species of shellfish can be found. Small periwinkles, dog whelks, mussels and cockles, and grey-top shells and a range of small clams are frequently found. An oyster shell bed would be a rarity today, though oyster shell dumps found in the islands dating back long ago, prove that they were once common and have also been fished out.

Razor shells (known locally as 'spoots', owing to their tendency to squirt water rapidly upwards as they contract and dive under the sand where they live) are still an item on many a crofter's seasonal menu. A 'spootie ebb', an exceptionally low tide, is still used by many for gathering razor shells. You may see people on a calm evening at very low tide, walking slowly backwards over wet sand exposed by the low tide and watching closely for a spoot, or spurt of water, as the shellfish under the sand senses pressure above and starts to contract, drawing itself deeper away from danger. With a rapid downwards thrust of a finger, they can be pulled out; a simple-sounding process, but trickier than you might think.

Crabs, lobsters and scallops are fished inshore and sea urchins (known as 'Scaddiman's heads' in Shetland dialect) are plentiful in Shetland waters and may well become a commercial item in the future, as they are a delicacy in Europe. Mussel farming is common in Shetland and other species of shellfish are being trialled, with a view to farming them in the future. Fish factories process shellfish in the islands and the range of different methods of preservation, packaging and storage has increased dramatically in recent years. Seafood products are sent all over the world. One enterprising business was set up to use most of the waste scallop shells and some are used by the craft industry for ornaments and art work.

Traditionally, freshwater as well as saltwater fish have been caught in Shetland. The place where burns meet the sea can be good for catching 'flukes', or small flatfish and eels too which swim up the freshwater burns in season to spawn. There are literally hundreds of lochs in the islands; many are well stocked with fish and much frequented by Shetland's keen anglers. There are well-maintained stocks of brown trout in many lochs and sea trout, although less common than they once were, still feature. Grilse too can be found, as well as increasing numbers of escaped salmon from sea cages.

Every loch in Shetland is different. Some are shallow and easily crossed in wading gear, others are boulder-strewn, or deep and treacherous. A new sport, 'loch-isleing', is gaining popularity, whereby anglers attempt to catch a trout in a loch on as many islands as they can. The Tourist Office in Lerwick has details of when and where to fish and how to obtain permits. They will have information on the best lochs, estuaries or shorelines and where to hire or buy fishing gear. There are also a number of sea-angling businesses. But there are mammals other than humans which depend on fish for their survival in Shetland.

SEA MAMMALS

Seals are possibly the only true native breeding mammals in Shetland. The ocean would have been no deterrent for this streamlined master of the seas.

Common seals have rather dog-like, snub-nosed profiles, tend to be variable in colour, often blotched and spotted, and are slightly smaller than the grey seals, which have domed, Roman noses. Both species are

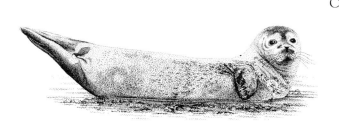

Common Seal.

numerous around the coastline, but other species do appear from time to time. Long-travelled strangers from far afield such as hooded seals, bearded seals, harp seals and even walruses have been found from time to time, hauled out on beaches or slipways and in some cases have been helped on their way back home.

Seals have become the subject of considerable controversy in Shetland in recent years. Traditionally, they were hunted for their fur and the sale of sealskins added to the family income for many folk. Following a serious decline in numbers, they became protected, since when their numbers have increased and their behaviour has become bolder and more confident. Where a seal might once have vanished at the sight of a human approaching the sea, they will now rise up and stare at you from amazingly close quarters. There are some who believe that seal numbers have grown so much out of balance that fish catches are affected. Seals seem to be fascinated by the sight of a party of humans and a walk along the banks can attract anything from one to several score seals at a time, all vying with each other to show off in front of their land-bound distant cousins.

Sometimes they swim remarkably close to the beach and just watch, 'bottling', or resting with their heads poking up out of the water, whiskers twitching, huge eyes goggling. They often make loud sneezing and snorting noises and, occasionally, moan like lost souls or wail like abandoned children. If you approach too close, they slap the water hard and dive, coming up again further out in deep water. But if you are good at sitting absolutely still for long periods, they will sometimes come right inshore to within a few yards of you. A party of children once settled themselves on some rocks right by the edge of the sea and waited, wrapped in black bin bags to keep out the spray and the cold. Several seals came so close that the group leader decided to call a retreat just in case. The nearest seal had been less than four feet from the group, so close that you could actually smell its fishy breath and almost count the eyelashes round each eye.

The common seal breeds in the summer but late autumn is the grey seals' breeding time. If you know your beaches, you can find the snow-white pups, waiting patiently, half-asleep, for their mothers' return with a new food supply. Young seal pups can be wonderful things to watch but only from a safe distance as bull seals will be patrolling the shore nearby. It is the young ones which catch at the heart; there is little more intensely appealing than these roly-poly waifs and it is easy to believe that they are marooned, abandoned, even injured, when all that has happened is that the approach of humans has frightened off their carers. Unguarded pups are greatly at risk. If approached, they turn wild with a vengeance; they will bite if touched, with fangs coated in germ-laden saliva, as seals carry nasty diseases. A frightened seal pup will often attempt to get down to the sea for safety, before it is old enough, only to die later. Mother seals can cover distance alarmingly fast, even on rough, bouldery beaches; they have immensely powerful jaws and no scruples. The father seal, the bull, is

Grey Seal pup.

never far away; angry and frightened seal pups make a terrific noise and seal hearing is sharp.

Whales are an increasing attraction in Shetland. Large numbers of cetaceans have been recorded in Shetland waters in recent years – a total of 23 different species, either alive, or dead and stranded. In times past, pilot whales, the commonest local species, were driven onto the shore and killed in large numbers for their meat, blubber and whalebone. Common porpoises, known as 'neesiks', are found in Shetland waters, though they are not as common as they once were. White-sided dolphins and Risso's dolphins turn up from time to time. But whales can be more difficult to plan for. Killer whales ('orcas') and minke whales (or 'herrin hogs') are the most likely species to be about, although sperm whales do make an occasional appearance and a white beluga whale was seen not many years ago. The Shetland Cetacean Group keeps detailed records of all sightings and there is now an annual whale-watching day in the summer which is well worth attending for the displays and videos, even if no whales actually turn up for the occasion! Humpback whales are sometimes seen surging out of the waves to turn, twist and crash back again, sending up fountains of spray. Equally dramatic, but less pleasant, are the sightings of killer whales attacking seals. Some bloodthirsty pictures have been taken by those who were in the right place at the right time.

Who are the Shetlanders?

O sing me a sang a da smack an da boom,
Gyaan aff ta da haaf idda simmer,
Whin da sails mirr an sing wi a fine room wind,
An da watter lachs back in a shimmer.

From *Löd a Langer* by Rhoda Bulter.

Shetland is home to a unique twenty-first century community, most of whom are still in close touch with their traditional crofting/fishing roots. The population stood at just over 23,000 as the twenty-first century began. Some Shetlanders consider themselves to be more Scandinavian than British, as these islands were home to Viking adventurers, farmers and raiders for some 800 years before the first formal Scottish rule was established. Shetland's native domestic animals – sheep, cattle, dogs, ponies and poultry – are special breeds, some closely related to those brought over by the Norsemen. Until Shetland became part of Scotland, 600 years ago, Norn, the Norse language spoken in the islands, was the only language. Norn songs, rhymes and sayings were still being used in some remote parts of Shetland as recently as a century ago.

The islands boast Europe's largest oil terminal on one hand, yet also one of Britain's densest networks of ancient archaeological sites on the other. Shetland is for ornithologists one of the world's most significant seabird breeding areas, the most important wild otter haven in the UK, a paradise for geologists, a key area for land and marine plant study, a magnet for traditional musicians from all over the world and a wonderful, safe and exciting place in which to live and bring up children.

Detail from the replica Viking longship *Dim Riv*, Lerwick.

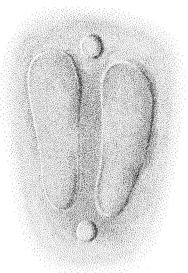

Carved footprints
at Clickimin Broch.

But life in the islands has not always been so good. Many periods of poverty, famine and oppression of various kinds throughout history – invasions, disasters, emigrations – have tested islanders to their limits, but somehow they survived. Those who left, or their descendants, frequently find their way back again, especially for the Hamefarin celebrations, specially arranged for Shetlanders living abroad, held every 25 years.

Today's oil reserves have transformed many aspects of Shetland, its society and infrastructure. But the modern and the old, the high tech and the prehistoric here lie side by side. At every turn, Shetland's ancient past confronts you. Here a castle rubs shoulders with a fish and chip shop; there an Iron Age broch faces a garage. Tractors and lorries rumble past ancient standing stones and occasionally, new 'standing stones' have been erected to mark the completion of a major new stretch of road. In Shetland, where people have lived for possibly 6000 years in the same areas, building and rebuilding over the house sites of former generations happens all the time. Old buildings were rebuilt again and again on the same sites, but their foundations remain and countless ancient sites await discovery.

You can spend hours just watching the comings and goings of the fishing fleet, the oil service boats and fisheries patrol vessels. 'Klondykers', or factory ships from former 'Iron Curtain' countries, used to arrive in large numbers, especially during the mackerel season. Occasionally, special cable-laying, seismic survey or even Greenpeace ships may call in. At night, larger seashore communities look out, not over the pitch-black, moonlit or starlit sea, but over a dark expanse filled with shimmering reflections and a dazzling array of lights, warning buoys, and coloured navigation lights, some flashing at different speeds. You need to travel to remote corners and tiny coastal hamlets to find the former dark stillness and peace of a traditional Shetland sea at night.

Aeroplanes taxi into Sumburgh airport along the runway, which was built over the earliest burial site ever found in the islands; the Aberdeen ferry entering Lerwick harbour follows the same course as the Dutch ships whose crews, almost half a millennium ago, set fire to the Cromwellian fort overlooking the town; salmon cages sit moored where longships once lay at anchor and the changes which have shouldered out the old ways await their own eviction by fresh changes as yet undreamed of.

Human History

Above the ruins the gulls are crying
Where once the Pict-folk stayed.

From *Burgawater* by Vagaland (T. A. Robertson)

Despite its remoteness, climate and exposed terrain, Shetland has attracted people to its shores for thousands of years, not simply to visit, but to stay. The settlement patterns have changed gradually through time, but themes of cultivation, fishing, crafts and husbandry remain common to all of them. Each year that passes sees both new revelations about early life in the islands, and new ventures by present-day islanders, all as keen as their ancient forebears to make an improved living here for themselves, their families and communities.

An astonishing number of ancient sites are found in Shetland, preserved probably because of the nature of land use, which has left much of the land undisturbed. It is fascinating to walk through the islands searching for sudden changes in vegetation, rectangular or circular outlines in even plant cover, or the occasional half-buried mound of stone. Many Shetlanders have become keen amateur archaeologists and walk systematically over their areas, noting and reporting on possible sites of interest. Since the mid 1980s Shetland has had its own professional archaeologist, Val Turner, and the sites and monuments list for Shetland has grown rapidly since field survey work has increased. Excavations take place whenever sites are threatened, and each one deepens our knowledge and understanding about the folk who lived here so long ago.

Research indicates that there have been critical times in the long distant past, when over-use has impoverished local soils, burning and grazing have drastically altered tree and other plant populations and, more recently, there has been a dramatic collapse of local fish stocks. Extremes of need, native ingenuity and rugged determination have ensured the islanders' survival before and it is hoped that, with new technology and information systems, disaster may be averted once again. The following section takes each period of ancient settlement in turn, in chronological order, and touches briefly on the buildings, agriculture, burial arrangements and trade, in so far as evidence has been found.

Clickimin Broch, Lerwick.

NEOLITHIC AND BRONZE-AGE SHETLAND

For me, there is nowhere better than Shetland in the whole of the British Isles for archaeology. The islands are believed to have several thousand prehistoric sites; more per square mile than anywhere else in the UK. Traditional crofting methods throughout many centuries have allowed vast areas of the islands to retain their ancient surface landscapes and skylines. Stripped long since of the tree and shrub cover which once grew here, the ground reveals traces of ancient habitation. Burial sites, cultivated areas and boundaries leave telltale patterns and undulations behind. Some areas have lost original soil and the ground with stones and rocks lies bare, with ancient foundations still visible. In other parts of Shetland peat has formed over old settled landscapes and buried the remains of buildings and field systems several feet below today's surface.

Following the ending of the last ice age about 10,000 years ago, the climate improved. Plants recolonised the denuded land and the presence of seabirds and fish, berries and scrub woodland may have made the islands attractive. Archaeological excavations in Europe have shown that travelling hunters and gatherers followed the migrating animals they depended on; making temporary camps, some of which have produced charcoal and evidence of tools and tool-working. Remains of dugout canoes found in Europe and ancient rock pictures of boats with skins stretched over wood from Sweden show that they were able to cross the sea. However, evidence of the Mesolithic, or Middle Stone Age, found in the Western Isles, and in Orkney too, has not yet come to light in Shetland. From the north of Orkney, people would just have been able to see Fair Isle, enticing them to travel further north. Any cave or seashore camp remains are almost certainly now lost to the rising sea levels, but evidence may yet come to light further inland, under the peat.

Carbon dating has so far placed the earliest Neolithic (New Stone Age) sites at roughly 3500 BC, or 5500 years ago. Archaeologists have discovered evidence of a remarkably mild climate during early settlement periods. A rise of even one or two degrees would make a big difference, with conditions at sea more conducive to crossings from mainland Scotland and the growing season extended, allowing more time for the ripening of cereal crops. Pollen analysis gives precise evidence of a large variety of plant species which grew at the time. Pollen grains can survive for thousands of years; some found deep in the present peat layers indicate that many plant, shrub and tree species once grew here where they can no longer exist under present-day Shetland conditions.

House sites of various sizes, mostly oval in outline, have been found throughout Shetland. Excavation of some sites has revealed a single room with recesses built into the thickness of the great walls. Traces of wood found beneath some Neolithic oval houses suggest that buildings of more perishable materials may well have predated the stone ones. Stone vessels have survived in large numbers. Charcoal and fragments of bone found during excavations indicate sites of fires and cooking. Pottery of various kinds has been preserved on some sites and recent research techniques enable far more information about Neolithic life to be gleaned from these fragments than was ever thought possible.

Where land is cultivated, stones are progressively cleared from fields and piled into heaps known as field clearance cairns, which occur widely throughout Shetland. Broken prehistoric tools have been found among stones at the base, while more recent items are sometimes found lying higher up. This suggests that some of these clearance cairns may have been used by Shetland farmers from prehistoric times right up to the present day. Ard points, or stone ploughshares, have been found and, on some sites, the deep scratches that they made in the subsoil, where ploughs have cut through the earth above, can sometimes be seen during excavations. On one site, a marvellously preserved hoard of charred barley was discovered in a midden where it had been buried. Some areas of Shetland which are currently covered in meagre, infertile soils, may in times long past have been intensively cultivated; the soils eventually becoming exhausted.

Evidence of land enclosure is widespread. Stone dykes or walls can be seen in many places, and some are thought to have been built to divide large tracts of land into smaller units, while others may have defined territorial boundaries. Shetland's native scrub woodland is thought to have been heavily used at this time.

Excavation at a Neolithic settlement at Scord of Brouster, near Walls, revealed several house sites spanning a period of 2000 years of habitation. Evidence of sheep and cattle was found and even a piece of red deer antler! The site of the biggest Neolithic building found so far, thought once to have been a temple or maybe a chief's house, is at Stanydale, close to a whole series of other smaller, contemporary house sites. These early Shetlanders were expert at working with stone. Some beautiful polished axes have been discovered. Look out for the remarkable 'Shetland knives', highly polished stone blades believed to have had great value, probably for symbolic or religious use rather than for practical purposes, in the Shetland Museum. Neolithic quarry sites have been identified in a few remote parts of the islands. Some stone tools found on the mainland have been traced back to Shetland quarries, demonstrating the extent of contact and trade during this period.

Some interesting burial sites from the Neolithic period are unique to these islands. Chambered cairns are found all over Scotland, but in Shetland they have a unique outline plan. They consist of a stone-built structure with an entrance-way leading to a small chamber with little recesses leading off it. The front is usually built into a flattened, slightly concave face of characteristic 'heel'-shaped appearance. The island of Vementry has a particularly fine one and there are many others, usually located on prominent hills. Heel-shaped cairns are thought to have contained the remains of a single individual. Burial cists or stone slab boxes appear to be a later method of disposing of the dead. Bones of several

Jarlshof, Sumburgh, South Mainland.

individuals have been found inside these cists, often accompanied by various items for their use in the afterworld. Shetland's earliest multiple burial site, dating from a little over 5000 years ago, was found at Sumburgh during the building of the airport and can be seen in the Shetland Museum.

About 4000 years ago a colder, wetter period began and farming seems to have become less dependable. Expanses of cultivated land became waterlogged and people abandoned them. Peat formed over much of the ancient landscape, obscuring many signs of habitation and cultivation. Evidence suggests that communities clustered into groups, often nearer to the sea. There are indications too that the population, which seemed to be high during the Neolithic period, began to decline. Round about 3800 years ago the first bronze appears on the scene and all sites and structures dated from this point on are termed Bronze Age.

Excavated in the 1950s, Clickimin Broch in Lerwick was found to have been built over a Bronze Age farmstead and Shetland Museum has extensive displays featuring the site excavation there. Jarlshof, Shetland's famous multi-period archaeological site, lies against the seashore at the southernmost tip of the mainland. Here, with almost the whole spread of Shetland's archaeological periods represented in one place, you can allow your imagination full rein as you follow the twists and turns of the paths. There are fine examples of Bronze Age houses and a smithy, where considerable evidence of bronze-working was found. You can borrow a torch from the interpretive centre and crawl into two souterrains, and be completely enclosed within the ancient stone-lined chamber. Wheelhouse and broch remains as well as Norse houses can be entered.

Scatness, a new multi-period site, is being excavated nearby and has even more metal-working remains including many moulds. Studies of Pictish and Viking remains from here are adding constantly to the understanding of this little-known period of Shetland's history. Over several summers, experts from The Living History TV programme experimented with local materials to produce tools, cloth and other items, demonstrating to visitors stone-working, weaving, iron- and copper-working and metal-working skills.

A remarkable feature associated with the Bronze Age is the 'burnt mound'. These intriguing, often crescent-shaped mounds of heat-shattered stones are found all over Shetland, always close to a fresh water source. Excavated examples have often revealed stone-and clay-lined trenches beneath them, as well as benches, conduits and other structures. Water may have been heated to boiling point by the throwing in of red-hot stones. Experiments have proved that it was possible, though extremely difficult, to cook whole animals in such trenches. Experts differ over the function of burnt mounds, believing they were group cooking places, or some form of sauna (common to many northern cultures) or perhaps locations for certain kinds of technology or treatment which required heat to process it. Perhaps they served a variety of purposes.

IRON-AGE AND PICTISH SHETLAND

The first evidence of iron working, bringing in the Iron Age in Shetland, dates from roughly 600 BC. Day-to-day agriculture and fishing may have continued much as it had before, but helped now by iron tools. A remarkable number of metal-working sites were revealed during excavations in the late 1990s. A variety of new features, including defensive sites, began to appear on the scene. This suggests that there may have been hostile groups against which communities needed protection, either from local, competitive groups in Shetland, or from raiding outsiders from across the sea. At this time, a number of seafaring raider groups were active. Although the Romans are known to have raided Scotland for slaves, there is as yet no evidence of their having reached Shetland.

The largest Iron Age buildings seem to have been brochs (double-walled stone towers or fortified houses), and blockhouse forts (defensive structures), the latter usually in very dramatic coastal sites. Some, like that on the Loch of Huxter in Whalsay, were built in lochs, connected to the shore by underwater causeways. Others, such as Scatness and Burgi Geos in Yell, were constructed on high cliffs. Where a broch was located within sight of another, should a suspect ship be seen approaching, fires (beacons) could have been lit as warnings, setting off a chain of similar fires as others saw and passed on the signal. Smoke signals could have been sent by day. Few brochs have been excavated as yet, but those that have been reveal an increasingly complex society, accustomed to trading and contact with people far away from Shetland. Finds indicate a wider range of material goods than people possessed in earlier times.

Mousa Broch.

Mousa Broch, the largest and most complete broch in Britain, survives on the island of Mousa, just east of Sandwick in the South Mainland, and was probably saved from demolition by its remote island location. There is an account in the *Orkneyinga Saga* of Erlend the Young escaping from Orkney with Earl Harald's mother Margaret and staying in Mousa Broch under siege until Harald and Erlend were reconciled and departed for Orkney together. Most prehistoric buildings survive only as foundations or floor-level ruins, usually covered by the heap of collapsed stone walls above. But in Mousa you may stand where people stood thousands of years before, completely enclosed by the same drystone walls. You can climb the same narrow stairs as they did, inside the thickness of the walls, to the lookout at the top of the tower.

A new, rather roughly constructed style of dwelling called a wheelhouse began to be built at about the broch-building period. Their builders possibly used broch masonry and sometimes built within the enclosing walls of an earlier broch. Artefacts found on these sites suggest a relatively affluent society, and include jewellery, fine pottery and evidence of the use of both gold and silver. There are wheelhouses at Jarlshof and more at Scatness, where one has been reconstructed in an experiment to understand Iron Age drystone construction methods. Interestingly, wheelhouses have so far been found only in the South Mainland.

Shetland was an established part of the northern Pictish kingdom, which was centred around Inverness. Pictish Shetland, often known as Shetland's Dark Age, dates from the late Iron Age. Artefacts left behind by the Picts certainly reflect an artistic side to their life and work. Pictish carvings and jewellery inspire designers to this day. Theirs was a literate society with a script known as Ogam, a series of short lines in groups, set across a long central line, the meaning of which has remained a mystery. However, recently progress has been made in the translation of Pictish Ogam by Kathy Forsyth in Glasgow and this may shed some light on our understanding of the period.

Excavated finds reveal the existence of good links with mainland Scotland, Ireland and Scandinavia at this time. A remarkable number of carved stones have been found in Shetland, a few of which have Ogam inscriptions, the first actual written records in Shetland's history. Many have been found in the vicinity of Cunningsburgh, a name thought to mean 'king's fortified settlement'. The purpose of intriguing painted quartz pebbles from this period remains a mystery, as does the material from which the marks were made.

The symbols and designs on some stones resemble those found on Pictish sites on mainland Scotland. A very old carved symbol stone, known as the Brake Stone, was found in the South Mainland at Brake near Quendale. The Mail Stone, found in 1992 at Mail in Cunningsburgh, shows an animal-headed figure and is thought to date from 700. The curious logo used to represent Islesburgh Centre is taken from the Islesburgh Eagle Stone, found north of Brae by a farmer, John Copland, when he was burying a sheep. All three of these ancient stones are displayed in the Shetland Museum.

Some Pictish houses, unlike the larger wheelhouses built earlier, were smaller and were informally termed 'jelly baby houses', thought to be possible to build in a day. They were rounded and consisted of two parts. Very few of these houses have so far been found, suggesting that more buildings may have been built out of wood and other biodegradeable materials, long since rotted away. The Viking word for Pict was *Petta*, found in place names like Pettadale, Pettifirth, Pettister and Pettawater. Some islanders like to refer to the Picts as the forebears of the Shetlanders we know today; rich in art, music, skilled in crafts, metalwork, stonework, farming and seamanship. Children in Lerwick have for generations (incorrectly) called Clickimin Broch the 'Picts' Castle'.

Clickimin Broch, Lerwick.

CELTIC SHETLAND

Christianity was brought to Pictish Shetland well before the Vikings first arrived. The journeys of the seafaring, missionary monks from Celtic, Christian communities in Ireland, Iona and the West of Scotland are well documented. They are known to have reached as far north as Iceland, so it is not surprising to find evidence of their arrival in Shetland as well, dated roughly at about the year 500. Some place names record the presence of places of worship or residence of priests, or *papae* (Norse for priests). Papa Little (little priest's island) and Papa Stour (big priest's island) Papil and the island of Papa near Burra, Papil Bay, Papil Ness and Loch of Papil in Yell all suggest that Celtic Christian influence was widespread throughout Shetland.

Surviving Pictish carved stone slabs sometimes depict both Pictish and Christian symbols. There have been a remarkable number of significant finds of carved stones from both Christian and pre-Christian periods in the islands. Papil in Burra has produced some wonderful finds including both carved cross slabs and carved stone panels from the sides of corner post shrines. The Papil Stone depicts four monks, two carrying books, a lion figure and two extraordinary bird-headed men pecking at a human skull. The Monks' Stone, also from Papil, is a carved side panel from a corner post shrine. Five monks are carved, one on horseback, all apparently travelling towards a cross. Beneath their feet is a row of nine linked spirals, rather like waves, possibly symbolising a sea crossing.

The Bressay Stone, a replica of which now stands where it was found at the churchyard of St Mary's at Cullingsburgh in Bressay, resembles the Papil Stone, having figures of monks with books and also strange beasts. Both stones have elaborate cross designs at the top. A number of carved stones have on occasions in the past been lost or stolen. There is a story of an ancient carved stone being found in North Yell many years ago, but it is now assumed to be lost. Another fine carved stone is recorded from Sandness but that too was lost, possibly stolen. A copy of the design survives. Perhaps they may turn up at some time in the future. New carved stones may yet come to light on excavation sites.

The name 'St Ninian's Isle' may or may not indicate that the saint actually visited Shetland, but the presence of the name at all is significant. In many cases surviving place names indicate the existence of ancient church sites and remains of earlier Christian buildings are sometimes found. A new church would be built on the site of an older one, thus covering all evidence of the previous building, itself perhaps having been constructed over an even earlier one. During excavations in the

The Bressay Stone.

1950s the famous St Ninian's Isle Treasure was discovered along with evidence of an earlier church. Eleven-year-old Douglas Coutts was helping out on the dig. He lifted a large flat stone and a wooden box containing the exquisite silver hoard was revealed. Shetlanders hope one day to see the treasure returned to the islands from Edinburgh where it was taken for safe keeping. In 2000, more of the site was excavated.

Yet another kind of religious site exists in Shetland. On some stacks and remote headlands very small, rectangular outlines can be seen. These, sometimes single, and in other places built in groups, are believed to have been monastic sites. Exactly how and when these sites were used is unknown. Their perilous and precipitous situations make them very difficult to excavate, but a site on an offshore stack in Papa Stour was investigated in the summer of 2000 by a team of archaeologists from Glasgow University. Other sites can be found at the Kame of Isbister, the Birrier at West Sandwick in Yell, Burri Geo at Culswick, Brei Holm and Maiden Stack off Papa Stour and Strandibrough Ness in Fetlar. In the summer of 2000 a pilgrimage was made to three of these sites, to celebrate 2000 years of Christianity.

Boat design and building skills must have improved greatly by this time, judging by increasing evidence of communications between Shetland and mainland Britain. But the real mastery of the sea belongs in the Norse lands to the east, where metal tools and unlimited fine timber led to the birth of the Viking longship. These superb vessels must have created quite an impression when they first appeared on the eastern horizon. It is tantalising to know so little about how their arrival into the relatively peaceful Celtic, Christian Shetland was received. But whether it was gradual or sudden, peaceful or violent, it heralded the end of an era and Shetland was soon to become a very different place.

VIKING SHETLAND

Viking/Norse Shetland began just as a period of warmer climatic conditions arrived in the early ninth century. For some time there had been a general migration 'west over sea' out of Norway and Shetland became a staging post *en route* to Norse colonies in Faroe and Iceland. It is known that in Norway population expansion was creating increasing problems. Inherited land, shared between sons, resulted in ever smaller and less viable units.

Perhaps the last straw that led to mass emigration was King Harald Harfager's unification of Norway, when for the first time he required payment of *scat*, a tax for the upkeep of government, and the provision of service when required for the defence of the realm. Many objected so strongly that they left Norway and settled in many different parts of Europe, including Orkney and Shetland, some reaching Greenland and even America. According to legend, Shetland rebels plotted to overthrow the king, but were foiled when King Harald actually landed in Haroldswick and dealt with them, presumably very effectively.

Until the 1980s evidence of Viking life in Shetland came mainly from excavations at Jarlshof in the extreme south, Papa Stour in the far west and Underhoull in northernmost Unst. More recent Viking excavations at Soterberg and Belmont in Unst and a number of new sites are bringing in new information and already a fuller picture of the period is emerging. Traces of rectangular Viking longhouses contrast with the previous circular and rounded prehistoric building outlines. Evidence of Norse occupation inside earlier buildings suggests that the Norse settlers very sensibly made use of existing houses as well as gradually adding buildings of their own. Field surveys so far indicate over 30 Viking sites in the islands and many more may await discovery.

Daily life in Norse times would have been similar to traditional Shetland crofting life in many ways. The tools and materials available were similar and the seasonal activities of fishing, cultivation, animal husbandry, harvests, pressures of weather, daylight and time are little different. Oats, bere (an old form of barley) and occasionally flax were grown. Sheep, cattle and pigs were kept and apart from metal, soapstone and jewellery, families would have been virtually self-sufficient. Blood feuds and raiding continued as recorded so vividly in the *Orkneyinga Saga*. Viking farmers sowed their cereal seed in the spring, and then set sail to spend their summers raiding coastal communities of northern Britain and its islands, returning in time to harvest the crops in the autumn. But despite the privations, life in general may well have been more comfortable and outward-looking than at any time in the preceding 3000 years.

Scattald, the Old Norse term for commonly held, open, unimproved land, is still used today and sheep can take shelter on whichever side of a hill is in the lee of the prevailing wind and rain. The different flocks mingle with each other as they feed and wander, making it difficult to sort them all out at shearing or lambing time. As with many aspects of traditional Shetland life, such as farming and fishing, a considerable amount of Old Norse vocabulary survives in the local Shetland dialects, and in terms for colours and patterns of colour in sheep fleeces: *moorit*, *shaela* or *sholmit*. A *crø* is an exclosure for sheep, *hentilaget* is a piece of shed wool.

A number of documents reveal tantalising glimpses of life in late Norse times. In *Shetland Documents 1195-1579* John Ballantyne and Brian Smith translate, among others, some wonderful property transfer documents dated from the very early 1400s. One list reads: '6 good beds with pillows of down which had good fringes...a rosary of pearls and silver...woven tapestries and glittering under-hangings and lace covers...jugs, dishes, pots...'. So there were spectacularly rich as well as poor even then. The Norsemen had access to iron, silver and gold, as well as the traditional materials, wood, stone, bone and leather. One kind of stone became very important in Shetland; steatite, or soapstone, had the advantage of being soft enough to carve, when quarried, and hardened later. It was worked in the quarry at Catpund near Cunningsburgh and exported all over Scotland.

A remarkable variety of burial methods have been discovered from the Norse period. The first Norsemen here, judging by their burials, were pagan, worshipping the Norse gods Odin, Thor and Freya and believing in the eternal life in Valhalla. Traditionally they buried their dead with grave goods, to equip them for the next world, a practice which was anathema to Christians. Several Viking graves were uncovered when Sumburgh airport was being constructed. The dialect names for bog cotton, *Luckie's oo*, and thongweed, *Loki's lines*, may have a connection with Loki the Norse god of mischief. Could it be that Viking children were warned off dangerous bogs, or swimming in places where thongweed could tangle round their feet and drown them, by associating them with a dangerous and powerful figure?

Norse incomers must have found Christianity already established in Shetland, and official conversion of the Earldom took place in 995. A bishopric of Orkney and Shetland was established in the eleventh century with a Shetland archdeacon who was based in Tingwall. Following this, churches were built all over the islands. Norse farms traditionally had their own small church. The church built at Tingwall in 1150 was magnificent for its time, larger than those at Papil in Burra and Ireland in Dunrossness, with a nave, chancel and a round tower of 60 or 70 feet high. The old chapel of St Olaf at Lund in Unst dates back to 1200.

Most of Shetland's place names are Norse in origin and are mainly descriptive. Wick, or *vik* in Norse, meaning bay, is found in scores of names like Lerwick, Haroldswick, Levenwick, Otterswick. Farm – *bolstadr* in Norse – gives the 'bister' suffix in Isbister, Fladdabister, and Outrabister. Pasture, or *saetr*, generates the many 'setter' names, such as Dalsetter, Aithsetter, and Culbinsetter. A Faroese philologist, Dr Jakob Jakobsen, carried out a detailed study of Shetland place names between 1893 and 1895, collecting over 50,000 words. His *Place Names of Shetland* was reprinted in 1993 and is still widely read. Ownership or function association generated other names, as did events or legends; they give the islands a very Scandinavian feel and are, in some cases, being translated on road signs, in an effort to assist interpretation and appreciation of the Norse heritage. A map of Viking place names was drawn up in the 1980s by Roy Grönneberg.

Many Shetland family names, too, derive from Norse names, notably those with a 'son' at the end such as Laurenson, Nicolson, Bairnson, Jacobsen, Anderson. The old system of patronymics required that each son took on his father's first name after his own. A girl took on her mother's surname. The language of Norn was Scandinavian and was spoken in Shetland long after the islands became Scottish. In 1774 Orkney minister George Lowe collected a few fragments of Norn in Foula. He wrote, 'nothing remains but a few names of things and two or three remnants of songs which one old man can repeat...'. Shetland, according to geologist Samuel Hibbert in 1822, was full of Norwegian ballads and had been 'from time immemorial, celebrated for its native poets'. Visitors often assume that Shetland shares with Scotland a Gaelic heritage, but this is far from the case. Some Pictish names have survived but Scottish Gaelic place names feature little, except occasionally as modern house names.

NORSE SHETLAND

Eventually Shetland and Orkney were given to Jarl Rognvald of More who became Earl Rognvald in the late 800s. He had several estates in Norway and so gave the islands to his brother Sigurd. The islands were used as a base from which Viking raids were made on territories further south. Shetland was only two days' sail from Norway, which was at that time evolving from free-booting Viking, to more organised and civilised Norse. The Norse estates were united and a separate 'earldom' of Orkney and Shetland was created. A tax, or skat, was paid to the Norwegian crown by all those who had land and all had to abide by laws which were drawn up. The system survived for several hundred years.

Norse rule was based on the *Book of Laws of St Olaf*. A 'Great Foude', or chief magistrate, appointed by the King of Norway, was assisted by a lawman to whom was entrusted the care of the *Book of Laws*. Shetland was divided into a dozen or so smaller units, each under the charge of an Under Foude who presided over local assemblies, and who was assisted by about ten local men of good reputation known as Ranselmen. The islands were visited in turn during each year and locally acceptable representatives called Lawrightmen in each district saw to the gathering of the land tax which was paid in material goods. Each year the Great Foude and his lawman went round every district, holding courts. Once a year the Lawting, main assembly of the parliment, was held at Tingwall; it continued to be held there until 1604: almost 800 years of Norse rule, several hundred years more than the Scots and English rule which has since followed. The ancient place name 'Ting' dates back to the Norse division of Shetland Mainland into manageable units, each with its own court, or 'Thing'. Six of the original names are still in use: Aithsting, Delting, Lunnasting, Nesting, Sandsting and Tingwall.

Udal law prevailed, wherein land was the property of the person who had first claimed and improved it, regardless of social status. If you come to Shetland in January to watch the Up Helly Aa fire festival, look at the very top of the mast of the galley before it is burned, for a severed hand motif. This is said to represent a Viking's hand, cut off and thrown onto the shore ahead of rivals when racing to beach their longships in a new country, the tradition being that the first to touch the land, laid claim to it from then on!

Land was valued in merks, a measurement based on productivity rather than physical size. This meant that however different in size two holdings might be, if they produced the same amount of crops, they had equal merks and equal land tax. Many people believe that this was a far fairer and more democratic system than any devised since.

Around 900 guizers with their burning torches surround the replica Viking
longship (galley) prior to its burning at the Up Helly Aa Festival in Lerwick.

Between 900 and 1100, Viking adventurers sailed ever further. From their
colony on Vinland in Newfoundland and Greenland in the north-west, to Russia
and Byzantium in the east and as far south as Spain and Rhodes, Vikings now
had access to goods from far and wide, whether traded or raided, and Shetland
remained a key northern base for their journeyings. Shetland Museum has lamps
and bowls, fishing weights, Norse bone combs and pins which have survived,
along with tools and items of harness.

The Earldom of Orkney and Shetland created a political and legislative
background to life in the islands and the two islands were closely connected for
several hundred years. In 1194 this changed suddenly. Olaf, a kinsman of the
then Earl, Harald Maddadarson, who had estates in Shetland, plotted with a
band of Shetlanders and Orcadians to overthrow the Norse King Sverre
Sigurdsson. The plot failed. Shetland was removed from the Earldom as a
punishment and annexed to the Norwegian crown. For the next 300 years, the
islands became a Scatland, or tributary province of Norway, overseen by a
'sysselman' or representative of the king.

While Shetland's ties with Norway strengthened, Norway's grip on former
territories to the south was gradually weakening. In an attempt to regain control
over former Viking territories, King Haakon fought King Alexander at the Battle
of Largs in 1263, but neither side won and both remained in dispute. In a treaty
drawn up in 1265, Norway ceded the Isle of Man and the Western Isles to
Scotland in exchange for an annual rent of 400 merks. Orkney and Shetland

were specifically exempted from this. Scotland failed to pay the yearly fee; had it done so, Shetland would still have belonged to Norway. But this was not to be.

Between 1200 and 1300 the climate deteriorated, greatly restricting the Vikings' northern sea routes to Iceland and Greenland. Ice floes would have blocked access to the north-west and increasingly bad weather would have restricted sailing ventures. The severe conditions must have had an impact on Shetland harvests and rural life and prayers may well have been said in the old churches in Shetland for a return to better weather and crops. Norse control over the seas was still strong, but other states and nations were edging into the trade and travel picture too. Fascinating and colourful stories from this period were told for generations and eventually written up in the fourteenth-century *Orkneyinga Saga*. Shetland's oldest surviving document is a letter written in 1299 by local lawmen, enquiring about allegations made by a woman from Papa Stour. The woman, Ragnhild Simunsdatter, had accused Thorvald Thoresson, then Sysselman in Shetland, of dirty dealing and claimed that he was a 'Judas'.

In 1319 Norway united with Sweden and in 1397 both united with Denmark. By the fifteenth century Shetland was divided up into five different land categories: Crown estates or Kingslands, Lordship lands of Shetland, udal lands, bishopric lands and kirklands, leading to complications and conflicts; one set of families rising to power, wheeling and dealing to maintain it and eventually being eclipsed by new ones. This period has been referred to as 'The Orkney and Shetland game of Monopoly'. Land ownership and sale can still be a contentious issue to this day.

A new method of preserving fish in barrels of salt was discovered which led to a big increase in fishing by the Germans who began to build up vast fortunes. Agents came to live in Shetland and built houses and trading booths, or 'böds', by the shore. Goods from far and wide were brought to Shetland and traded either for cash, or for butter, woollen garments, fish and livestock. Local people must have looked forward to the trading season and these booths, Shetland's earliest shops, were built by successions of traders over the next few centuries.

In the mid fifteenth century King Christian I of Denmark and Norway realised that there was little chance of retrieving the Scottish debts unless by force, which his own lack of funds prevented, and a strategic marriage was arranged as a substitute. In 1468 a marriage treaty was drawn up, setting at 60,000 florins the dowry required for Margaret his daughter to marry the young Prince James, shortly to become King James III of Scotland. This effectively cancelled the Scottish debt and placed Denmark 10,000 florins in debt instead. Two thousand florins were paid promptly, the remaining 8000 were to be paid in due course, and Shetland was pledged by way of a surety until the debt was settled. All subsequent efforts by Denmark to do this were deliberately ignored and sidestepped by Scottish officials, who thus skilfully enabled Scotland to retain the Shetland islands to the present day. There are still some in Shetland who feel strongly that the islands should be restored to Denmark.

Shetland was administered in much the same way as it had been under Norse control for almost another century, with Bergen as the most influential source of control. But eventually, things began to change. During this time, the traditional Shetland trading links with Bergen were shifting in favour of direct trading connections with Germany and later, Holland. The Hanseatic League dominated Shetland trade for many years. It had its own laws and conventions and on the whole was used and appreciated by the islanders. When changes in trading laws were introduced by the English king and parliament, the new requirements were largely ignored by Shetland and for many years things went on as they had done before. Norse influence is still much talked about in Shetland. Scottish influence spread only slowly, as the islands held on to their Norse laws and language for a long while. Norse manuscripts relating to Shetland were still being written several hundred years after the islands became effectively Scottish.

SHETLAND FROM 1500

An interesting insight into this time came when the foundations of a large stone building were revealed during an archeological excavation at Kebister, which proved to be a *teind*, or tithe barn, belonging to Henry Phankouth, Archdeacon of Shetland in 1500. The report which was published later is well worth reading by those who have an interest in this period.

The reformation of Shetland churches in 1560 was handled by Adam Bothwell, Bishop of Orkney, and Jerome Cheyne, the Archdeacon of Shetland. The Sinclair family too held powerful positions in the islands. James V's illegitimate son, Lord Robert Stewart, was granted the Earldom and Crown lands of Orkney and Zetland in 1564 by Mary, Queen of Scots, his half sister. Robert Stewart had a big house built at Sumburgh, the ruin of which was seen by Walter Scott on a visit to Shetland. He was inspired to write *The Pirate* and named the ruin 'Jarlshof', and the site has been known by that name ever since. In 1571 Robert Stewart delegated his position of Foude, or chief magistrate, to Laurence Bruce of Cultmalindie, a disaster for Shetland by all accounts. Complaints flooded in, resulting in the arrival of two royal commissioners who interviewed 760 people at Tingwall. But after a brief spell in prison, Bruce returned to Shetland, a far from reformed character. He built Muness Castle in Unst and many a tale of his ill-treatment of islanders can be read in the island's interpretive centre.

Shortly after Mary granted the earldom to Robert Stewart, she conferred on James Hepburn, Earl of Bothwell, her third husband, the title of Duke of Orkney. His enemies were numerous and when things began to get hot, he tried to take refuge in Orkney. This failed, so he sailed to Shetland, but, learning that he was being followed, he struck a deal with a Dutchman, Geert Hemelingk, who took him to Norway in his ship *The Pelican*. In a dramatic escape, the ship took a devious course out of the north mouth of Lerwick harbour, thus luring the

Muness Castle, Unst.

pursuing ship, *The Unicorn*, onto a dangerous rock, which has borne its name ever since. Bothwell finally arrived in Denmark, but past crimes caught up with him; his attempts to win favour failed and he was imprisoned. Bothwell died in prison and his corpse remained a gruesome visitor attraction until only a few decades ago, when his bones were finally buried.

The Spanish were at war with England in 1588, and after the Battle of the Armada a number of Spanish ships, attempting to return to Spain round Scotland, were wrecked on the Shetland coast. Stories of Spanish survivors still exist in various parts of Shetland. Some concern the building of chapels of thanksgiving. One records a Spanish ship dragging her anchor until her prow ground a huge, glass-smooth groove in the rough cliff face near Islesburgh which can still be seen. Another tale tells of a party of Spaniards landing, executing and burying a shipmate, then returning to sea. A Spanish supply ship from the Armada, the *El Gran Grifon*, was wrecked on Fair Isle and an account of the fate of the survivors was found among archives in Madrid. The short but fascinating piece graphically describes the physical appearance and meagre existence of the islanders of the time.

Robert Stewart handed the lordship over to his son Patrick and Earl Patrick Stewart took up his new position in 1593. He ordered the building of Scalloway Castle, reputedly using forced labour, where he lived in grand style by comparison with the Shetlanders. The court, held for so many years in Tingwall, was moved to Scalloway Castle. Experts differ over the degree to which Earl Patrick's reputation was manipulated by jealous contemporaries, but massive amounts of

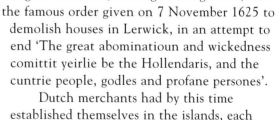

land and wealth were certainly accumulated. The *Court Book of Shetland 1602-4* records heavy fines imposed for minor offences and the confiscation of land and property. There was public anger at the increasing number of injustices and in 1609 Earl Patrick was arrested and his lands confiscated. In 1611 an Act of the Scottish privy council banned the use of Norse laws; only the newly revised Scottish laws were to be used. The old *Book of Laws* has been lost. After a failed attempt by influential landlords to regain their lands by force, both Patrick and his father were executed in Edinburgh in 1615. Sadly there were plenty of powerful clergy and landowners to continue and even increase exploitation and oppression of the islanders for generations to come.

Growing concern about the lawlessness of Scotland's poor led to resolutions to educate the people in the scriptures and to increase literacy throughout the population. A number of wealthy islanders appear to have had private tutors for their children, but an Act was passed in 1616, instructing the establishment of schools in all the parishes of Scotland. The Act had no powers of enforcement and little seems to have happened in Shetland as a result. Fragmentary references to schools appear in records, but nothing formal was organised for the best part of another century.

Gordon Donaldson's edited transcript of the *Court Book of Shetland 1615-29* makes enthralling reading. Cases of theft, gruesome accounts of assault and murder, the settling of disputes, unpaid debts, rent recovery, land ownership and details of inheritances, create vivid images of the life of the period. The best-known extracts concern cases of alleged witchcraft, leading to the gallows, and the famous order given on 7 November 1625 to demolish houses in Lerwick, in an attempt to end 'The great abominatioun and wickedness comittit yeirlie be the Hollendaris, and the cuntrie people, godles and profane persones'.

Dutch merchants had by this time established themselves in the islands, each with his own corner of suitable sheltered natural harbour and piece of land, for which they paid rent to the local landowner. In the stone trading booths which they built, various local goods such as knitted socks and caps, butter, fresh meat and eggs were traded for tobacco, spirits, cloth and meal. A number of their elaborate gravestones can still be seen in a few of the older graveyards. The riches reaped by the trade in salt herring helped to fund the Dutch East Indies ventures and Amsterdam was said to be 'built on herring

Window detail from
Muness Castle, Unst.

bones'. Claes Jansen, a Dutch sea captain, was buried at St Mary's, at Cullingsburgh, Bressay, in 1636 and the tombstone can still be seen. His ship had struggled into Bressay Sound after a dreadful crossing from Mozambique, plagued by gales and disease. He died the following day.

These were times of great unrest in Europe and Shetland felt the ripples from battles and sea chases over many years as the focus of the fighting switched between the English, French, Dutch and Spanish. In 1640, four Spanish frigates surprised four Dutch men-of-war in Bressay Sound as they were waiting for a fleet to arrive from the Indies. A ferocious battle ensued and several ships were sunk. A cannon from one of them was dredged up in 1922 and now stands in Fort Charlotte in Lerwick.

In 1653 a Dutch East Indiaman, *Lastdrager*, was wrecked off Yell and in 1664 the *Kennermerland* was wrecked off the Out Skerries. Visit the Pier House exhibition in Whalsay to picture the busy scenes of the day. A fascinating glimpse into the lives of the poorer people at the time is provided by a young Dutchman, Jan Camphuijs, who survived the wreck of the *Lastdrager* and was washed up on the coast of Yell. He was given shelter by an old man and his son who shared what little they had without hesitation. He describes a large stone being rolled towards the fire as a stool and records how an oxhide bag carrying all the food they had was taken down and offered to him.

Shetlanders benefitted from their Dutch trading contacts and there must have been considerable resistance to the growing interference from the British government, for whom the Dutch were the enemy. National government concern about the Dutch led to the building of Fort Charlotte in Lerwick in 1665. The Dutch got their own back by burning the fort to the ground, along with part of the town, and hostilities continued for years. After 1667 Shetland's Scottish land tax was collected by the Commissioners of Supply, consisting of the landowning and power-wielding élite of the day, who also decided how it should be spent. It must have been agonising for local folk, accustomed to their seasonal friendly relations with the Dutch, to stand and watch while more of their ships were burned in 1677. Token storming of Scalloway Castle by Lerwick gentry is chronicled from the period. Troubles mounted up as the fisheries themselves began to decline and, as if this wasn't bad enough, French pirates began to

The south gate into Fort Charlotte, Lerwick.

make raids on Shetland, causing considerable disruption to trade. To add to the general misery, smallpox broke out, there were several bad harvests and serious famine hit the islands in the 1690s.

An Act for the Settling of Schools was passed in 1696, which enabled a fresh effort to be made towards the educating of the young people of the time. Some wonderful characters and individuals committed themselves to campaigning and working towards the setting up of schools in many parts of Shetland, sometimes helped and sometimes hindered by the Scottish Society for the Promotion of Christian Knowledge (SSPCK), the local presbytery and the Church authorities in Scotland. Shetlanders, despite (or maybe because of) their poverty and wretched circumstances, famine, disease and general suffering, proved to be very keen to see their children learn. Astonishing sums were sometimes raised in areas where money was desperately scarce. There is a vivid insight into this period in *A Vehement Thirst after Knowledge* by John Graham; particularly inspiring is the story of Happyhansel School in Walls.

In 1700 there were developments in the Christian arena between Presbyterian and Episcopalian factions within the church. A commission of ministers was sent to Shetland by the General Assembly of the Church of Scotland. Among these was the Revd John Brand, who wrote in an account of his visit (a wonderful, if not wholly accurate account of Shetland at the turn of the eighteenth century): 'The people are generally discreet and civil, not so rustic and clownish as would be expected in such a place of the world...'!

More wars in Europe affected Shetland and its trading patterns. During the War of the Spanish Succession, a fleet of French warships came on a large fleet of Dutch herring busses and cruisers in Lerwick harbour; 100 Dutch ships were burned.

In 1707 the Act of Union between Scotland and England sealed the fate of Shetland. Now, as an economic part of Great Britain, it would never return to Denmark. With the introduction of a stinging tax on imported salt, the keystone of the Hanseatic fish trade, money no longer flowed into the hands of Shetlanders and the era of Shetland-Holland alliance was over. As this resulted in removing the only source of income for the people to pay their rents, some lairds began to take over the role of merchant themselves. One of the most adventurous was Thomas Gifford of Busta, many of whose letters have survived and form a valuable insight into the problems and ideas of the time. Many of the gentry disapproved of the idea of actually handling money and dealing directly with the common populace!

Potatoes were introduced to Shetland in 1730 and other agricultural experiments and improvements were set up. The Greenland whaling began in the same year, attracting hundreds of men away from the islands for months at a time during the season, away from the drudgery and poverty, where even if you worked hard to improve your croft or your lot, the rent would simply be increased, as often as not, to reflect the added value. Lairds were much opposed to their tenants going to the whaling as each man who left was one less to join their fishing fleet.

Gifford built up markets in Spain for hard dried, lightly salted cod and ling, a trade which lasted into the next century. More Shetlanders turned to trading, some buying large ships and selling fish widely throughout Europe. The rise of the Shetland merchants had begun. Smuggling became widespread on these voyages. The Revd John Mill travelled to Shetland in 1754 and kept a detailed diary of his life as a minister in the islands. The diary makes very interesting reading and includes some vivid accounts of Mill's view of the depravity of the time.

The Greenland whaling was building up by 1750 and nearer to home, the Haaf fishery was beginning to gain momentum. Gradually, as well as owning the land and the crofts, lairds owned the boats, fishing gear and homes, and also the shops which provided every essential item for the survival of their tenants. Large families were encouraged, to breed more young fishermen, and extra land to feed the growing population was taken out of the hills. People worked all hours to catch fish, weave cloth and make butter simply to exchange it in the shop for the basic necessities of life. This was the infamous 'truck system'.

New smallpox epidemics killed large numbers of people, reducing the rise in population to 15,000 by 1755. It was still early days in preventive medicine. Links with the Scottish mainland were improving and after several years of a limited and irregular service, the first regular post began to travel between Lerwick and Leith, taken by the open packet ship *Isabel* on 6 May 1758, and the service continued for two years. Today E-mails fly between Shetland and the rest of the world every second of the day and night. In those days a journey to Aberdeen could take days or weeks, if the weather was bad.

By 1760 inoculation against smallpox had been developed, but a single dose cost more then than a whole year's wages for many. In 1761, 200 people died and severe frosts and loss of cattle added to the suffering. It was then that a remarkable Shetlander, John Williamson, developed a cure of his own for smallpox. He treated infected matter with peat smoke and buried it in camphor. A tiny amount was inserted under the skin and the cut wrapped in cabbage leaves. According to the medical practitioner in Lerwick at the time, 'Johnnie Notions', as he came to be called, never lost a patient.

While ever-larger boats were plying between Shetland and mainland Scotland, smaller sixereens, six-oared open boats, were working the Far Haaf (the open sea), rowing for 40 miles and more out to the west to catch ling. Boats from all over Shetland were working flat out between mid May and mid August. All round the coast, on gently shelving pebble beaches, especially in the north and west, fishing stations were set up where the split fish were dried and stacked. The men lived in small huts or lodges. Sometimes artificial beaches were built; stones were laid up on the grass until there was enough area of 'shingle' to lie the drying fish. Productivity rose dramatically and in 1763 a new method of curing fish was pioneered by Bruce of Symbister.

By 1770 Lerwick was growing fast, as was the population, which had begun to increase since the smallpox was brought under control. The industrial revolution began to get underway in Shetland in 1780 with a number of experimental ventures undertaken. Flax was grown for linen, copper was mined and kelp burning was tried along suitable stretches of coastline; the sale of the rich ash augmented many incomes. It was hard work for little reward and the labourers may well have stopped to rest their aching backs and gaze out to sea where the Haaf fishing was bringing in record catches. There are still remains of kelp-burning pits in places. Despite all the innovation and change, repeated bad harvests created high levels of poverty. George Lowe was commissioned to travel through and report on Shetland in 1774 for a writer called Pennant who had just completed an Orkney account. Lowe's Shetland writings were finally published in 1879, 85 years after his death.

By 1790 the Lodberries, small stone warehouses built out from the shore, were being constructed in Lerwick, trading and commerce having taken over a large proportion of the town's foreshore. For the first time, some Shetland merchants became richer than the landowners and tension between them began to mount. This dynamic time saw the production of one of Shetland's most important documents, A *Statistical Account of Shetland*, compiled from questionnaires sent to every parish minister in the islands. In 1809 Arthur Edmundston wrote his *Views of the Ancient and Present State of the Zetland Islands*.

The Napoleonic Wars saw an increased demand for seamen in the British navy. Captains knew that Shetlanders were superb sailors and despite the fact that the quota of 100 men (and more) was regularly met, sailed their men-of-war into every voe, lay in wait and resorted to the vilest of deceptions and brutalities in order to 'press' more and more men and even boys into service. Around the shores of the islands in 1810 the press gang were in action, sailing stealthily into bays and anchoring offshore, ready to launch small boats and capture as many

Old fishing station, Stenness, Eshaness.

young skilled Shetland
seamen as they could
surprise. Men were taken
from their own weddings,
boys taken out of school.
Stories abound of incidents
with the press gang; escapes,
hiding places, women carrying
food and provisions across the
hills and along dangerous cliff
paths in the dark to their menfolk.
Now and again successful tricks were
played against the officers by local men,

Shetland Croft Museum, Boddam.

betrayed by unpopular landlords who knew which
men were home from the fishing and which were not.

Samuel Hibbert, a geology student, arrived in Shetland in 1817 where he
found chromite in commercial quantities. He explored Shetland thoroughly and
in 1820 published a geological account of Shetland, complete with a colour map
and then in 1822 published A *Description of the Shetland Islands*. A wonderful
collection of extracts from his and other historical writings can be found in
Derek Flinn's *Travellers in a Bygone Shetland*.

There were developments on Shetland's spiritual front at this time. The
first Baptist Church was built in Dunrossness; Methodist preachers arrived a few
years later and a number of other denominations added to the variety of
Christian witness in the islands.

In the 1820s the first tenants were forcibly removed from their crofts to
poorer land. *Rigga rendal*, or runrigs, which had fed families for a thousand years
were ploughed up into large fields where fodder crops were grown. Cattle and
vast numbers of sheep grazed over traditional croftlands. This was the start of
the infamous Clearances. Sandlodge and Sumburgh farms were laid out.
Landowners, no longer able to make their fortunes through the fishing, for
which their tenants provided the labour, looked to sheep-raising as a more
lucrative business. Over a quarter of the population of Shetland left the islands,
most of them in the second half of the century, settling far away, often in New
Zealand, America and Canada. Some merchants began to buy fish directly from
local fishermen and lairds were said to keep watch on their small fleets, to
prevent private sales of fish.

Shetland fishermen ventured as far as Greenland and Norway's North Cape
looking for cod. Improved boats with decks enabled the men to split and salt the
fish on board. Landlords no longer controlled the fishing scene and income
increasingly went to the fishermen themselves. Chromite quarrying opened in
Unst, and Hay and Ogilvy were established as shipbuilders, from which grew the

twentieth-century Hay and Co. a business success story. The Shetland Bank was set up in 1821, producing its own notes, an indication of just how much money there was around by this time, at least in the coffers of a few. The Haaf fishing was still providing catches for processing at the fishing stations at Fethaland, Stenness, Gloup and Haaf Gruney. In 1832, disaster struck and 105 men were lost in one deadly gale, while out at sea. The boats afforded no shelter from the weather and there was nothing in the way of the safety equipment and rescue services we take for granted now.

In 1832 the Reform Bill was passed, giving some Shetlanders a right to vote; and in the same year communications to the mainland improved when the paddlesteamer *Sovereign*, the first steamer service to Shetland, began fortnightly summer calls into Lerwick. Shetland's first newspaper, *The Shetland Journal*, was launched. By the 1840s the Scottish landlords were beginning to derive more income from farms than from fishing and ceased trading in fish. Crofters could no longer sell fish to help pay the rent. Many moved to other districts or emigrated. Those first emigrants had no chance of returning. Now, many generations later, more and more of their descendants visit Shetland in search of their roots. Every 25 years a special 'Hamefarin' event is held to welcome them back. The Prime Minister of New Zealand in 2000 was Helen Clark, whose family originated from Cuckron in Stromfirth. She follows in the footsteps of emigrant and teacher Sir Robert Stout; born in Lerwick in 1844, he became Prime Minister of New Zealand in 1884.

The autumn of 1846 was the first of four years of failure of the potato crop, reducing the islanders to deeper levels of famine and poverty than ever before. Relief was sent up from Edinburgh in the form of supplies of meal in return for work building stone walls, or 'dykes', and also proper roads, for which there was a growing demand. The work was to be supervised by the army. All transport had previously been by sea around the coastal settlements. Overland journeys across the hills were made on foot or by pony. Over 100 miles of 'meal roads', as they came to be known, were built and in Papa Stour you can still see part of one. Many have disappeared under modern routes.

Gas lighting was introduced to Lerwick in 1856 and new technologies began to transform the traditional ways. A Lerwick man, Arthur Anderson, who started as a beach boy drying fish in Lerwick, proved a dynamic and creative businessman and philanthropist. He became the first Shetlander M.P. and made a great

Mill stone.

Contemporary painting of Arthur Anderson's fishing station at Vaila in the 1840s.

impact on the lives and fortunes of Shetland people, the effects of which linger still. He devised an improved system for drying fish, jointly set up the P&O shipping company, started Shetland's first newspaper and in 1862, perhaps most importantly of all for Shetland, founded the Anderson Institute, a first-class school for Shetland's children.

In the same year, more Clearances took place, some families moving to Orkney but many opting to go further afield. In just ten years from 1871 close on 5000 people emigrated from Shetland. An attempt was made at last to bring relief to Shetland's poor and the unfair system of the lairds' shops was examined by the Truck Commission. The landmark Education Act was passed in 1872 requiring all children to attend school. Schools were built all through the islands, replacing the previous private and church schools.

In 1881 disaster struck the fishing communities again when another 58 fishermen were lost in a single night, this time off Yell. There were other smaller losses and gradually the Haaf fishery began to come to an end. The communities had been devastated by the deaths of so many young, active men, and some families had lost all their menfolk, leaving women and children destitute. In 1883 the Napier Commission visited Shetland to investigate the conditions of crofters. The reports made by Shetlanders were so grievous that they led to the setting up of the Crofters' Holdings Act of 1886. This gave crofters security of tenure, compensation for improvements, and a new, fair rent. In 1889 the Local Government (Scotland) Act established Zetland County Council as a representative body, to be elected by the Shetlanders themselves. This period marked a turning point in the security and welfare of the islanders.

A new insight into the times became possible as photography arrived in the islands. Prints reflect contemporary Shetland with views of people at work, crowds of steam drifters, rural scenes, villages with thatch-roofed houses and women with heavy 'kishies', or baskets, strapped to their backs, hands busy knitting while they walked. The new computer database in Shetland Museum enables you to select photographs from their enormous collection, glimpse life in hundreds of Shetland scenes and even buy a print to take home.

Woman knitting, with a kishie on her back.

The Shetland Pony Stud was established in 1890, reflecting the respect with which the breed was regarded.

For some time the herring fishery had been expanding with dramatic increases in catches of herring. Herring are a migrating species and in the summer months, move into Shetland waters. Alistair Goodlad's *Shetland Fishing Saga* covers this period very thoroughly. There were hundreds of herring boats and boat-building and repair businesses expanded rapidly. Herring stations multiplied along the Lerwick seafront during the great Shetland herring boom.

The Public Health Act of 1897 enabled a sanitary inspector in Lerwick to put assistants to work in every district to report on the conditions of houses and people's health. The Gilbert Bain Hospital was built in the same year.

THE LAST HUNDRED YEARS

By 1900 the herring fishery was prospering while the cod fishing was coming to an end. In 1905 the sail fleet is said to have peaked, with 1000 sail boats and nearly 300 steam drifters landing their catches at an incredible 170 fishing stations spread around the coast of Shetland from Boddam in the south to Baltasound in Unst in the north. A. Halcrow's *Sail Fishermen of Shetland*, reprinted in 1994, captures some of the atmosphere of this period.

The Smallowners (Scotland) Act passed in 1911 gave the Board of Agriculture power to establish smallholdings, with or without the landlord's consent. The current of reform and redistribution which had been in full flow was interrupted by the First World War. Shetland played a strategic role in the British defences. Great guns were built on Vementry and Bressay to guard the most important approaches to Shetland and large numbers of servicemen arrived to man the many military locations around the islands. Equally large numbers of islanders left for service abroad and many never returned. There were especially devastating losses on the Somme, with some families losing several members.

In 1919 the Land Settlement (Scotland) Act came in, giving the Board powers of compulsory purchase. In 1923 Veensgarth farm and a number of others in Shetland were broken up and the 19 new holdings and ten enlargements virtually restored the valley to the state it had been in 100 years before. This was revolutionary change for the better in the fortunes of the ordinary folk of the islands. It was hundreds of years since the last period of true independence had been enjoyed on the land.

There was an outbreak of scarlet fever in 1930. TB was still present in Shetland, but islanders' health and welfare generally were improving. Mains electricity, generated by a small diesel power station, was introduced in 1932, almost 80 years since the introduction of mains gas in Lerwick. Shetlanders saw their first aeroplane, which landed in 1933, followed in 1934 by the first commercial flight carrying passengers.

In 1939 the Second World War broke out and Shetland again assumed national importance. Once more servicemen flooded the islands and large numbers of Shetlanders left to serve in the forces. Casualties, despite being fewer in number than in the First World War, were, as before, higher in relation to the local population than anywhere else in the UK. Massive military construction work took place, building military air strips, barracks, various sea defences, air-raid shelters and gun emplacements. Public access to certain areas was restricted and the islands braced themselves for several years of wartime conditions. Echo sounders and Decca navigation systems were introduced at about this time, which were to have a major impact on the fishing.

A new chapter in relations with Norway opened with the 'Shetland Bus' resistance network, described later in the Scalloway section, page 189. Every Shetland family has a story to tell about the war and a full account of this period has still to be written. Shetland in many ways benefitted economically during the war and when the troops finally left, there was a period of real hardship.

By 1942, 63 miles of road had been constructed in Shetland, effectively bringing to an end the old pattern of communities linked only by sea. Some hamlets still without road access began to shrink, as first one, then another family left to live somewhere a little more accessible to the road network. The North of Scotland Hydro Electric Board was formed in 1946 for 'promoting social improvement and economic development...throughout the Highlands and Islands' by providing electrical power. The Board took over the old generating station, running it for nine years before building a new diesel power station out at Gremista. By 2000, there were over 1000 miles of supply lines in Shetland, compared to just ten in 1947!

Russian and Polish trawlers began to fish off Shetland. Lobster fishing increased significantly during the 1950s. In 1955 work began on a major redevelopment of Lerwick's waterfront and harbour facilities; a plan which had taken many years to draw up. Construction of a covered fish market was begun in 1959 and in 1960 the whole completed works were opened by Queen Elizabeth. Herring and mackerel processing, consisting of gutting and packing in salt, had been a familiar industry for decades but refrigeration in the 1960s created an expansion in fish processing. In 1965 the first Norwegian purse-seine netters arrived in Shetland. Almost every new development to the earlier ways of fishing met with resistance from the old guard; but the purse-seiners went further than usual, often catching 100 tons at a single cast in contrast to the five tons caught by a Shetland drifter in one night. Shetland's fishermen could not have survived against this degree of competition. By 1967 Shetland had its own purse-seiner and others followed.

There were some very different types of boats operating off Shetland during the late 1960s. They were oil survey vessels, testing the seabed and the geological formations below for the presence of oil. The increase in shipping around the islands began to present safety problems and in 1969 VHF radio sets were installed in the harbour office and the pilot boat in Lerwick. The pelagic (fish that swim in shoals of the same species, e.g. herring and mackerel) fishery took off, benefitting from continuing developments in catching technology, and other countries joined in the race. Fish-processing factories were doing well but by the early 1970s indications of over-fishing were becoming obvious. The herring stocks were so low that a total ban on catching them was imposed between 1977 and 1983.

New technology, as well as transforming fish catching, entered the world of accounting in the 1970s. The Computer Age arrived with the introduction to the Shetland Council's finance department of a Burroughs B 80 system which involved pre-programmed sheets with magnetic strips. MacDonald Douglas micro-computers were introduced in 1979 and they in turn were replaced. The current system consists of AS 400 PCs and covers all departments. Computers eventually entered the machine-knitting arena and designs can be typed onto a screen at one end of the process and emerge in a finished garment at the other.

Oil was eventually discovered to the east of Shetland and the oil boom which hit soon afterwards had a major impact on the course of development in the islands. Shetland had been experiencing a period of relative economic well-being just prior to the discovery of oil. Only a short time before this, things had looked pretty bleak, and an oil bonanza then would have been instantly welcomed. But coming when it did in 1971, there was considerable suspicion of its likely consequences. Traditional industries of knitwear and fishing had been helped to new levels of profitability with changes in economic support and marketing. A boom in the sale of knitwear to France made a real impact on the income in that sector; Shetland knitwear had become fashionable. The revival in the economy was paralleled by a growing confidence within the community.

Then local government reorganisation came in 1969. The first proposals for Shetland suggested that the islands be merged with a large part of mainland Scotland. This was vigorously and successfully opposed and Shetland along with Orkney and the Western Isles achieved all-purpose status in 1975. Thus they secured the powers of both tiers of local government, regional as well as district. The stakes rose, with opportunist incomers on the prowl for speculative land acquisition. These were exciting times and key local figures steered Shetland towards one of the best deals ever achieved with oil companies by a small community. The Zetland County Council Act was passed in 1974 and enabled the council to have greater control over new developments in the 'first phase of oil'. Shetland MP Jo Grimond was instrumental in driving the project through parliament. Land for an oil terminal was acquired and development plans drawn up. The Council drove a hard bargain with the oil companies, persuading them to contribute to the cost of port infrastructure and a disturbance fund, as well as fixing income per barrel from oil and agreeing on high standards of care of the environment through which the pipeline construction would pass.

SOTEAG (Shetland Oil Terminal Enviromental Advisory Group) was set up to monitor the impact of oil activities on the environment. Construction camps complete with self-contained catering and leisure facilities for up to 7000 workers were installed at Toft and Firth, with built-in safeguards for removing all buildings and restoring the land to agricultural condition after the phase was over. The oil terminal produces its own electricity from a power station built at Sullom Voe. It is the largest building in Shetland and has a capacity of 125 megawatts fuelled with waste gas from the oil fields, as well as diesel. The hordes of workers and incomers brought with them new foods and locals still chuckle about the courgettes and celery, green peppers and other 'unken' foods that 'cam in wi da oily men.'

By the end of the decade the 'oil invasion' was in full swing with the construction of the oil terminal, and new air and marine infrastructure. The oil companies courted popular approval and their funds supported many local projects. High wages paid for very basic work such as cleaning and bed making were tempting people out of their previous jobs and even luring older teenagers away from school. Skilled workers – electricians, bakers, plumbers and men and women from all walks of life – left their jobs in droves, heading for the terminal and the money! Shetland infrastructure rapidly began to feel the pinch and soon businesses were having to close. The island population swelled by 35 per cent with the families of oil workers from the south and the demand for new housing and schools, better roads and health facilities grew more urgent. Housing schemes for oil staff at Brae and Mossbank necessitated enlargement of local schools.

The advent of oil didn't end the use of other energy sources. Commercial extraction of peat, despite some misgivings, was introduced in the 1980s, and became widespread in Shetland. Between the wars 'windy lights', or small wind-driven generators, were installed privately across much of Shetland. Private diesel generators produced power for outlying islands and private homes until very recently and many people still hang onto their generators in case of winter power cuts on the mains. Only a few solar panels have so far been installed in new buildings despite the latitude with its long hours of summer daylight. The Council built a Waste to Energy plant during 1998 which supplies hot water to a district heating scheme. This sells and distributes piped hot water to a number of houses and other properties in Lerwick, including the hospital.

The first roll-on-roll-off ferry, *St Clair*, arrived at Holmsgarth terminal on Tuesday 5 April 1977. In the same year Radio Shetland went on air for the first time and has since become something of an institution. People see the radio as 'their' service, not the BBC's! There are regular news reports and special programmes on music, wildlife and archaeology. There are interviews and outside broadcast reports as well as opportunities for new poets and writers to have a wider audience. Shetland also has its own commercial independent radio station, Shetland Independent Broadcasting Corporation (SIBC), which went on air in the 1980s after a long campaign by its founder, Ian Anderson. Some Lerwick shops leave their radios tuned in to this programme all day and many of them use it for advertising. There are frequent breaks for weather and local and national news items.

The 1980s were a time of peak activity. Computers were used in schools for the first time. Many social and economic changes in Shetland had been predicted. A total of 9000 oil-related jobs had been created. The oil terminal was officially opened by the Queen in 1982. New airport facilities were completed at Sumburgh, and at Sullom Voe the major construction activity of the 1970s came to an end, resulting in an increase in unemployment, and the population fell. However, the Council made use of its oil revenues to help develop the traditional sectors, as well as supporting new business ventures. Thus by the end of the 1980s the population had stabilised and many new jobs had been created. In particular, fish farming was proving very successful and grew from nothing in 1983, to a major source of income by the end of the decade. Agriculture and fisheries also benefitted from new investment. One unexpected bonus from the ending of the construction phase was the 'Grand Scran' or scavenge, when the workers' camps were dismantled and all the materials were gathered and carted off for use on crofts and around the homes and gardens of hundreds of local people. Vans, lorries, tractors and trailers made many a sortie, even across the sea to other islands before the available wood, metal, fittings and prefabricated sections had all gone.

Tourism was expanding and a wide range of new leisure facilities and interpretive attractions appeared. Individual craft businesses and small knitwear and jewellery firms were helped to promote their products and combine forces on Shetland stands at some of Europe's major trade fairs. Oil reached a turning point of activity in its 'fourth phase' and from this point on, a gradual decrease in jobs and services began. One benefit of incomers who stayed was their visitors, who seldom returned home without buying Shetland knitwear and other craft items. Shetland's unique wool and knitting designs received a boost with the registering of a trade mark and new designs were tried, as well as the traditional Fair Isle and Unst lace patterns. Young knitters excelled themselves in the college knitwear courses and showed their goods far and wide.

There was a significant oil spill in 1978 when within a month of the oil terminal opening to tankers, the *Esso Bernicia* lost 1174 tons of bunker oil into the sea. Some 4000 seabirds died and the seashore from North Brae to Fethaland was polluted. Ironically the most serious oil-spill disaster before 2000 was the wrecking of the *Braer* in 1993, a vessel which had nothing to do with Sullom Voe at all, but was simply passing by the islands. The ship broke her back on Garth's Ness near Sumburgh and sank, releasing 86,000 tons of oil. The emergency response arrangements were initially hampered by an almost total blocking of transport into the islands by media hacks, competing for disaster images and copy. Nineteen days of almost continuous gale-force winds followed the wrecking of the *Braer*, resulting in far less coastal damage than might otherwise have been the case.

Many questions remain unanswered about aspects of the accident; the condition of the ship, the suitability of the crew, the possible consequences and nature of the oil dispersants used. Many claims for compensation had still not been settled by 2001. It was seven years after the *Braer* that shellfish harvesting restrictions were lifted on the inshore areas where the spilled oil was believed to have collected and contaminated the seabed. There was a call for a special tug to be kept in Shetland in case of future tanker breakdowns at sea. It was several years before the government agreed to fund a suitable tug in the Northern Isles during the winter months. After the *Braer* oil spill, Shetland played a key role in European initiatives to tighten control over maritime safety.

Many of the gloomy predictions of the negative impact of oil on the Shetland way of life proved groundless. Many newcomers contributed to the revival of music and language. Improved roads and transport facilities increased mobility and people travelled about the islands for enjoyment as well as necessity.

Arts and leisure centres attracted growing numbers and sports activity increased. Teams attended the Inter Island Games. Community centres were built with the 'oil moneys' as well as extra support facilities for the elderly and disadvantaged. New groups and clubs sprang up and local community history projects gathered momentum. The Council's Leisure and Recreation department assisted the visits of many theatre groups, music groups and orchestras to the islands. Shetland Amenity Trust was founded to further interpretive, conservation and environmental work and the Shetland Arts Trust was established a few years later.

The 1990s saw yet another local government reorganisation. All the larger authorities were split into many smaller ones, but Shetland remained largely unchanged, retaining all-purpose status. Fire and police services continued as before but water and drainage services were hived off into separate quangos. In 1999 the first Scottish Parliament for 300 years was established and Shetland elected Tavish Scott as its first MSP. Jim Wallace, the former Westminster MP for the North Isles, became the MSP for Orkney and Deputy Leader of the Coalition. Alistair Carmichael became the Westminster MP for Orkney and Shetland. A number of government departments have offices in Shetland, such as Customs and Excise, Employment, Social Security and Agriculture and Fisheries.

Since the early 1980s, a steadily increasing impact of European Union assistance and support has been felt within the islands, despite the overwhelming rejection of entry into the EEC by Shetland in 1975. The EU now has a major effect on daily activities in Shetland through various policies on agriculture, fisheries and the environment. Perhaps the biggest impact has been through the access to funding for infrastructure and business developments. Now, EU grant aid acknowledgement signs can be found in many places; beside newly aligned, improved roads, outside factory premises and beside piers and interpretive facilities. Further education centres including the Shetland College and the North Atlantic Fisheries College have received considerable funds. Up until the end of 1999, it is estimated that well over £200m has come into the islands. There has also been EU funding for exchange projects involving island energy issues and school projects under the Comenius scheme which suports links and visits between UK and other European schools.

Shetland was in a strong position to dictate terms to the oil consortium in the 1970s. However, the tables were turned in the mid 1990s when the oil was said to be running out. One interesting item, apparently overlooked in the early and effective pre-oil negotiations, was the subject of rent of the terminal. At the negotiations which led to the Busta House Agreement in the late 1980s, the Council was in a much weaker position than it had been before the lease for the terminal was agreed and fared less well than many hoped. Similarly, in the mid 1990s, urgent negotiations to secure Sullom Voe in Shetland, rather than Orkney or other Scottish locations, as a base for the new oil extraction zone 'west of Shetland' met with far less success than the original deal in the 1970s.

Conservation (now a term included under the umbrella of 'environmental issues') became a major element in Shetland towards the end of the twentieth century. Initially introduced as a measure to prevent the extinction of rare birds (too late for the sea eagle, the peregrine falcon – and the Shetland pig!) it now has a part to play in almost every island equation. Government legislation and, more recently, European directives have placed statutory requirements upon all regions of the UK to set in place various protection, interpretation and monitoring systems. Scottish Natural Heritage has a base in the islands, which is jointly managed with Orkney. As time goes by, there is a growing appreciation of the complexity of conservation issues and of the rarity and value internationally of many of Shetland's habitats and wildlife species. The Council has its own Environmental Services department and other agencies and organisations play various parts in the growing debate including Shetland Crofting and Farming Wildlife Advisory Group, the Shetland Amenity Trust, The RSPB, Shetland Bird Club and an increasing range of special interest clubs, groups and trusts. A Biological Data Recording Unit was set up in 1998.

Growing concern over radioactive particles found near the nuclear reprocessing plant at Dounreay on the north coast of Caithness resulted in some very imaginative initiatives being taken in the islands. Shetland and other North Atlantic countries belong to KIMO (a Norwegian acronym), an organisation set up to discuss concerns about nuclear contamination and other factors governing the health and safety of northern seas.

Shetland Field Studies Group, set up in 1981, researches local areas in detail and provides interpreted guided walks which are regularly written up in the magazine *Shetland Life*, and produce leaflets and maps for each walk undertaken. They welcome visitors on their programmed walks, which can be booked at the Tourist Office. They publish a small journal, *The Shetland Naturalist*, in which new research is presented to the general public, rather than remaining in academic obscurity. In 1983 the Shetland Field Studies Trust was established to promote and provide environmental and local studies in Shetland schools. Shetland Conservation Volunteers organise voluntary projects to enhance sites of special wildlife interest. The next decade may well see a growth of local interpretive initiatives based in local communities. Coastal paths and scenic way-marked routes are currently under consideration.

The annual Environmental Award scheme highlighted a wide range of environmentally friendly ventures and thus encourages people to attempt more still. You may see 'Dunna Chuck Bruck' signs, meaning 'don't throw litter', and stickers on sale in some places, designed to combat litter in the islands. Despite anti-dumping-at-sea legislation, tons of sea-borne litter washes up around the coasts every year. Inevitably, the wind picks it up and blows it all round the islands. Each spring since 1982 the Shetland Amenity Trust has organised a massive islands-wide litter collection day called 'Da Voar Redd Up' and an astonishing number of people join in. The Shetland Bird Club maintains detailed records of native and migrant birds in Shetland, publishing an annual *Shetland Bird Report*. The more recently set up Cetacean Group and Shetland Entomological Group follow a similar form, publishing reports of sightings and identifications in their newsletters. A growing number of businesses have been set up to help visitors enjoy the wild environment. Boat trips, tour companies and special holidays spring up every year as interest in wildlife tourism grows.

The last decade of the twentieth century saw a gradual consolidating of economic and interest groups through the islands. Oil money looked set to flow for a good few years yet, and a healthy debate was in full swing on the subject of fish stocks, quotas and protection measures. There was help for new businesses with assistance from Shetland Enterprise, the EU and local and national government. Welfare and health-care provision was at an all-time high and the older generation was cared for and valued. There were a number of social problems with drugs and alcohol, just as there were throughout the rest of the country, but youth workers and special projects were being well supported. There was a real celebration in 1999 when the Tall Ships Race visited Shetland, leaving behind unforgettable images of masts and sails and a general air of festivity.

SHETLAND TODAY

The new millennium found Shetland in good shape. The quality of life in the islands was arguably the best that it had ever been, for the population as a whole. The economy was healthy, unemployment low and the population stable. A network of wide, well-maintained roads, good air and sea links with the mainland and excellent services to the islands enabled people to travel more easily and quickly than ever before in the islands' history. Air and sea transport and freezers allow food of any kind to be ordered and delivered from Aberdeen often within hours. But island economies are very fragile and local people know well how quickly the picture could change.

Shetland Aerogenerators installed three 750-megawatt wind turbines in 2001, overlooking Dales Voe, and the beautifully tapered, curved blades began to turn, feeding clean power into the Shetland grid. They were a fitting symbol of confident 'green' progress for a new century, visible from far away in many directions.

The built landscape is vastly different from that of 50 years ago. New houses, built for views rather than shelter or good productive soils, lie scattered across increasing numbers of accessible, attractive seaward-facing hillsides. Efforts have been made to group dwellings and limit grossly out-of-character styles, with mixed success.

There is a strong tradition of right-to-build where and how people wish, born perhaps out of the surviving feelings of determination never again to be bullied by those in power which date back to Shetland's centuries of oppression. There are many fine new buildings, however, and some traditional crofthouses have been restored and gracefully extended. Norwegian 'kit' houses are common, and here and there curious little dwellings have been constructed as shells around an inner caravan. A number of imaginative, well-designed clusters of new dwellings have been built for low-income groups.

Support for Shetland dialect has grown and a steady increase in both poetry and prose writing has resulted in many tapes and books of Shetland poetry, children's stories and novels on sale. A Shetland Literary Award is presented each year to the author judged to have produced the finest new work. Local concert parties produce first-class local comedy and command large audiences. More serious work is reflected in the quarterly *New Shetlander*. A rich mixture of verse, stories and historical writing can be enjoyed every month in *Shetland Life* magazine. The end of the twentieth century saw a revival of live story-telling which is gaining momentum. Autumn 2001 saw Shetland's first Story-Telling Festival. A range of some of the best literature is well represented in the book *A Shetland Anthology*.

Each new generation is encouraged to keep cultural traditions alive, and the Council provides resources for traditional fiddle tuition, knitting and even Shetland dance in Shetland schools. Despite increasing numbers of closures during the last century, there are some 35 schools in Shetland. Of these, 29 are primary schools and eight are junior high schools, which have both primary and secondary departments. Nursery school provision is increasing and well-resourced and staffed playgroups still fulfil a major role in pre-school education. A number of small communities have single-teacher schools, but visiting specialist staff increase the staffing provision overall. The Further Education College in Lerwick provides a wide range of training services every year and the arts department has helped produce some of Shetland's best new knitwear designers. In Scalloway, the North Atlantic Fisheries College is at the forefront of developments in aquaculture, marine and and fisheries research, attracting many students from all round the world.

There remains a tangible Shetland warmth, a generosity and openness which affect all who visit the islands. This generosity and positive approach is reflected in particular in the involvement in third-world and other charities; with special commendation frequently given to local groups of national charities, for raising vastly over the national average in funds, for the size of area and population. Shetland Aid Trust helps projects in Albania and other countries and lorryloads of goods are driven there each year.

The islands have an energetic, forward-looking society, which still retains strong links with its past. As a small community situated in a remote location and a hostile environment, it has triumphed over the many and rapid changes forced upon it in the past 30 years. The survival instinct is strong and the environment demands a toughness and vitality which are found not only in young and old, but in natives and incomers who have stayed as well. These qualities will be tested to the full with each fresh challenge which the new millennium presents; conservation of fish stocks, future employment problems and the ever-present risk of marine accidents.

SHETLAND TOMORROW

A number of exciting and controversial changes in transport, energy and industry are appearing on the horizon as the twenty-first century begins. Inter-island ferries in some cases may be replaced by 'fixed links' (bridges or tunnels) and the long-campaigned-for new road out west will be built. The new Aberdeen ferry service started and prompted mixed feelings as P&O's long service to Shetland came to an end.

More renewable energy projects, both wind, wave and tidal, are being designed and trialled, but there is a growing realisation that 'green' energy developments will remain limited unless a mains cable link to mainland Scotland can be laid. New oil developments west of Shetland promise a reprieve for the island economy in the short term, provided that safety measures prevent more accidents from occurring. Sustainable industry is a goal to which many agencies are directing their support.

Fish farming is broadening out to include other species including cod, halibut, lobster and oyster farms and knowledge about how to control the sea lice without poisoning the seabed is increasing. Fears remain in some quarters that, in a search for employment, even bigger quarrying projects might lie ahead, as minute traces of both gold and platinum are found here, which would require vast amounts of rock extraction in order to recover economic quantities of these precious metals.

The market for cholesterol-reduced meat is growing, favouring traditional breeds such as Shetland sheep and cattle. The amount of organically grown and locally produced food is increasing and climate change may help or hinder this in times to come.

A brand new Anderson High School, designed and planned during the 1990s, will eventually be built. The new Shetland Museum will be built in Lerwick. New excavations will uncover yet more of Shetland's past, maybe even solving the riddle of the Bronze Age burnt mounds. Experts may discover just what was used to paint the Pictish pebbles and even decipher their mysterious Ogam inscriptions.

Wildlife agencies and enthusiasts watched with concern as, despite conservation measures, certain birds and rare plants declined during the 1980s and '90s. Growing public awareness of the problems and education could well bring a change for the better in terms of habitat and species protection, leaving Shetland a richer and more precious place for posterity.

Looking across Cribba Sound and the island of Vementry towards Neeans Neap, West Mainland, with Papa Stour in the distance.

The Islands

Sometimes I tink whin da Loard med da aert,
An He got it aa pitten tagidder,
Fan he still hed a nev-foo a clippens left ower,
Trimmed aff a dis place or da tidder,
An He hedna da hert ta baal dem awa,
For dey lookit dat boannie an rare,
Sae He fashioned da Isles fae da end o da aert,
An med aa-body fin at hame dere.

From *Shetlandic* by Rhoda Bulter.

There are many guides which begin their journey in Lerwick, but it is all too easy to drift into a view of Shetland as a big town with radiating minor routes, dotted with items of interest. The organisation of this Guide seeks to value each community and settlement in its own right and to visit Lerwick as a part of Shetland's whole in passing. Shetland, though small, is a lot bigger than many visitors realise. Finding your way around can be a challenge if you don't have good maps, and to avoid missing some of the less well-known highlights of the islands' treasure store of features, the following gazetteer is designed to help you explore with confidence. Shetland, being the furthest north of the British Isles, sees, in turn, Unst as its northernmost outpost. So this Guide begins with Unst and takes the reader gradually south through the outer isles, taking in village after village, feature after feature until we reach Fair Isle at the furthest southern limit.

In a book of this size, it is impossible to include every hamlet and settlement but most of Shetland is here. References to geology, botany and wildlife are made where particular locations merit a special mention, but not in any great detail, as these subjects have been covered in the introductory sections. Archaeological sites are mentioned in context, in order to make it easier to visit them when in the area. The routes from place to place are chosen to help those travelling by car, bike, or even on foot, to find their way, gain an understanding of and make the best use of their time in each area. Where appropriate, incidents from history are introduced roughly where they are believed to have happened, as a means of bringing the past to life.

From Unst, the Guide travels to Fetlar and then Yell. Whalsay and the Out Skerries follow, as these too count as northern isles. Northmavine comes next and introduces Mainland Shetland. The Guide breaks off at this point and focuses on the West Mainland, including the islands of Papa Stour and Foula. The text then returns to Brae and covers Mossbank and Voe, followed by the central and eastern landscape as far south as Tingwall. The Guide then leads the reader north-west to Weisdale and Kergord, to link up with the West side section covered earlier. Returning to Tingwall, we head south to Scalloway and the Scalloway islands, including Trondra and Burra, before covering Lerwick. Bressay and Noss then take centre stage, concluding this section of the Guide. The final part of the text is a broad scan southwards from Gulberwick to Scatness. Fair Isle forms the concluding elements of the islands-wide tour.

A short section on travel and holiday information follows, covering briefly a range of current topics, sports, music, exhibitions, eating out and other facilities with general advice for visitors. The final section consists of appendices, with lists for reference on Shetland's chronological history, plants and birds and other items of interest, including a best beach guide.

Out Stack
Muckle Flugga

Herma Ness
The Noup
Brei Wick
200
Hermaness Hill
Saxa Vord ·285
Skaw
Holm of Skaw
Wick of Skaw

Hermaness National Nature Reserve
Burra Firth
Grunka Hellier
Lamba Ness
Nor Wick

Tonga
Tonga Stack
Visitor Centre
Norwick

Orknagable
170 Burrafirth
Unst Heritage Centre
Skeggie

Libbers Hill
B9086
Hill of Clibberswick

North Holms
Wood Wick
Hevda Hill ·116
Haroldswick
Boat Haven

Loch of Cliff
Nikka Vord
Harold's Wick
The Nev

South Holms
Baliasta
Halligarth
The Rett
Buness
Hagdale
Chromate Quarry
Keen of Hamar
National Nature Reserve

Baltasound
Balta Sound
Balta

·216
U N S T
Huney

Spoo Ness
Newgord
Valla Field
Hill of Colvadale

Loch of Watlee
Brough Taing

Westing
Colvadale

Gloup Holm
Gloup Ness
Wick of Breckon
Lunda Wick
Underhoull
Sobul
Vord Hill 112
The Vere

North Neaps
Breckon
St. Olaf's Kirk
Gunister
Framgord
Sand Wick

Gloup
Memorial Mid Breck ·116
Kussa Waters
Papil Bay
Lund
Loch of Snarravoe
Mu Ness

West a Firth
Cullivoe
Blue Mull Sound
Uyeasound
Clivocast
Muness Castle

Hill of Vigon
Stonganess
Belmont

Y E L L
97 ·
B9082
Wick of Belmont
Uyea Sound
Skuda Sound

Gossa Water
Linga
The Ward
Uyea
Haaf Gruney

Dalsetter
Gutcher
Wick of Belmont
Wedder Holm

Hill of Dalsetter 95
A968
96 ·
Sellafirth
Sound Gruney

Lochs of Lumbister
Colvister
Cunnister
Urie Lingey

Kirkabister
Burra Ness
Tressa Ness
Stack of Birrier

Basta Voe
Hamars Ness
Urie Ness
East Neap

Loch of Vollister
Basta
Oddsta
Vord Hill ·159
Strandburgh Ness

The Camb
North-A-Voe
Basta Ness ·94
Brough Lodge
RSPB Reserve
Wick of Gruting
Head of Hesta

Windhouse
Camb
Kaywick
Hascosay Sound
Sands of Sand
F E T L A R
Skutes Water

A968
Mid Yell Voe
Hascosay
105
B9088
Houbie
Interpretive Centre
The Tind

Mid Yell
Hill of Lussetter
Vatsetter
Colgrave Sound
Papil Water
Tresta
Aith
Funzie

Loch of Vatsetter
Lamb Hoga
Wick of Tresta
Loch of Funzie

Laxa Burn
Birrier
RSPB Reserve

North Aywick
Aywick
Head of Lambhoga
The Snap

B9081
South Aywick
Queyon
Rams Ness

Hill of Arisdale 205
Otterswick
White Wife

0   5 km

0   5 mile

Unst

You cannot get any further north in the British Isles than Unst. Only the stacks of Muckle Flugga with its famous lighthouse (built by Thomas Stevenson, father of Robert Louis Stevenson, and David Stevenson in 1858) and the battered rocks of the Out Stack lie a little further to the north – the only 'land' between here and the Arctic. The island, famous for its exquisite lace 'wedding ring' shawls, is just 12 miles long from north to south and five from east to west.

The ferry to Unst leaves from Gutcher in Yell and sails east across Blue Mull Sound to Belmont. This stretch of sea is thought to be the channel carved by a glacier towards the end of the last Ice Age. While you cross, keep an eye open for unusual birds swimming or fishing in the Sound, including white-throated divers which are sometimes seen here. The crew may know if there is anything interesting about. As the ferry approaches Belmont, it passes an ancient broch site on the left, high on the cliff-top. Iron Age Picts may have kept watch from here as the first Vikings arrived.

There is a substantial modern pier at Belmont, very much like one at Ulsta in Yell, but instead of having been excavated from schist, it is built out of the yellow/green and blue/green blocks of serpentine taken from the quarry behind the carpark. Belmont House, one of several old lairds' houses in Unst, stands four-square above the shore to the left as you approach the pier. Built in 1777 for one Thomas Mouat, the house has many architecturally interesting features and additional farm buildings behind it. Funds are being raised for its renovation through the Belmont House Trust.

A short way north from the ferry, the Loch of Snarravoe comes into view to the west, with its ruined houses and outbuildings, last inhabited in the early 1950s. A windlass was used here to bring water up from the loch. This must have saved much back-breaking carrying of buckets. Old rig lines run down the green slopes to the shore of the loch, where anglers regularly catch trout. You can walk across the moors northwards to a second deserted homestead at Snabroch, with its ancient

broch site and more scattered ruins, as far as Lunda Wick.
A number of prehistoric sites have been found in this area and
recent excavations have revealed much information about
ancient settlement in Unst.

The road for Uyeasound turns right a mile or so north of
the ferry, the isle of Uyea with its derelict house and chapel
ruin visible across the sea to the south. A stranding of killer
whales caused some excitement here in the early 1990s. There
is a small hostel and a busy shop opposite the substantial pier,
which is in constant use. The ruin of an old trading booth,
Greenwell's Booth, still stands here and the houses facing the
sea are thick-walled and sturdy. The Church of Scotland was
built in 1843 originally as a United Free church, and has a
belfry. Children at Uyeasound school were among the luckiest
in the land when at one time they could watch a snowy owl
from their classroom windows.

As you head east out of the village, look out for a tall
prehistoric standing stone on the right. A few miles further
along the southern coastline is Mu Ness, a headland full of
interest for botanists, geologists and archaeologists. Explore
Unst's most notable historic building, Muness Castle, which
stood originally three storeys high. It was built in 1598 for
Laurence Bruce, half-brother of Robert Stewart, the notorious
illegitimate son of King James V, whose reputation for
tyrannical rule he shared. Local fishermen say that some of the
huge building stones fell into the sea while being unloaded and
can still be found underwater. A key to the
castle can be obtained from the
nearby cottage.

Bordastubble Standing
Stone, Unst.

If you have time and
enjoy walking, there are fine
views and much to
discover on the coastal
route north from
Muness to Baltasound.
Sandwick was the site
of a large amount of
Norse settlement, and
artefacts are
periodically washed up
by the sea onto the
wonderful sandy beach

here. Local fishermen claim that there are remains of walls under the waves, which snag their nets from time to time. Recent excavations on a Norse house site managed to establish a considerable amount of information before the last of the steadings was eaten away by the waves. The site of the old church of St Mary's at Framgord dates back to Norse times and there are some interesting old 'keel stone' gravestones and also the grave of Laurence Bruce from Muness. You can walk north along the coast from here to the deserted settlement of Colvadale, where the ground is still green and fertile, after centuries of human habitation and land improvement. Among the ruined crofthouses and stone walls can be found signs of prehistoric sites, earth banks, lines of once-cultivated ground and clearance cairns.

Head north from the Uyeasound junction, and turn left along a side road signed to Westing. About a mile along, turn left again, past the great standing stone of Bordastubble, said to be the largest in Shetland. The ruined house of Lund, built for John Ross in the eighteenth century, stands here. It was said to have been haunted and a number of wild tales exist about the place. The devil is said to have left an imprint of his hoof in the fireplace. The road continues down towards the sea and ends at the kirkyard of St Olaf's, built around 1200 and still being used in 1785. In the graveyard are two very old memorial stones belonging to merchants from Bremen in the days of Hanseatic trading; Segebad Detkin and Henrik Segeleken the Elder who died in 1585. There is a lovely, peaceful beach down here at Lund which is little used and is sheltered from the prevailing south-westerlies. You can retrace your route and turn left past the Stone of Bordastubble.

Underhoull Broch earthworks lie to the left of the road just before it dips down into the Westing approach. Several ancient sites can be found locally, including a Norse farm and prehistoric house site as well as the broch. An excavation was undertaken here in the early 1960s which shed light on life and farming in Viking times in Shetland. The road carries on, ending at Westing itself. Here there is a fine shingle beach which forms the start of an interesting walk north along the coast past several abandoned townships. Not far offshore is a small island with yet another broch site on it. A burn runs down into the sea at Westing and a few hundred yards upstream, an old water mill can be seen. As you retrace your

Lunda Wick from
Underhoull Broch.

route to the main road you appreciate how this whole area is
sheltered from the east and south by the massive ridge of
Vallafield.

A short way north of the Westing junction on the way to
Baltasound, you can detour left to Gunnister where you can see
another of Unst's remarkable prehistoric stones, but this one
isn't standing. It lies rather like a massive cushion, well
plumped-up in the middle, but with curious scalloped
depressions like small bowls all round the outer edge. The
purpose of this stone is unknown, but, however fanciful, ritual
sacrifice springs to mind when you study those strange hollows
and imagine them full of blood.

Baltasound is a large settlement clustered around the
shore. The harbour is greatly protected against the worst of the
heavy seas by the barricade of Balta Isle, which lies a few miles
out to the east. At the beginning of the twentieth century
Baltasound was a seething hive of commercial activity with all
the herring traffic: boats, fishing stations, gutters and coopers
and their accommodation sheds. Unst has never seen busier
times. At that time, Balta itself had many fishing stations and

working piers. Now only tattered fragments of concrete and iron remain to poke up from among the rocks and sand. Today, salmon farming is in full swing, a growing element of the local economy.

Baltasound is the main village in Unst, with a hotel, shop and garage in the centre of the village. High hills to the north shelter the community from the worst of the northerlies. On their south-facing slopes lies a circle of ancient stones. These were said to have been the place to which, long ago, people accused of certain crimes could run for sanctuary; that is if they managed to survive the gauntlet of violence meted out to them *en route* by a gathering of hostile individuals!

A fine leisure centre was built in Baltasound in 1988; an ideal solution to a day of bad weather. The junior high school has a wood and large pond, one of Shetland's first school wildlife areas. The primary school children from the recently closed Haroldswick school now attend here. An airport at Baltasound served both island and oil rigs until the end of the 1990s, when the oil companies which used it shifted their operations to Scatsta. Scheduled flights ceased in April 2001.

There are many pleasant walks around Baltasound and some interesting buildings to be seen. Buness dates back possibly to the seventeenth century and is an old haa (laird's or merchant's house) which has been considerably added to. It was here in 1817 that the Frenchman Jean Baptiste Biot carried out an experiment into gravitational acceleration at high latitude. The experiment was repeated in 1999 at a local festival. St John's Church is built on the site of an earlier church and several others have stood in the village in the past. Hillside Church at Balliasta, now a ruin, was identical to the Uyeasound church and the Old Kirk built in 1764 is also roofless, standing in its old graveyard. There is an ancient church site in Balta, too, but long since lost under the sand dunes and no one knows exactly where it stood.

Halligarth, in the north-east corner of Baltasound, once home to the Saxby and Edmondston families, is the site of Britain's most northerly woodland. In its heyday, the wood boasted many scores of different tree and shrub species, an avenue and gardens. In spring the ground beneath the trees is carpeted with bluebells. Migrant birds make straight for the sheltering branches when they struggle into Unst from the east after hours or days of battle with south-easterly winds. The shelter the trees provide is considerable and rare breeding birds have been recorded here on several occasions. Halligarth is part of a large estate which has been gifted to the National Trust for Scotland and includes many buildings, both historic and traditional, as well as croft land and peat moorland.

Woodwick, once the site of a fishing station, makes a lovely place for a walk west from Baltasound. As the name suggests, the sea here has washed in flotsam and jetsam, forcing it high up onto the beach. Immense quantities of timber can be found here, especially after westerly gales. The valley approaches are beautiful and in summer are full of birds and flowers.

Heading east and north from Baltasound, the land rises up to Hagdale, where chromate was once quarried. Signs lead you to the restored horse-mill which is well worth a visit. Just to the south is the Keen of Hamar, a National Nature Reserve, famous for the flora which grows on the Serpentine Fellfield here. Just as Shetland has greater geological variety than any other county in the UK, so Unst has the greatest variety in Shetland. These rocks break down to form interesting, mineral-rich soils which support some unusual plant species. At the Keen of Hamar these tend to grow smaller than usual, possibly because of the cocktail of minerals in the soil. Among the rarities found in early summer are Norwegian sandwort, northern rock cress, early purple orchid and a species of arctic chickweed, an exquisite flower unique to the island. The significance of the Shetland chickweed was first appreciated by the famous young Unst botanist Thomas Edmondston, who published a paper about it in 1843 at the age of 18, and the flower has been known as Edmondston's Chickweed ever since. Thomas was a remarkable young man who became a Professor of Botany at Glasgow University at the age of 20. Son of doctor and naturalist Laurence Edmonston, he died in a tragic accident barely a year later while on a scientific trip to Peru.

The road continues north,

Norwegian Sandwort.

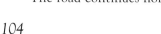

descending past more quarries and Haroldswick comes in sight. This is said to be the site of a battle when King Harald Harfager landed here and slew the exile rebel Vikings who had taken to raiding the Norwegian coast. Here, opposite the community hall, was the most northerly school in Britain. This has been converted into the new Unst Heritage Centre and is a 'must' for every visitor to the island. There are several displays about life here in the past, including excellent displays of Unst's famous lace knitwear. An archive of local history, families and houses is also kept and worked on here. The centre holds a wealth of information and hundreds of fascinating items from times past to examine.

You can walk for hours along the tiny roads which thread through the island here, and enjoy a snack in the do-it-yourself café in the shop. Behind the shop is the Unst Boat Haven, a splendidly designed and locally run maritime museum. For long a collector of old boats, Duncan Sandison dreamed of and worked towards the establishing of a museum to safeguard and interpret them for the future; this museum is now a reality. Look for the massive mural of an old fishing station painted by Liam O'Neil and wander among the boats, the exhibits of marine gear, shells, accounts of famous voyages and expeditions and model life-size fishermen. There are many fine walks north along the coastline, with superb views and more archaeological remains.

Early settlers quarried here, though only on a small scale, as was discovered when the talc quarry at Clibberswick was extended. Signs of ancient quarrying came to light, where the softer, freshly exposed rock had been chipped out into large bowls and troughs and hewn out intact for use in the ancient steadings in the isle. Other ancient steatite workings in Shetland are found at Catpund and Fethaland on the Mainland and in Fetlar.

Haroldswick had, until recently, Britain's most northerly post office, which sold postcards of itself and also franked letters with a special postmark. Now Baltasound has assumed the title and the service.

Norwick, to the north-west, has a beautiful beach, with interesting serpentine outcrops, giant boulders and expanses of sand. You can have a fine walk on a sunny day starting here and following the cliff-tops right round to the south, ending up back in Haroldswick. Remember to keep well back from the

cliff edges, use stiles whenever they are available and, if you have to use them, avoid damaging any gates or fences, taking great care to leave them exactly as you find them, whether open or closed. From Norwick the road leads up past Lamba Ness, a dramatic headland chosen for a radar station during the last war. Many of the structures still survive, but take care if you venture close, as floors are rotten.

Urda Stack and Flodda Stack, Hermaness, with Neap and Tonga in the distance.

Britain's northernmost house at Skaw, Unst.

At the end of the road from Norwick lies Skaw, literally the last and most northerly habitation in the UK. Minute shells strand along the beautiful beach where a stream runs out to sea. Prehistoric sites near cliff-tops in Shetland have sometimes been eroded by the sea and occasionally you may find items washed up on the beaches. A number of stone tools have been found here, so keep your eyes open.

Muckle Flugga and
The Gord, Hermaness,
from Saxavord.

Should you come across an ancient artefact or something
which might be, remember to take it along to the Shetland
Museum or the Archaeologist, as certain stones, if they prove
to be prehistoric in origin, are classed as treasure trove and
must be registered.

Saxavord is crowned by an RAF early warning station
which had a massive white radar dome, which was blasted into
the sea in 1991 by the 200 mph winds. The RAF base near
Haroldswick contributed greatly to the population and
employment in the island, even providing it with electricity, a
dentist and a cinema, long before other Shetland communities
caught up. Improvements to the buildings at the base include
some houses with interesting architectural features and there is
a beautiful new chapel built of wood. Recent cutbacks of staff
have been a serious blow to the island. The future use of the
base, once most of the personnel had left, is the subject of great
concern and debate.

Burrafirth lies at the head of a long north-facing inlet
sheltered from west and east by the high cliffs of Hermaness
and Saxavord. The long sandy beach has to be accessed by

track but is beautifully peaceful. Drift seeds – tropical plant seeds washed across the Atlantic by the currents – have sometimes been found here. The former lighthouse station now belongs to the RSPB and has a splendid interpretive centre for birdwatchers, complete with recorded bird calls of several different bird species. Shetland's largest loch, the Loch of Cliff, is surrounded by lush vegetation and rich flora in summer and is a favourite haunt of anglers.

Hermaness, a National Nature Reserve, is arguably Unst's most spectacular feature. According to one local legend, two giants, Herman and Saxa, fought, hurling huge rocks across Burra Firth at each other from their respective headlands. In the summer hundreds of thousands of seabirds congregate here to raise their young. Follow the well-marked route down the centre of the reserve, with footbridges and walkways built neatly over the boggiest parts, during the breeding season. Or you may choose to branch off to the cliffs and walk along the western or eastern margins of the Ness. A black-browed albatross from the southern hemisphere took up residence among one large colony of gannets here in the 1990s and stayed for some years. The relatively silent cliffs of winter become scenes of such thronging, screaming hordes in spring that they simply take the breath away. This is a time of great danger for the birds, with enemies at every turn and the endless battle for food and survival to be fought. There is murder in the air and in the water, with great skuas (bonxies) and great black-backed gulls (swaabies) attempting to steal food, chicks and even adults from among the ranks of puffin, guillemot and smaller gull colonies.

The cliff approaches require extreme care; remember in particular to stand or sit when using binoculars. It is all too easy to look through them as you walk, without realising how close you have come to the edge. Up on the high moorlands different species breed. Here you are constantly under surveillance, and often under attack, from the skuas and gulls. Bonxies tend to dive on you from a height, Arctic skuas tend to fly fast at ground level and head straight at you. But all of them, great black-backs too, can switch tactics occasionally. Keep a hat on, or hold up a stick or an arm and they are unlikely to cause a problem. However, they can sometimes strike you in passing, so avoid their nesting territories, or walk in a group where possible.

Fetlar

Fetlar takes a little planning to get to, but the rewards for making the effort to read the ferry timetable are endless. You need to get to Gutcher in north Yell, from where you will be taken to Oddsta in Fetlar, usually via Belmont pier in Unst! The island had a population of 900 during its heyday, but just under 100 live here today. Fetlar, which means 'fat land', is traditionally called the 'Garden of Shetland' and is roughly five miles by two and a half in size. There are public toilets at the ferry terminal; a camp site, a museum, a shop and a tiny primary school. The island rocked the bird establishment with the discovery by Bobby Tulloch in 1967, of a pair of breeding snowy owls. The RSPB have a bird reserve here with resident staff to protect the rarities and to help visitors watch and appreciate the bird life safely. A wonderful hide was built near Funzie, for watching the phalaropes feeding in the pools a few feet away. Apart from rare birds, Fetlar has spectacular geological features, wild flowers and a wealth of archaeological and historical remains.

Great Skua ('Bonxie').

The geology in Fetlar is very varied. A combination of metamorphic schists, serpentines and ancient conglomerates have left a rich legacy of fascinating and rare rock types. These have formed as great blocks and lie jammed together along fault lines. Where they are visible in cliff faces there are some stunning effects. The underlying drama of rock has created some very varied scenery and a wealth of different habitats. There are gentle rolling moors and high, bleak plateaux; wide sandy beaches and narrow shingle strands, low rocky shores and spectacular high cliffs and stacks. Beaches in Fetlar are full of interest and contrast.

Tresta, with its wide curve of sand, has striking pebbles banded with a kind of graphite with which you can actually draw on paper. A massive stone wall runs from Papil Water out along the edge of the ness, constructed under duress by semi-slave labour. Funzie (pronounced 'Finnie') has cliffs made from ancient pebble beds, greatly deformed by millions of years of heat and pressure. These pebble beds are thought to be almost 4000 ft (1200 m) thick. Aith, which was once the scene of a busy fish-curing station, has lovely green and yellow patterned serpentine pebbles. Talc and steatite or soapstone are also found in Fetlar and some of the outcrops show signs of having been worked in prehistoric times.

Soils vary over the different rock types, with acid peat moorland forming over the schists and marvellously green fertile areas over the conglomerate and lime-rich rocks. Wild flowers are at their best between late May and August, with especially fine displays along the roadside verges, sea cliffs and beside the burns. There are native willows and juniper, albeit very small and low-growing, and a host of mosses, sedges and rushes. Much of the pasture is surprisingly green. Apart from

Towards Papil Water, Lamb Hoga and Wick of Tresta, Fetlar.

The northern cliffs of Fetlar – Il Holm, East Neap and Busta Hill.

wild flowers in natural habitats, there is a history of famous gardens as well. Both Brough Lodge, now derelict, and Leagarth House were renowned for their extensive gardens in times past. Their cossetted plants flourished while many of the crofters' rigs, deprived by the Clearances of their seasonal tending, reverted to the wild. A few garden flowers have invaded wild places; look out in summer for the rich bronze double-flowered mimulus in some stream banks.

Fetlar's resident and summer-visiting birds attract large numbers of birdwatchers. Among the summer-visiting birds are rare red-necked phalaropes which nest among the freshwater loch margins in the Mires of Funzie, and new pools have been added to help boost their numbers. These birds are remarkably tame and you can watch them from quite close quarters as they swim and feed among the marsh plants. One of Britain's rarest waders, the whimbrel, breeds here too. Look out for golden plover, Arctic and great skuas, oystercatchers and curlews. Remote lochs are favoured breeding places for red-throated divers and ringed plover and dunlin will be seen along the shorelines. It should be possible to see fulmars, black

111

guillemots, kittiwakes, shags,
several species of seagulls and
puffins around the coasts on
most days throughout late
spring and summer. You might
see otters playing around
quiet piers and among
seaweed-covered rocks at low
tide. The less-frequented beaches
around the north coast are havens
for seals; some canoeists camping on a
remote north-facing beach were woken by
the screams of seals being attacked by killer whales.

Ringed Plover
('Saandy Loo').

There are many prehistoric house sites, standing-stone
features and ancient stone walls. Perhaps the most impressive of
these is the Finigert dyke which begins at the cliff-top above
Muckle Funziegord Geo in the north and runs south between
Vord Hill and Stackaberg. The intriguing Hjaltadans is a stone
circle north of Skutes Water, which, according to legend, is
made of stones which were once trows, who turned to stone
when the sun rose and caught them all still dancing. Look out
for a standing stone, known as the 'Ripple Stane', close to
Leagarth House; further along the road to Funzie, an elongated
mound known locally as the 'Giant's Grave' is thought possibly
to conceal a Viking ship burial. Traces of a Neolithic
chambered cairn remain on Vord Hill.

At Strandburgh Ness an offshore stack bears traces of
buildings thought to have been an early Celtic Christian site.
Monastic settlements were not uncommon in the Western and
Northern Isles in the fifth and sixth centuries AD and this one
has similarities with other sites in Shetland. The monks would
have lived simply, by their faith, and would probably have
grown their own food and had a small church and possibly a
library in order to be self-supporting, not unlike the twentieth-
century equivalent establishment founded in the early 1980s,
now very much part of Fetlar. The Episcopalian religious
community of SOLI (The Society of Our Lady of the Isles),
stands at Aithness; the modern, almost boat-shaped chapel and
house visible from miles around. People come and stay in the
self-catering chalets here for the peace and quiet which is
found in Fetlar, supported, if they wish, by the services of the
religious community.

Today large areas of Fetlar still bear the scars of the Clearances. Many ruined buildings can still be found, along with the green vegetation over their once-cultivated land, clearance cairns, drains and walls. Countless stories survive in Fetlar of bitter quarrels, forced labour, particularly brutal evictions and revenge hauntings by resentful spirits. There are traces of early fishing industry ventures, old fish-drying beaches and fishing stations, as well as modern boat gear and facilities lying nearby. The 'big houses' still remain, as do those of some of their factors, agents and local merchants, and some extraordinary follies. Brough Lodge was built in 1820 for Arthur Nicolson. It was he who built the folly, resembling the castellated round tower of a small fort. He later built another oddity, a summer house with classical columns topped by a wooden structure, long since collapsed. The pillars survive, standing at rakish angles in a sea of nettles. Leagarth House, which had its own private electricity supply, was built in 1900 as the home of Sir William Watson Cheyne, assistant to Lord Lister.

The Fetlar kirk was built in 1790 and its graceful manse, with its beautiful landing window, stands nearby, surrounded by trees. The name of the nearby loch, Papil Water, or priest's water, suggests a place of early Christian influence. There are remains of 15 more old and ancient kirk sites in Fetlar, some visible, others remembered only by their place names. The span of Christian influence here goes back well over a thousand years.

Wildlife events are regularly held in the summer, with guided walks through the reserves and birdwatching hides available for use by the many visitors in the spring, summer and autumn. Do not miss the Fetlar Interpretive Centre which has developed into a marvellous exhibition, archive and information nerve-centre for visitors and islanders alike. Legends and traditional stories abound, as do a number of wonderful songs, fiddle tunes and poems. Here you can meet Fetlar residents and read about many of the island's more colourful and interesting characters and their lives.

Red-Necked Phalarope.

Yell

The ferry for Yell leaves from the pier at Toft on Mainland Shetland and heads north across the notoriously moody stretch of sea known as Yell Sound. It takes a course halfway between Bigga to the west and Samphrey to the east, the two largest of the islands in the Sound. A number of other islands lie scattered between Yell and the Mainland and all are now uninhabited, save for sheep and seabirds. Each, though, has a unique history, with many stories of hardship and privation, as well as of adventure and heroism. Some have sites of prehistoric houses and ancient chapels.

The south coast of Yell stretches out ahead, with Copister, the southernmost settlement, in the foreground and the high hill of Arisdale beyond to the north. To the east and south as you cross, you can get fine views of Lunna Ness, Mossbank and other islands, while behind you, across Mioness, the flare stacks of the oil terminal at Sullom Voe glow fiercely as they burn off unused gases. Look out for seabirds as you cross Yell Sound. There are always a good selection busy fishing and if you are lucky, you may also glimpse dolphins, porpoises or even whales. The ferry lands you at Ulsta, where you can, if you need to, book a return ferry at the booking office. There are public toilets next door to the office. Make use of the splendid shop and filling station should you need fuel. The ferry assembly area is carved out of a hillside of iron-stained schist which gleams silver and red-gold when the sun shines onto its wet faces.

Yell is largely composed of schist and gneiss which lie now beneath peat – which is as much as 40 ft (12 m) deep in some places in the island. Blanket bog and heather moors cloak the hills from south to north, through which run channels of brown water between vivid banks of sphagnum moss. Here and there lochs and streams catch the light, lacing the landscape with silver trails. In places the streams turn suddenly into foaming torrents and rush through steep-sided gorges. Among these habitats you can find a wealth of wild flowers and birds can nest here in peace.

In spring, peat banks are flayed (stripped of turf) and cut, often by machine, but many still cast by traditional methods with the tushkar, a tool designed centuries ago for slicing regular blocks of wet peat and lifting them into courses to dry. Yell boasts some of the best peat-stacking skills in Shetland and if you are fortunate, you may still see expertly built, intricately patterned low walls of peats arranged to allow free passage of air between them. No two are quite alike, each reflecting the particular tradition or style of the caster.

From Ulsta you can choose whether to head north along the fast, improved A968 road to Mid Yell, with detours off to the west, or to take the smaller, quieter east route to Mid Yell via the B9081. The first is faster and wider, useful for drivers heading for the Unst ferry and it gives you easy access to several of the more interesting south-west corners of Yell. This Guide takes the east route first.

Copister, a settlement with a fine shingle beach that played an important part in the days of the Haaf fishing, is signed to the right just as you leave the ferry at Ulsta. There are remains of a broch just off the point of the Holm of Copister. Arisdale with its fine burn, almost a small river at its mouth, a favourite haunt of trout, lies a few miles further along the road towards Burravoe. Hamnavoe, a scattered hamlet, overlooks an exceptionally sheltered stretch of coastline, protected by the mass of Ness of Copister to the south and west. The small church of St Magnus stands here, built in 1838. The name 'Hamnavoe' occurs frequently in Shetland, and derives from the Old Norse for safe or sheltered harbour; a good description of the curving tongue of sea sheltered by the Ness of Galtagarth.

It is tempting to imagine the longships of early Viking settlers gliding in, sails being lowered and the scuff and drag of keel on shingle as they beached and settled against the land. Today a whole range of salmon farming buildings and gear dominates the scene. These shallow waters can often provide excellent birdwatching. Waders and many kinds of migrant duck feed here at different times of year. Beyond Hamnavoe and Houlland, the road curves round the Loch of Littlester on Burra Ness. The name 'Burra' frequently indicates the presence of a broch and there are several near here. One is sited very strikingly on a small island in the Loch of Kettlester about half a mile inland to the north.

Burravoe appears next, facing south and well sheltered by the protective arm of Heoga Ness from the ravages of south-easterly seas. The village, with its great variety of buildings, was one of Yell's most important in the days of the Hanseatic trade. More recently it was a major link in the former Shetland-wide ferry service, and the next stop after Whalsay for passengers from Lerwick.

Especially interesting is the wonderful local museum, garden and interpretive centre in the Old Haa. This striking building has arched buttresses through which the road once passed. The buildings to which it was joined were demolished when the road was widened. The house dates back to 1672 when it was built by a Scottish merchant, Robert Tyrie. It was lovingly restored in the 1980s and a local group produce regular exhibitions of changing themes. As well as a café and craft shop there are thousands of carefully stored and catalogued items. Many local people work to save and study everything that can be found of Yell's past.

From Burravoe head north, deviating right into Gossabrough which has a fine, sandy beach. You can enjoy warm shelter should a fine day be plagued by westerly winds. A large mound marks the site of the broch and you can see the sadly neglected buildings of the two old haa houses, once grand and imposing.

The road towards Mid Yell splits north of Otterswick, and you can choose whether to take the high road, with its marvellous views down over the east Yell coast, or the low road through the settlements themselves. A quiet, peaceful place, Otterswick was the scene of a dramatic shipwreck in April 1924. The German ship the *Bohus* mistakenly entered the bay in poor visibility and was unable to turn round in time to avoid smashing into rocks on the north shore below Queyon. Brass portholes and items made of wood from the ship are among a

number of relics still treasured from the ship but the biggest relic of all, the figurehead, was erected just above the rocks as a memorial to those drowned. It is well worth visiting the recently restored figurehead, known as the *White Wife*, which was carved holding a Bible and gazing out to sea.

Horse of Burravoe on the east coast of Yell, with Fetlar beyond.

If you have time, explore Aywick, a community clustered in a half circle around the tiny bay, with all the rigs radiating out from the shore in a design as picturesque as it was practical. Another broch site remains here, on a magnificent setting above the cliffs a short way along the north coast. A mile or so north of the broch site is another important prehistoric site, that of an ancient fort at the Birrier, not far from Vatsetter with its excellent views of the islands of Hascosay and Fetlar beyond. This site, like that north of West Sandwick on the west coast of Yell, is inaccessible now, after centuries of erosion from the wild winter seas which rage here every year. Only a couple of miles north, the coastline turns sharply west, below Lussetter Hill towards Mid Yell.

Yell's largest village, Mid Yell has a secondary as well as a primary school, several factories, shops and many other

Loch of Scattlands and West Sandwick on the west coast of Yell.

facilities. A particularly beautifully designed care centre was built recently. St John's Kirk was built in 1832, but the old kirkyard down near the shore has the graveyard, where fragments of the earlier kirk can be seen, including part of a stone arch, and several interesting old memorial stones can be found.

Some old buildings still stand in Mid Yell, including Linkshouse, a merchant's house, near the pier, built in 1770; Lussetter House (former home of the late Bobby Tulloch, Shetland's famous naturalist) is an eighteenth-century manse with castellated outer walls. The Haa of Gardie at Gardiestaing dates back to the mid 1600s. Many events take place during the year in Mid Yell and it is always worth checking dates so as not to miss one. Whether fishing, sailing, lectures or sales, they are excellent opportunities to meet and talk with Yell folk. Make good use of the free information magazine when you come.

Yell is almost cut into two here, as Mid Yell Voe from the east and Whale Firth from the west almost meet below Windhouse, the dramatic ruin on the skyline, built in the early

Windhouse, Yell.

1700s and said to be haunted. At the foot of the track to Windhouse stands a camping böd converted from the old lodge. Mid Yell Voe is overlooked by Camb and North-a-Voe to the north, opposite and facing Mid Yell itself. You can walk north round the coast here, past the secluded bay of Kaywick and round Basta Ness to Basta, set above the massive arm of Basta Voe, and beyond to Dalsetter and Sellafirth. The sea can be very shallow here at times, and I learned from one Yell resident that as a child, he and his friends had sometimes waded across the sea to the old school at Colvister, often with younger brothers and sisters on their backs, to save over a mile of walking.

The steep-sided gorge of Lumbister and the old ruined settlement nearby make an interesting walk across the moors to the west past the Loch of Colvister. You will need waterproof footwear and a map, but will be well rewarded if you make the effort. There are some mysterious stone alignments here and local legends tell of strange events relating to drowned sailors buried nearby.

At the head of Basta Voe, there was once a choice of routes to the far north of Yell but the westernmost route, to Cullivoe, has been allowed to deteriorate, and is definitely a walking, not a driving option. Burra Ness, famous for otters, stretches out to the south-east and has a broch site. Substantial amounts of lichen-cloaked wall still stand, in which storm petrels nest in summer. The deserted settlement nearby tells another part of the sorry story of the Shetland Clearances. The road leads to Kirkabister where one of Shetland's pony studs once flourished. The curious stone pony enclosure with its four raised corners is one of several in Shetland. Whimbrel frequent this corner of Yell.

Gutcher is the ferry point for both Unst and Fetlar and there is a splendid café and shop, as well as a post office and public toilets. Cullivoe has a shop, too, and now boasts improved marina and harbour facilities. Further north, the road bends left heading for Gloup, but first there is Breckon.

Take a walk over the links to Breckon. The ancient kirk of St Olaf, dating back to pre-Reformation times, stands amid the gravestones at the recently refurbished cemetery here. But beyond these to the north lies a stretch of ground inhabited at various points throughout several thousand years of history. Archaeologists believe there to have been prehistoric as well as Norse dwellings. Many tantalising features still survive, poking through the dense dune grasses and the large, rocky beach stones to the east. The area is full of a sense of the past. Whole human skeletons were discovered during the excavation of an eroding grave site. One, it was claimed (by a local man of considerable standing, who was present at the excavation as a boy), was seven feet long and had two identical bony outgrowths, like short horns, on his skull, one above each temple.

Take the narrow road west, past the modern strawberry farm with its tough polythene tunnels, noticing the Haa of Houlland on the skyline to the left, built around 1735, as was the Haa of Midbrake to the right. The road ends at Gloup, a busy farm whose fields overlook a historic scene of tragedy. Here the Gloup memorial, the stone statue of a woman and child, stands gazing blankly out to sea where, on 20 July 1881, 58 men lost their lives in a horrific summer gale. It brings into sharp focus the harshness of Shetland life in former times. The event still shadows many families today, whose forebears were among those lost. Gloup Haa, built in the eighteenth century and much restored, stands on higher ground to the south.

Gloup Voe strikes south here, following a fault line, in a steep-sided fjord-like slash through the coast. There are beautiful gorges and stream gulleys at the head, with wild roses and honeysuckle growing in abundance, but the walking can be a strain; steep-angled ground surface and narrow path. There is wonderful moorland above and beyond with many lochs, some thought to have been dammed by ice during the retreating

glaciers in the last ice age. Across the voe can be seen the deserted settlements of West-a-Firth and Graven. The more hardy walkers can take a long route west as far as Yell's west coast past the remote ruin of Vigon. There was a shop right out here, long ago. The precarious remnants of a prehistoric fort are found at Burgi Geos.

The Guide now returns to Ulsta, and describes the western route to Mid Yell. The road heads north from the ferry terminal with its pier, toilets, shop and garage and runs along between the cultivated land with the old settlements of Clothan, Freedom and Setter and the steeper hills to the east. You could walk down to the attractive Ness of Sound with its tombolo, the wide strips of shingle connecting it to the shore like a sheep on a tether. The uninhabited islands of Uynarey and Brother Isle just beyond lie a short distance away offshore and away across Yell Sound you can see Ronas Hill and take in the impressive seascapes towards the eastern cliff faces of Ollaberry, North Roe and Fethaland on Mainland. To their north lies the seldom accessible, wild cluster of the Ramna Stacks, an RSPB bird reserve. To the south is the distant

Sands of Breckon, north Yell.

expanse of Mioness and moorland stretching out of sight between Graven and Voe. A little to the west stand the massive, cylindrical tanks of stored oil on Calback Ness, and the flare stack from Sullom Voe oil terminal flickers and surges above the scene.

The road carries on north, overlooking West Yell, Newhouse, Foreland, Kirkhouse, Everhoull, Laggins and Westbrough with its ruined broch on a small, projecting headland. Stone-walled enclosures and scattered dwellings lie below the road, some with remarkable gardens and surprisingly mature trees. Here and there the lines of old cultivation rigs and fenced or stone-walled strip fields bear witness to the intense agricultural labour of former times. Now the road begins to descend as Southladie Voe and West Sandwick come into view.

Southladie Voe, protected by the Ness of West Sandwick, was a safe anchorage for ships in days gone by and the eighteenth-century North Haa still stands, surveying the sea approaches. West Sandwick is well worth a picnic stop, with its magnificent sand dunes, sandy beach and the burn where otters often play. There has been considerable sand extraction here in the past and the issue has been the subject of much debate in the islands. Sand dune and machair habitats are relatively rare in Shetland and they support several rare plants. A short way to the south there is an impressive broch site, accessible with extreme care. A mile or so to the north of West Sandwick beach you reach Heracle, or Harkland, and the Loch of Birriesgirt, where another broch site still stands. A mile or so north along the coast, connected to the cliffs by a tortuous tumble of rocks, are the remains of an ancient monastic settlement at Birrier, from which the loch gets its name. Hardy walkers might like to continue north to the Stuie of Graveland, the headland which narrows to a point opposite Gorset Hill in North Yell. The return route then cuts back to the Herra and to West Sandwick either via the road or the hills through some of the finest cliff scenery in Yell.

From West Sandwick the road veers up, away from the sea and cuts through moorland to the south of the Hill of Bouster, descending towards the head of Whale Firth. Windhouse is now clearly silhouetted against the skyline and the road soon meets the Mid Yell junction. The Yell circuit is now complete, from both approaches.

Out Skerries

Bruray

Grunay

Housay

Mio Ness

Benelips

Filla Sound

Filla

Little Skerry

The Vongs

Muckle Skerry

Outer Holm of Skaw

Skaw Taing

Nacka Skerry

Nista

Mooa

Isbister Holm

Grif Skerry

Inner Holm of Skaw

Skaw

Yoxie

Isbister

WHALSAY

East Linga

Rumble

Vaivoe

Brough

Loch of Houll

Loch of Huxter

Ward of Clett

Sandwick

Muckle Fladdicap

Muckla Billan

Linga Sound

Symbister

Bremen Böd

Lunna Holm

Lunna Ness

Stanes of Stofast

Outrabister

89

West Linga

Hunder Holm

Stava Ness

Lunna House

Lunning Head

Lunning

Longa Water

Lunning Sound

Herra

Fora Dale

Levaneap

Bellister

Iron Age Fort

Hill of Neap

Lunna Kirk

Lunna

Lunna Voe

Ness of Setter

L U N N A S T I N G

98.

Housabister

Kirkabister

South Nesting

Fish Holm

Linga

Vidlin

The Cabin

Skelberry

Muckle Ness

Dury Voe

Bretabister

Fiska Bay

Samphrey Nature Reserve

Mossbank

Firths Voe

Wether Holm

Noness Head

Swinster Voe

Swining Voe

Swining

Laxo Water

Laxo

.129

B9075

Laxfirth

Dury

N O R T H N E S T I N G

Loch of Skellister

Flamister

Toft

Tofts Voe

Firth

Fora Ness

Dales Voe

Collafirth

Collafirth

Quhamm

Muckla Moor

A968

B9076

Ube

Seggie Burn

B9071

Gossa Water

Hoo Kame 209

A970

B9075

LERWICK

Whalsay and Out Skerries

WHALSAY

Whalsay, five and a half miles by two, with a population of just over a thousand, lies to the east of Shetland Mainland. The tiny Out Skerries lie to the north-east of Whalsay. The ferry to Whalsay usually leaves from Laxo but in certain windy conditions it goes from Vidlin. Signs at both ferry terminals always advise visitors when there is likely to be a change. The crossing, if conditions are reasonable, is one to enjoy, rather than to spend sitting in the car or the passenger lounge. You can sometimes see unusual migrant birds, rare divers and seabirds from the ferry and, unless the weather is poor, there are marvellous views of the eastern faces of Lunning and North Nesting and down as far as Bressay and Noss. In late spring, the small, uninhabited islands which you pass to the north – Hunder Holm, Bruse Holm and West Linga – are ablaze with sea pinks and thronged with birds. Whalsay's western face with its crofted landscape, clustered houses and backdrop of hills is a lovely sight as you approach Symbister and you can see why the nickname 'Da Bonnie Isle' has been applied to Whalsay for generations.

Most of Whalsay consists of ancient sedimentary rock, eroded from long-vanished mountains, buried hundreds of millions of years ago and altered by intense heat and pressure into the metamorphic schists and gneisses we see today. They have long since been forced above sea level into their present forms, along with slices and blocks of other rock masses, by earth movements. Through these layers of metamorphic rocks, jets of molten rock were forced in some places, ripping off jagged fragments of local rock, known as xenoliths, which can be found lying embedded in the solidified granite. Tourmaline and felspar crystals can grow very big in some rocks and beaches can prove wonderfully rewarding places to potter among. Fault lines run through parts of Whalsay where different rock types have slid against each other and there is a strip of limestone along a section of the east coast where Isbister has developed, its cultivation patterns marking the presence of more fertile, lime-rich soils. Wild flowers and seabirds dominate the coastline during spring and summer and sea asters grow on a few remote cliffs and small offshore islands.

The island is higher at the south, the Ward of Clett rising to 390 ft (119 m) and commanding splendid panoramas all round. At the summit are the remains of Second World War buildings, offering shelter from the wind, from whichever direction it comes. Sturdy cliffs gradually lose height as they run north, facing the eastern seascape with its scatter of uninhabited islands and skerries. There are a dozen or so good-sized freshwater lochs in Whalsay and four coastal settlements. You land in Symbister in the south-east corner, close to Sandwick which faces due south. A mile north of Symbister you reach Marrister, with Brough and Challister further north still. The old runrigs are still visible all round the houses and reaching up from the west-facing shore into the moorland behind. On the west side, at Kirk Ness, a sturdy church with a small belfry stands on the site of a much earlier church at the north end of a loch. In the summer, Tirricks (Arctic terns) often swirl around above the relatively sheltered shallows. The road rises further to the north as it crosses Challister Ness and swings into Skaw with its windswept airstrip and the most northerly golf course in Britain. Just north of Symbister, a branch road crosses the centre of the island to the east and drops down into picturesque Isbister.

Whalsay has more ancient prehistoric sites than might be imagined for its size. They tend to be well scattered through the landscape; house sites closer to cultivated land, burial sites higher up in the hills and there are the remains of a defensive site or blockhouse fort built out into the Loch of Huxter. North along the coast from here you come into the deserted settlement of Treawick, abandoned within living memory. On the southern coast of Whalsay, a remarkable number of ancient sites can be found all fairly close together at Sandwick, suggesting some intensive settlement at one time. There is a cup-marked stone near Brough, with 40 or so small bowl-shaped cavities cut from sheets of bedrock. But perhaps the best known of all Whalsay's prehistoric treasures is the Neolithic house site at Yoxie, north of Isbister on the east coast. The structure is impressive and, like the one at Stanydale on the west side of

Shetland, has been loosely called a 'temple', but many experts consider it more likely to have been a large house. It was excavated in the 1950s by archaeologist Charles Calder and a local historian, John Stewart.

Symbister House, once the seat of the Bruce family, is Shetland's most imposing Georgian building and towers above the village. The mansion, built in 1823 for the then massive cost of £30,000, is said virtually to have bankrupted the family, though one colourful account claims that this was in fact the intention, so as to deprive the descendants of their inheritance! As ever in Shetland, stories of oppression by the lairds abound and many present-day families can recount grim incidents from several generations back. Now the mansion, stripped bare of its interior finery, houses the island's secondary school. Among the many outbuildings are the office of Whalsay's local history society, one of Shetland's only two dovecots, and a three-seater toilet. There is a new primary school not far away and beside it, the local sports and leisure centre with its heated swimming pool. Not far from here, the Scottish poet Hugh MacDiarmid once lived with his wife and son in a cottage now converted into a camping böd. Fishing dominates island life more than anywhere else in Shetland save the Out Skerries and Burra Isle. Some of Shetland's biggest and most technologically advanced fishing boats can be seen in the main harbour which has been considerably enlarged and modernised. A fish-processing factory provides local employment. A range of smaller craft – dinghies, yachts and traditional 'Shetland model' rowing boats – lie moored in the inner harbour. The Pier House exhibition in Symbister is in a beautifully restored Hanseatic Booth, with excellent interpretive displays about the Hanseatic League and the merchants who lived here several hundred years ago – a trade which lasted for several centuries. Other historic buildings, docks and stone store houses and a man-made drying beach, indicate that the whole area must have been a hive of maritime and commercial activity. Stories of local fishermen's wealth, however apocryphal, abound. Whalsay today retains its strong individuality with its rich and distinctive local dialect and customs. Whalsay wedding celebrations can last as long as three days.

Hanseatic Booth,
Symbister, Whalsay.

127

OUT SKERRIES

Out Skerries, Shetland's and Scotland's easternmost landfall, is a cluster of small, rugged islands, roughly two and a half miles long by one and a half miles broad, 24 miles north-east of Lerwick. The islands make up tenfold in quality what they lack in quantity and a visit here adds something very special to a holiday in Shetland. The Skerries, as they are locally called, consist of heavily metamorphosed rocks with a band of limestone cutting through the centre of the group from east to west giving the soils added fertility. Although glaciation may have ground down the islands to some extent, it left a number of pockets of clay behind. The three main islands, Housay, Bruray (which are joined together by a bridge) and Grunay enclose a perfect natural harbour. The people of Out Skerries share with Whalsay folk the richest surviving form of Shetland dialect in the islands.

Settlers must have found the harbour several thousand years ago, as a number of prehistoric sites remain, among them a possible burial site on Mioness, two Neolithic house sites in Queyness and the remains of a probable broch on Grunay. Many other puzzling remains and stone features have survived the centuries, most famous of all being Skerries' Battle Pund. This curious stone circle (or rectangle) is said to have been an ancient site for solving disputes. Archaeology is not confined to the land; underwater exploration has revealed the locations of many shipwrecks. Artefacts retrieved by divers from the *Kennermerland* and other wrecks feature in the Shetland Museum.

Looking east from Housay across South Mouth towards Grunay, Out Skerries.

128

Shipwrecks have decreased greatly since the building of the lighthouse on Grunay. A German plane crashed onto Grunay during the last war. An engraved wristwatch, found welded to some melted wreckage, enabled the pilot to be traced and eventually islanders joined his descendants in a special service of remembrance. A memorial has been erected on the site.

From the earliest times, the Skerries were extensively cultivated, but as in the rest of Shetland, much of this has now returned to the wild. The many acres of rough grassland now support magnificent displays of wild flowers from May into August. The scent on a still, warm summer's day is unforgettable. A particularly deep-red eyebright grows here and among the tormentil and lousewort keep an eye open for the tiny green frog orchid.

Those arriving by plane on the tiny airstrip miss the thrill of reaching the Skerries by ferry in rough seas. Cliffs seem to bar every approach, but at the last minute a channel appears and the ship is skilfully steered through into calm water and arrives at the large modern pier. Apart from the shop, church, village hall, post office, lighthouse and fish factory, the island has one of the smallest, most interesting schools in Britain. In this tiny primary and secondary school pupils enjoy a freedom of shared association and creative play, natural skills long since removed from the majority of school children by the separation of their schools and age-group segregation. I will never forget seeing the 'big ones' racing into the primary classroom to collect their younger brothers and sisters and taking them outside, lifting the tiniest and carrying them on their shoulders. When the end-of-play bell rang, back they all trooped, excited and breathless after their shared break.

Nowhere in Shetland, except perhaps Whalsay and Burra Isle, has been so dependent upon the fishing for its survival as the Out Skerries, right up until today. Salmon farms are the most recent chapter in the long, colourful history of fish. But there are many difficulties and risks in all branches of fisheries. Ingenuity, tenacity, dedication and teamwork of Skerries folk will be put to the test in the years ahead if the island community is to survive the coming decades.

Out Skerries by Joan Dey, a former head teacher, is well worth reading if you visit these islands. It is full of humour and history, stories of famous fights, shipwrecks, sailing tragedies and battles for survival.

Northmavine

The gazetteer now begins to unravel the corners of Mainland Shetland, from Northmavine southwards. In fact, returning from Unst and Yell, Toft and Mossbank are the first villages touched, but to simplify the progression, we begin with the furthest north.

One of Shetland's most popular walks is from Isbister to the most northerly point on Mainland Shetland, Fethaland, with its deserted fishing station, prehistoric sites and spectacular scenery. It is relatively straightforward, but fairly long, and can be gruelling in poor weather. A track leads from Isbister, the most northerly point of the A970, where the road ends, along past an old graveyard. There are interesting old wooden headstones here which are worth a detour from the path. Continue past crofthouses old and newly restored, northwards across the grassy moorland, until just before the land tapers away to a narrow point. In places along this route, purple mountain saxifrage, one of Shetland's botanical rarities, blooms in early spring.

Isle of Fethaland, Ramna Stacks and Gruney from Fethaland.

Fethaland has beaches facing both east and west, making it an ideal site for a fishing station. During the days of the Haaf fishing, men would stay in small stone huts during the summer fishing season; between June and mid August, around 60 boats would have been in use. Over 20 buildings stood during its heyday in the late 1800s and just behind them is a prehistoric house site. Traces of old fish bones can sometimes be found in the upper beach strata, remaining from the split fish which were salted and laid out to dry. A prehistoric steatite quarry was once worked here. The marks of bowls and troughs can still be seen cut into the cliff face slightly north and east of the fishing station. A small modern lighthouse stands on the furthest point of the headland. The cliff tops are precipitous and indented here, so be very careful, especially if it is windy. When you reach the northernmost point, stand and take in the view for a while. The sea-lashed Ramna Stacks lie to the north and away to the east beyond them is the northwest coast of Yell, with the tip of Hermaness in Unst and Muckle Flugga far beyond.

Gannet ('Solan').

There is an early Christian site on the inaccessible headland of the Kame of Isbister on the east coast, half a mile along the track north from Isbister. The best place to see the structures is from the high cliff-top of Virdifield to the south. A number of small square foundation outlines remain just visible, marking the locations of missionary cells on the level grass-covered summit. They stand directly opposite the monastic site at Birrier in West Yell. It is quite possible that they were contemporary and that there might have been some form of communication between them. Services were held near both sites in the summer of 2000, commemorating 2000 years of Christian worship in the islands.

The settlement of Sandvoe is about as remote from Lerwick as it is possible to get on Mainland Shetland. The Voe of Sandvoe itself is exquisite, especially when glimpsed for the first time from the North Roe to Isbister road. The sea reaches deep inland, round a curving inlet with great cliffs rising up on either side of it adding a majestic frame to the scene. The beautiful beach at the head of the voe is a particularly good place to spend a fine day when Shetland's prevailing strong south-westerly wind is blowing. In summer, meadow cranesbill grows in several places nearby, adding a rich purple-blue to the dazzling native flora.

Uyea is one of the most isolated corners of Shetland, a deserted settlement at the extreme north-western tip of the Mainland. You can walk along the coast from Sandvoe, but it is worth going on the peat track from the coastguard hut in North Roe. A Neolithic axe factory, old mills and the remains of a fishing station add to the interest. A sand causeway connects the island of Uyea itself to the mainland but is only crossable at certain times of the tide and even then, recent storms may have shifted the sands away, so access cannot be guaranteed. Even when the weather is fine, the ascent is awkward and in places very unsafe.

There is something of a magical quality to this tiny island, set among dramatic sea stacks. It has a lush growth of grass and a tiny flock of sheep are grazed on it each year. Grey seals give birth to pups among the boulders on the more inaccessible beaches here in October and you can sometimes see them from the cliffs above. The baby seals with their silver coats and enormous dark eyes are immensely appealing and it is easy to convince yourself that they are abandoned and need rescuing. But they are very closely supervised by their parents and are well adapted to their strange, harsh nursery. Take pictures if you wish, but don't approach too closely. The creatures can give ferocious bites and can move surprisingly fast. They often carry diseases, some of which can be contracted by humans. Mothers can be even more dangerous, so don't go anywhere near a mother with a young one nearby.

From Uyea you can walk southwards along the west-facing cliffs to the dramatic sea-carved pool at Fugla Ness. Here, way out at the westernmost tip of the North Mainland, a small section of cliff has been eroded by winter seas to reveal rare secrets from the past. Under a thick layer of glacial till lies a narrow seam of fine, dark material. A small stream trickles down to the sea through a corner of the seam and in its bed are found remarkable fragments of Shetland's ancient, pre-human landscape. Tiny pieces of wood lie among peat particles and clay from the stream. These fragments are thought to be at least 40,000 years old. Pollen analysis indicates that at one time, there would have been open coniferous woodland here, with birch, oak and elm among other species and areas of heather and marsh nearby. The climate must have been far milder than

Uyea and Garmus
Taing from Fethaland.

that of Shetland today. Evidence of oak, of Scots pine and even a Mediterranean species of heather has been found among samples taken by experts. None of these species remains in Shetland, nor do they appear in pollen found in soil core samples from prehistoric sites in the islands. Somehow, although the whole area must at one time have been covered with ice, tiny pockets of an earlier landscape have survived beneath the crushing weight and bulldozing action of the later glaciers. Only one or two other sites of pre-glacial peat, as this is called, are known in Shetland.

Retrace your steps to North Roe and begin the long, meadering route back to the south. Nestling under the lee of the massive Beorgs of Skelberry, the small hamlet of Skelberry has a busy, cheerful air. Beyond, close to the road are a standing stone, now fallen, and a burial site known as the giant's grave. The Housetter road turns off left just south of the loch of the same name and continues to Lochend where a haa was built for the Nicolson family in the 1700s overlooking a long beach, with splendid views across the sea towards the east-facing cliffs of the Ness of Queyfirth.

The main road runs on south, bending sharply into the inlet of the Voe of the Brig, past the new Collafirth fishing pier, site of a former whaling station. The Burn of Roerwater runs out to sea here and the fit and adventurous can follow it up into the loch-scattered wilderness to the west where at the

Lang Ayre and
Gruna Stacks to
the north-west
of Ronas Hill.

extremity, a waterfall cascades into Lang Clodie Wick. Several
Neolithic house sites exist in the area.

Ronas Hill is Shetland's highest hill and is composed
almost entirely of granite of about 355 million years of age.
Frost and wind action have created a fragile ground cover of
gravel and tiny plants, known as Fellfield habitat, over the
upper slopes. Deep peat hags have formed lower down. From
the top you can see from the Out Skerries to Foula and from
Fair Isle to Muckle Flugga. The best approach is to take the
steep access road from Collafirth to the former signal station
and set off across the bouldery, heather moor to Mid Field, the
smaller summit visible to the west. From there you descend a
shallow valley and climb up to the top of Ronas Hill itself,
which has a large and impressive chambered cairn at the top.

Across the boulder-strewn plateau to the west, the going
can be dangerous, with deep crevices and crumbling edges to
the massive, sheer cliffs. But many folk venture down the Burn
of Monius to experience the grandeur of the Lang Ayre, with its
mile-long shingle beach. Mountain azalea, bearberry, club moss
and ferns survive in the harsh local conditions, amongst many

other species. Rare sea
eagles have been seen
here on occasions, and
in summer the rocky
slopes chime with the
plaintive calls of golden
plover. Anglers enjoy
fishing among the remote
lochs to the north and few
other places in Shetland have
the same freedom and wild spaces.
To the south, the slopes intensify and
certain parts are precipitous, so be really
careful especially if the fog comes down. From
Ronas Hill north, some of Shetland's wildest and least
hospitable terrain can be found. There is no shelter and
weather can change very quickly.

Male Eider Duck
('Dunter').

The A970 skirts Colla Firth, and passes a small
community at the neck of Queyfirth. The main road forks just
as Ronas Voe swings north-west, the right-hand branch leading
to Heylor and the left towards Urafirth and Hillswick. But at
this point, before following the route right into Hillswick, we
take a detour into some of the settlements to the east. A side
road branches to Leon and rises up the Hill of Ollaberry, and
there are fine views over the Loch of Queyfirth with its shingle
bar, before crossing over into the village of Ollaberry itself.

Ollaberry faces east across the sea towards Yell and
clusters around an old centre close to the pier and beach. Some
very old buildings have survived, as well as a primary school,
shop, church and some more recent houses, producing an
attractive blend of old and new. The Ollaberry Hall, one of the
venues for the Northmavine Up Helly Aa, serves teas on some
summer Sundays. A local crofter, John Williamson, was among
the first to experiment with greenhouses and fruit cultivation.
For many years his peaches, plums, apples and cherries were
something of a legend, and at blossom time there was never a
shortage of visitors.

North of Ollaberry the ground slopes up slightly, then
levels off at a point where a shallow depression crosses the end
of the rounded headland from east to west. This looks at first
sight like an overgrown, deep drain, but it is in fact the line of
a geological fault which is called locally the Back of Ollaberry

136

Fault. Geologists believe it is a continuation of the Great Glen Fault, which is exposed on the beach to the west. If you are agile and suitably clad for a rough, muddy adventure, follow the depression to the cliff-top and clamber down (with care) the gulley to the simitar-shaped beach. The tear fault forms the face of dark, hard rock to your right, which cuts clean across the beach like a great door. Exposed tear faults are rare features.

The B9079 winds south from Ollaberry over the moors and skirts Eela water, with its water treatment plant, and joins the main A970 from Collafirth, passing several branch roads which lead off to quiet, old settlements, each full of interest. Fiblister, lying to the east, comes first and is a particularly attractive farm with lovely views across to Gluss Isle. Next a road turns left for Gluss itself, and curves through a beautiful valley where Turvister, Nissetter, Bardister and South and North Gluss lie amid fenced and cultivated land. You can walk over to the gently domed Gluss Isle, with its long shingle tombolo and peaceful views west over the trim croftscapes. Seals and maybe otters, quietly murmuring eider ducks and scuttling waders will watch you should you spend time walking over to the isle. It is one of the best places from which to see the oil terminal across the sea to the east. Tankers slide slowly by, eased alongside the jetties by tugs. You can also walk south from here, round the Ness of Bardister, round Fugla Ness and the Houb, coming out into the village of Sullom.

Sullom is a quiet and peaceful village, facing south-east across the sea to the North Ward of Voxter. There has been a mine here, now a quarry, where magnetite was extracted. A super quarry was proposed for the Hill of Hagrister in the 1980s and though it hasn't come yet, many local people fear that the threat may return. Two roads leave the village, the south road joining the A970 at Islesburgh, near Brae, and the north leg joining the A970 at Johnnie Mann's Loch, almost opposite the Gunnister junction.

The Guide now returns to Ronas Voe, where the east coast communities were described, and takes you out to Hillswick and the north-west before returning to the A970 south and the settlements on the west side of the area.

Ronas Voe, Shetland's only true fjord, is very deep, and runs in under the southern lee of Ronas Hill. It is overlooked by the tiny settlement of Voe at its head. Along the shore can be found traces of the old whaling stations which once stood

here. Further out along the south side of the voe, there is a fish factory. The north side of the voe is very beautiful and you can clamber along from the head of the voe, at least as far as the ruins of Feal where otters are sometimes seen. Ravens nest in early spring, relict trees and plants cling to the sheltered low cliffs. The road along the south shore swings south as the voe turns north, a branch leading on along the coast to Heylor.

A strenuous but superb walk begins here, following the massive headland past the empty crofts of Sannions and Sumra, right round to the point at The Faither and then south to the deserted township of Ockran, green amid the brown landscape. History records a sorry tale of local folk. The 1851 Census recorded 99 inhabitants in the ness in 14 separate crofts. Then in 1865 two locals, who had earned a fortune in the Australian gold mines, bought the tenancy from the landowner for twice its annual rental. They then evicted their own neighbours and families and built the big house of Newton which still stands at Tingon today, and introduced sheep, attempting to grow even richer. Many ruins remain as witness to this Clearance. The brothers eventually fell out with each other and went bankrupt.

138

The Isle of
Westerhouse and
The Drongs from
Hillswick Ness, with
Papa Stour and Foula
in the distance.

The area is full of geological interest, as here the Ronas
granite meets the Eshaness volcanics and there are superb
exposures along the Villians of Hamnavoe. The village of
Hamnavoe has a magnificent broch site and the camping böd
known as Johnnie Notions. The settlement here overlooks the
sheltered Hamna Voe, with Hoohivda on the far side. From
here a road connects with the B9078 to Eshaness and back to
Hillswick.

The road which curved left at the Heylor junction passes
Assater and joins the A970 at Urafirth. Hillswick is situated a
mile or so along to the right. The village was once the furthest
north point on the Mainland for the West Side steamer, a ferry
and cargo boat, which brought passengers from Leith. The
St Magnus Hotel, built in 1900, dominates the village. The
wooden construction material was imported from Norway.
Nearer the shore and allegedly formerly the oldest pub in
Shetland, *The Booth* is said to date back to 1684 when a
Hamburg merchant, Adolf Westerman, is recorded as having
had a booth in Hillswick. It was converted in the mid 1990s
into a vegetarian restaurant. Behind it, there is the Hillswick
wildlife sanctuary, where oil- or storm-affected seals and otters
are sometimes brought and treated. This facility was set up
with funds raised after the grounding of the oil tanker *Braer*.

The large church, built in 1733, had a gallery built in 1825 and the manse about 30 years later. A shop and post office and small garage facility add greatly to the village amenities.

Hillswick Ness must number among the best of places to walk in Shetland, with virtually no fences or barriers to speak of at the outer end. Nearer to the farm there are walls and access on the western side is difficult. The easiest place to start is just outside *The Booth* itself and follow the shore west. The flowers are wonderful in summer and for those interested in ancient sites, the ness is full of them, none instantly obvious, but all there for the sharp-eyed to spot and examine. The ground rises gently as you make your way out towards the end of the ness with its tiny lighthouse. Beaches on the eastern shore have some wonderful pebbles, but the western face of the ness is much higher with massive cliffs and stacks. There is superb cliff scenery, with wide panoramas across Shetland's western coast and islands.

A short way back out of Hillswick the road for Eshaness turns left just before the village hall. It cuts uphill, overlooking the beautiful beach of Sandwick with the Drongs, sea stacks shaped like dragons' teeth, beyond. The road crosses Watch Hill and suddenly the whole Eshaness plain comes dramatically into view; a small world of its own. The road is like a spine, winding out to the west, with small rib roads branching off in both directions to reach outlying settlements, Hamnavoe, Hoohivda, Cross-Voe-Sand, Braehoulland and Leascole among those to the right, and Breiwick, Tangwick, West Hogaland and Stenness to the left. To the south, the curiously shaped stack of Dore Holm, rather like a drinking dinosaur, stands out starkly against the sea.

Eshaness has to rank among the top ten of Shetland's beauty spots. The dramatic 150 foot high cliffs are wave cut through extrusive volcanic rock from the Middle Devonian period. Massive sea stacks rise up from turbulent water and seabirds wheel and call. Tour buses call here endlessly in the season and locals take their visitors and relations to the lighthouse and car park just to stand and soak up the scenery. The North Atlantic roars against the land here, exploding in white mountains of spray on a wild day in winter and bursting up like geysers through many blowholes, yet in spring there can be days of totally windless, warm silence, with the sea nudging the rocks like a seal pup its mother. Seabirds abound here and

Tangwick Haa,
Eshaness.

seals spread themselves out to snooze on the rocks below the cliffs, turning their heads to gaze inquisitively up at you as you gaze down. But the cliffs are very high and often have dangerous overhangs.

Calder's Geo cuts inland in a deep slash in the cliffs, the edges of which are frequently crumbly. When the sea is high, unexpectedly fierce waves could break and, at the very least, soak you to the marrow with ice-cold salt water. At worst you could be knocked down or washed over. It is advisable to keep well back at all times.

On a fine day you can walk north, passing the gaping Holes of Scraada where two blow-holes at the head of a long sea cave collapsed, leaving a tunnel 100 yards long to the sea. A small stream runs down from the Loch of Houlland with its ancient broch and causeway, and three old ruined watermills are found alongside it. A number of other ancient sites have been found in the vicinity. You can walk right along to where the coast bends east towards Hamnavoe just beyond Da Grind o da Navir, a particularly dramatic chasm in the stark ignimbrite cliffs where the sea breaks through in wild weather, hurling great rocks through the gap onto a storm beach high above.

Stenness today is a cluster of houses above a large pebble beach, with some ruins ranged around the shore above it. Here in the 1800s, 40 to 50 open boats were worked, setting off for 'da far haaf' and bringing back their catches of cod and ling to be cured. The fish were split, salted and laid side by side on the pebbles and stacked when dry, ready to be transported for sale. It would have been a hive of activity, with boats, boys and men, fish drying, seagulls crying; now the waves lap the deserted shore, rattling the igneous, multicoloured pebbles against each other. Take care on the steep grassy slope as you walk down to the shore and contemplate the sheer grim determination, the desperate need, which must have driven those fishermen to row out up to 40 miles west to set their lines. The long, cold, wet wait, then the hauling, and the rowing back, reading the skies for signs of bad weather and the ever-present risk of disaster.

A visit to Tangwick Haa museum is a must during the summer months. Staffed and run by volunteers, the standard of display and interpretation is first class and each year features a newly researched topic of local history. The building which houses the museum has been sensitively restored, with particularly fine woodwork inside. Nearby are the remains of an excavated burnt mound. Here in the early 1990s, experiments were carried out to see just how these ancient burning sites may have functioned. Visitors brought eggs to be boiled and great fun was had by all. Much was learned but many questions still remain as to the exact purpose of burnt mounds.

Dore Holm from near Stenness, Eshaness.

Urafirth lies at the head of a peaceful voe, and has a fine new school. In February, the Northmavine Up Helly Aa procession starts in Hillswick and parades all the way from the Hillswick beach to the edge of Urafirth, where it stops for the burning. The torches flicker and flare, songs rise up to a dark sky and then waves of arrowing flames fly through the air into the old ship, which is launched and pushed out to drift away over the water, burning into its own reflection. On occasions, Caain whales have swum into the shallow and accidentally beached themselves.

Deep inlets, such as Hamar Voe, feature in several places around the western sea coast. Olnesfirth, Scarpy and North and

The battered cliffs of Eshaness – looking across Calder's Geo from South Head of Caldersgeo.

South Lees face the Hamar Voe where, apart from the sound of sheep and the odd car in the distance, you are undisturbed. But half a century ago the scene would have been very different. There was a constant flow of ships and small boats here during the herring boom. At the head of the voe, Orbister presents a quiet and peaceful face to today's visitor, but 100 years ago it was a place of hustle and bustle. You can walk out around the shore past Hamar to the south and find traces of the busy fishing stations and shop where at one time several hundred telegraph messages a day were sent and received. The main road south of the Orbister turn is joined by the B9079 from Ollaberry.

Several other settlements lie on this stretch of coast, their tiny roads threading west from the main road to Brae. Just south of Punds Water a road winds over to Enisfirth which overlooks Gunnister Voe. You can walk the circuit of the Ness of Hamar, which is rugged and dramatic, with Hillswick Ness visible across Ura Firth to the west. A mile or so further south along the A970 another road turns off west to Gunnister and Nibon beyond. Near the junction, among the peat banks, the body of a man was found in 1951, buried in peat. Known now as the Gunnister Man, this person was dressed in homespun garments and is thought to have been a rent collector who came to grief somehow during the late 1600s, judging by the coins found in his knitted purse.

The small, scattered hamlet of Gunnister at the head of Gunnister Voe is set among some of Shetland's loveliest scenery. A wide arm of sea reaches deep inland past several small islets. The tiny Gunnister hall used to resound with the noise and laughter of dances, concerts, sales and auctions. There is a remarkable degree of shelter in the valley here and some unusual garden plants grow surprisingly well despite the latitude and climate.

A favourite place for Shetlanders to go on a Sunday afternoon, Nibon is an exceptionally beautiful spot. Otters often appear here and seals will watch you from the shallows, following your progress along the shore. Only a handful of houses stand here, sheltered from south-easterly winds by the high moors and inland cliffs which stretch right over to Mangaster, and from the ravages of the sea by the Island of Nibon to the west. Beware, though, the long, winding, single-track road which has to be negotiated first, and if you come by car, drive slowly in order to avoid having to reverse considerable distances, maybe even up hill or round a bend or two to allow other vehicles past.

The next small road to the west goes to the croft of Mangaster, tucked into the lee of Gruna Vird and the solid mass of high, craggy moorland to the north. There is a challenging walk here round to Nibon and back along the road past Gunnister. You would need a good six hours and more, even on a fine day. In poor weather it is easy to get lost on the tops. Mangaster Voe, sheltered on both sides with Islesburgh Ness to the south, was found to be an ideal site for salmon farming and considerable development took place in the 1990s.

Islesburgh Ness is a headland a mile north of Brae, full of geological and botanical interest, with superb views from its irregular coastline. Islesburgh Community Centre and Islesburgh House with its youth hostel in Lerwick, owe their name to this little corner of Shetland. A Smith family who farmed at Islesburgh, owned the house in Lerwick which they named after the ness. Islesburgh Ness, which means 'isle's broch headland', is well endowed with prehistoric features. An Iron Age house was excavated some years ago and a fine chambered cairn and Neolithic house site stand not far away. Some intriguing circular features around a small loch have never yet been fully explained. When the farmhouse was built near the site of the broch, many prehistoric tools were unearthed. A Pictish symbol stone was found here some years ago by the farmer John Copland. He was determined that the stone should not leave the islands and it can still be seen in the Shetland Museum. The 'Islesburgh Eagle', as it is called, seems to depict an eagle in flight, with something in its claws. The image has since been adopted as the symbol of the Islesburgh Centre.

In the 1970s the farm at Islesburgh was renowned for exceptionally good quality seed of the Shetland cabbage, a larger, tougher variety of cabbage than the conventional variety. Shetland's first garden nursery was established next door to the farm in the 1970s by John Copland when he retired. People visited the beautiful garden first, deciding which of the superb flowering and foliage plants they wished to have in their gardens, then bought specimens from the sales beds. Later he wrote a very popular gardening book, *Hardy Plants of the North*, which sold out twice. The farm has received many agricultural awards in recent years and in the 1990s had the reputation of producing some of the finest wool from Shetland sheep.

Just south of Islesburgh, the road rises a little, then dips downhill and bends slowly round to the east. For a moment, the sea appears simultaneously both to the left and the right of the road. This point is known as Mavis Grind, or *Maeve Isthmus*, a narrow gateway. The whole of Northmavine here is almost severed from the rest of Mainland Shetland. A good over-arm bowler can hurl a pebble from the Atlantic Ocean to the North Sea just by throwing it across the road from one shore to the other! Great craggy cliffs rear up to the right, their unstable faces still shivering down quantities of loose stone several decades after they were blasted to provide road-building materials for the oil terminal. The road follows the line of sea below them as it heads south towards Brae and the turn-off towards Muckle Roe and Busta.

Muckle Roe is a particularly lovely corner of Shetland. A mass of granite, wild and beautiful on the west, fertile and settled on the east, it is connected to the Mainland by a bridge across a short sea sound. If you have plenty of time, you can enjoy long walks around the coast from Otter Ayre on the north-eastern corner southwards as far as the Hams of Roe, a well-loved area of quiet beaches and spectacular cliff scenery on the west where many Shetlanders make frequent summer trips.

Cormorant ('Muckle Scarf').

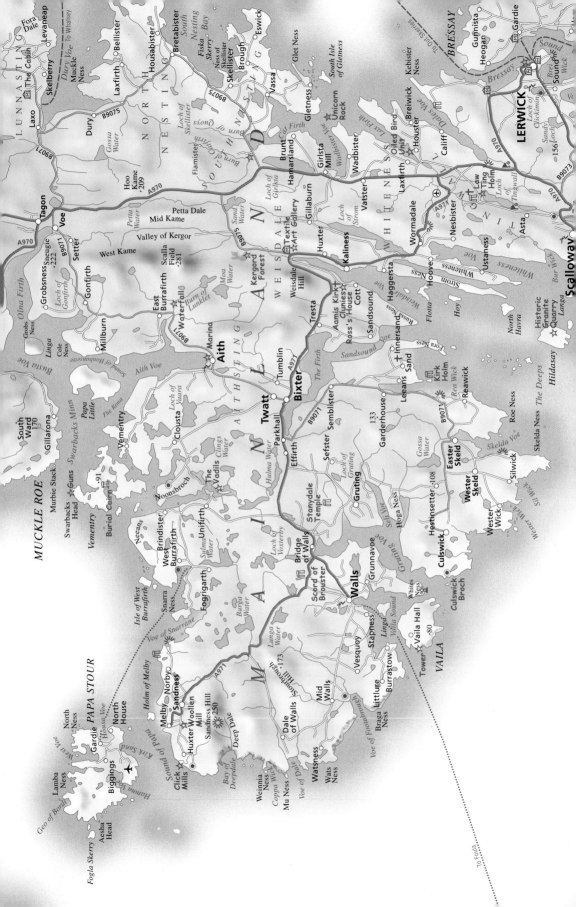

West Mainland

The Guide now describes the route out west, starting at Weisdale at the head of Weisdale Voe.

Skirting the head of the Voe, the road begins to climb towards the *Norseman's Inn* and the end of the road into Cott. Down here you can find Clunies Ross's house, now completely ruined, but still imposing, as are the remains of the old harbour on the shore. Here John Clunies Ross was born to a wealthy couple, Elizabeth Ross and George Clunies. After a career in the Royal Navy, in 1827 he became governor of the Cocos Islands in the Indian Ocean. His enlightened improvements to economic and social conditions earned him the islanders' title of 'King of the Cocos'. Just near the old house is a graveyard, site of an old church known as 'Da Aamis Kirk'. Money or gifts were deposited here when someone hoped for a special prayer or wish to be granted. Despite official church disapproval, the tradition survived long after the original kirk was demolished. As recently as the 1940s Shetlanders *en route* for war service brought their *aamis* (money or gifts) here before they left the island, hoping that this would speed their safe return.

The Cott road ends just beyond this point but at one time the community was much larger and crofthouse ruins can be seen far down the length of the ness. You can walk right round the western headland and back on the other side into Sandsound. There are fine views across the sea to the Scalloway islands from the ridge above. If the weather is calm, a ridge walk can be marvellous, with extensive views both east across Weisdale and west over Tresta, Bixter and the Skeld hills.

The road to Tresta goes up the west side of the valley out of Weisdale. A layby near the top provides a safe stopping place from which you can see for 30 miles south towards Fitful Head, across a foreground of islands and hills. The road turns sharply west as it levels out and if you feel like stopping there is a track at this point up to the mast on top of the hill above. From the summit you can see almost the whole of Shetland and if the weather is fine, the panorama is unbeatable.

The road crosses Weisdale ridge and a whole new landscape comes into view. A great expanse of sheltered water reaches from Tresta Voe into the wide firth, narrowing to Bixter Voe and finally Effirth Voe with the hills of the 'west side' for a backdrop. The sea here enters through Sandsound, a relatively narrow gap between headlands, out of sight to the south.

Just over the brow of the hill, the winding Burn of Tactigill flows south under the road as it emerges from a beautiful gorge, hidden from view to the north. Clay similar in some of its properties to kaolin can be found here and a representative of Wedgewood's potteries is said to have surveyed the place with the idea of extraction. But the deposits are relatively small and so factories were never built and the gorge was left to its wildlife, sheep and walkers.

The road descends gently into Tresta with its old house and walled, wooded garden. Other houses have been built along the shore and under the lee of the lower hills to the north, their cultivable land raking down the slope towards the sea. During the 1980s Lea Gardens were established here around a small crofthouse and became one of Shetland's most interesting gardens with an extensive plant collection.

A single-track road turns off to the left in Tresta and winds south past Lung Ness above the sea to Sand. Houses, some old, some new, have been built along the face of the slope here, enjoying wonderful views to the west and south. A long, pleasant walk can be taken from the end of the road here right round Russa Ness and back over the ridge to Cott and Weisdale.

Just before Bixter, a road branches north, signed to Tumblin. A winding single-track road connects scattered houses and crofts, some placed at the end of further branched tracks, and eventually ends at a turning place. The whole road is untypical of Shetland, lying out of sight of the sea. Interesting valleys, their stream banks concealing in places half-buried remains of planticrubs and other stone structures. The name 'Tumblin' is said to originate from a local incident many years ago, when the tiny church roof tumbled in.

Bixter, a sizeable hamlet, with new houses scattered among older ones, well above the sea, has grown up at the junction between the main road link to the north and the road out west. The village has a veterinary practice, doctors' surgery, a shop, garage and public toilets.

This gazetteer now breaks off from the road to the west and describes the route to Aith and Voe with its many fascinating side roads.

The hills are wide and curving as the B9701 rises north from Bixter. A side road turns west to the quiet crofting settlements of Twatt, Clousta and Noonsbrough. There is a lot to explore in this out-of-the-way corner of the 'West Side' and few visitors manage to penetrate its secret corners, with their archaeological sites and rich bird life. A large hotel, long since burned down, was built here in the nineteenth century to service the requirements of the holidaying sportsmen who came in droves to shoot waterfowl in the 'Vadils', a salt-marsh and muddy shingle area much frequented by waterfowl. This habitat has recently been awarded special European conservation status.

The road to Aith continues to the north, rising slightly then dropping down towards Aith Voe and its fringe of densely settled slopes. As it bends sharply to the right, there is a fork north to Vementry. This route makes a rewarding detour, with many miles of cliff and seashore scenery to enjoy. As you approach the farm of Vementry at the end of the road, look out for a small loch on the right with a rowan tree growing on a tiny island, and ivy and honeysuckle growing along a fenced embankment. A short sea sound lies between the mainland shore and Vementry itself, which has not been inhabited for many years.

Redshank ('Ebb-Cock').

The Island of Vementry, sometimes described as 'little Shetland', has a bit of almost everything that Shetland is well known for: glorious scenery, wild flowers, superb archaeological sites and even First World War features. At the top of the highest point stand Shetland's finest ancient burial cairns. Beyond, at Swarbacks Head overlooking the seaway westward, stands an enormous gun complex, quietly rusting away above a series of underground bunkers and shelters which were part of Shetland's coastal defence system during the First World War.

Aith, overlooking the sheltered waters of Aith Voe, is a large village with a junior high school, shop, garage and a sheepskin business. The village has a new leisure centre, marina and one of Shetland's two lifeboats is based here. Look out for activities based in the hall during the summer, where local folk set up a splendid catering venture during the late 1990s. One of the highlights of the Aith year is the regatta with its multitude of events.

The road continues north, then curves round towards East Burrafirth, crossing the Burn of Lunklet. A signed path here leads to Ramnageo, a spectacular gorge and waterfall. In summer, honeysuckle and wild roses bloom here in abundance among bell heather and a dozen other wild flowers. The scene is one of Shetland's most photographed and is well worth seeing.

East Burrafirth has grown up along the coast facing south-west across Aith Voe. Evenings can be lovely here, with sunsets tinting the water and night time bringing reflections of lights on the farther shore. It seems hard to believe that the side road which leads into the hamlet is one of the most recent features in the landscape. But the construction of the single-track link in the 1920s across the upper grazings of the seashore crofts is still remembered. The road men got 6d (2 1/2p) per hour and had to walk or cycle to the job and stay in an old house all week. The nearest shop was in Grobsness, several miles across the hills and back again, often walked by children carrying messages.

South Voxter, a mile or two further north, is signed off the main road to the left. The short road gives way to a track and forks, one branch leading over to the old settlements of Houbansetter, Ladie and Quiensetter on the western shore of the ness opposite the island of Papa Little. Here, many years ago, during a visit to Shetland by the Royal family, the young Princess Anne and Prince Charles were ferried with their escorts and spent a blissful day playing among the heather and along the shore while their parents went about their official business. Above South Voxter the ruined crofthouse of Moon stands starkly against the horizon, its empty windows gaping against the sky.

Grobsness, at the end of another short road to the left, overlooks a sheltered stretch of water where salmon farming was established in the 1990s. An old Haa house ruin stands a short distance down the slope from the road, facing old and

East Burra Firth and
Aith Voe at dusk, with
Aith Ness, Papa Little
and Muckle Roe
beyond.

new crofthouses. A shop and busy fishing station once stood
here. There are fine views across the settlement of Gonfirth
below and across Gon Firth itself towards South Voxter and
Cole Ness. Views are even better half a mile further on, when
the road curves round the face of the hill. It descends very
steeply before ending in a large turning place, beyond which
the access to the Grobsness settlement is gated. Linga and
Muckle Roe and Wethersta fill the scene to the west and north,
with Papa Little and Vementry to the south.

The road rising up to the Loch of Gonfirth is narrow and
twisty, so take care and be prepared for oncoming traffic.
There is a strangely remote and bleak feel to this loch, with its
pewter-grey water and dark rock-strewn margins. A young girl
once found a finely worked white quartz arrowhead here, a
great rarity among Shetland's archeological treasures. The road
levels out, following the curves of the shore, then drops
steeply down towards Voe. You can glimpse long vistas to the
south along the valley between West and Mid Kame before the
road crosses a fast, full stream near a large old quarry and
enters Voe itself.

151

The route north via Aith from the road out west, now meets the main north-south Voe to Lerwick road, which is covered in the North-East and Central Mainland chapter.

The Guide now returns to Bixter and continues west to Park Hall, where a small road leaves the A971 heading south to Effirth and Reawick, west to Skeld and eventually rejoins the main road shortly before the Bridge of Walls. Park Hall stands forlorn and shabby now, having been empty so long that all traces of former glory are lost. The big house was home to the Bowie family, from whose ranks came many notable scholars and enterprising Shetlanders over the years. In its heyday it was very grand with some unusual features and extensive gardens.

Effirth with its scatter of crofthouses overlooks the head of Effirth Voe below. The road skirts higher moorland to the west, through Semblister, where a small side road branches east to Sand. Notice the old, but well-preserved hill dyke to the right of the road as it rises up the hill towards Sandhoulland. The road forks here, the right fork leading to the imposing Haa of Sand, built in 1754 for Sir Andrew Mitchell of Westshore in Scalloway, which has windows allegedly taken originally from Scalloway Castle. The Haa overlooks Sand Voe, with its splendid beach sheltered by the narrow finger of Fora Ness beyond. Near the old pier and former fishing station is a cemetery and the complete chancel arch of St Mary's pre-Reformation church, which is linked with local legends concerning Spanish sailors shipwrecked here.

Surviving chancel arch of St Mary's Church, Sand.

Experimental tree plantations and ponds were introduced into the old crofting landscape here during the 1990s. You can go as far as Inner Sand overlooking the narrow Sandsound Voe and the high bulk of Russa Ness beyond before returning to the B9071. Turn left, passing Garderhouse, which overlooks Seli Voe, with its salmon farm and the island of Kirk Holm on which ancient foundations remain. Reawick comes in sight, set above a

lovely crescent of warm, russet sand fringing the shore here. A fine walk along the precipitous cliffs and round the headland, passes Deepdale and the Hill of Swartagill before leading you back to Easter Skeld.

Easter Skeld overlooks Skelda Voe and has a splendid modern hall, housing estates, a new school and imaginatively sited sheltered housing with views across the sea for all the residents. The village was a hive of industry in the late 1800s as a centre for the dried salt fish trade, exporting to Spain. Remains of old buildings stand near the pier. Today the state-of-the-art Shetland Smokehouse produces fine salmon and other fish delicacies, sending them all round the world. A side road left goes to Scarvister where a scatter of houses face the early morning sun, above Tarasta Ayre. You can walk from here right round the dramatic headland of Skelda Ness with its magnificent sea stacks and geos. At the T-junction the road turns left to Wester Skeld and then divides.

Ignoring the right fork to Westerwick, you reach Silwick with its peat stacks, tiny fields and string of old crofthouses set above the shallow valley and shingle beach. Some of the most dramatic sea stacks in Shetland can be seen when walking out to the coast from here, one of which supports a cormorant colony. A truly splendid walk along the cliffs to the west takes you right round to Westerwick, guarded by a protective curve of scapolite-rich cliffs leaving wonderfully framed views out to sea. A handful of houses, marshy fields and the site of an old mill beside the burn grace this tiny valley. There is very little space for cars however, so ask and park sensitively if you come by vehicle and intend walking. A quiet hour spent on the beach here heals many a weary spirit. From here, if you feel like a longer walk, you can continue west to Culswick, or you can return to Wester Skeld.

From Wester Skeld the road now goes due north, meeting the one from Easter Skeld at Hestinsetter, meaning 'settlement of horses'. Turn left and after a mile, take the left fork into Culswick, one of Shetland's most attractive corners. It is an area of stunning cliff- and sea-scapes, seabird colonies and superb archaeology, set in an old crofting and grazing landscape under wide skies. There are some unusual wild flowers among the marshy fringes of the loch here and the small community cherishes the unspoilt, peaceful atmosphere which pervades the valley. A fine walk out to the west passes deserted, enchanting

Sandness Hill,
Hill of Bousta and
Snarra Ness across
West Burra Firth.

Sotersta, and reaches Culswick Broch, still one of the largest broch remains despite considerable robbing of stonework. It has a doorway capped with a huge, triangular lintel stone. The area is among the finest for coastal walking with views across to Vaila, Whites Ness and Gruting. Retrace your route to the junction where the Culswick road turned off. You can now turn left and head north, cutting across bleak moors, past Ola's Voe and Hoga Ness where you may notice some remarkable old double dykes, stretching east across the hills in a die-straight, east-west line.

Keep an eye open for grouse as you descend towards Seli Voe with its fringe of habitation, old, deserted and new. The road curves up and round to a crossroads; go left for Gruting itself, straight ahead for West Houlland with its broch site and reach Bridge of Walls, or right for Stanydale.

Gruting is one of the richest areas in Shetland for Neolithic sites and has an air of antiquity with numerous settlement sites, ancient walls, burial sites and clearance cairns. If instead of turning left to Gruting you had turned right at the crossroads, you would have crossed a wide stretch of moorland, passing Loch of Gruting and the road to Sefster and Heathertown, and come to Stanydale.

You are signposted to the famous 'Stanydale Temple' site, the dramatic and massive stone Neolithic building which far exceeds the normal house size of this period. Stand within those sturdy walls and you are standing where some of the earliest settlers in the islands stood, over 5000 years before. A glance at the 1-50,000 Ordnance Survey map will show you several other sites nearby. The present landscape here is thought to have been influenced by Neolithic overfarming, which impoverished the land and led eventually to a period of depopulation.

The road continues north from here and rejoins the main A971, completing the loop begun at Park Hall.

Turn left at the A971 with Hulma Water lying below to the north. After a mile or so, a road is signed off right to the Papa Stour ferry. Papa Stour is described on page 161. This road threads its way through some of the most mysterious and varied scenery in Shetland, linking the scattered settlements of Unifirth, Brindister, West Burrafirth and Fogrigarth right out as far as Snarraness. Those who like really wild places will enjoy exploring the rugged headland of the Neans, with its scores of tiny lochs and craggy outcrops, which was home to the legendary 'Tief o' da Neeans', a thief who lived in a cave here long ago. There are great views north from here, of the West Burrafirth islands and Vementry as far as Hillswick and Stenness in the distance.

When the Papa Stour ferry point was moved to West Burrafirth from Sandness, it gave this corner of Shetland a new lease of life. There is a pier, carpark and toilets. The entrance to the sea is guarded by treacherous skerries and stacks and a safe passage past them has been secured with leading lights. You can see small, white huts in two places on the coast here, which, when viewed from out at sea, shine lights which change colour if the boat steers a fraction either side of the central beam, thus shining a perfect course. A ruined broch stands on a holm below Engamoor and few places are more peaceful. The rocks of the area have been heavily faulted; split and fused many times so that sandstones, breccias, conglomerates and metamorphic outcrops can be found alongside each other.

The narrow road winds on past West Burrafirth and peters

out above a shingle beach at Snarra Ness where the sea has
almost cut right through, nearly turning Snarraness into an
island. A fault cuts through the metamorphic rock where the
land is narrowest. The Ness widens beyond into hilly terrain,
forming an ideal bastion to the forces of wind and sea to the
west. The old house has been beautifully restored and you could
ask before leaving a vehicle, or walking further out. A glorious
walk starts here which leads right round the Ness and back,
with wonderful sea views and cliff and seashore scenery. The
cliffs are sliced by geos and inlets, full of caves. At one point a
series of massive rocks has tumbled from a high cliff face and
among them nestles the Snarraness press-gang cave in which
local men hid from the press gang during the Napoleonic Wars.
From Snarraness there is an old way round the coast to
Sandness, through the deserted township of Kellister.

Returning to the main A971, the road continues south for
a mile, then curves west into Bridge of Walls overlooking the
Voe of Browland, meeting the branch road from Skeld.

The Guide now follows the road south into Walls and the
neighbouring settlements, before returning to this point and
continuing to the west.

The old centre of the village of Walls, or Waas, as it is
called in Shetland, still clusters round the pier and the old
harbour and the old haa, with its charm intact despite many
visual changes over the years. Walls is a lively community, with
a school, swimming pool, and village hall. The Walls bakery
has raised the status of traditional Shetland products, especially
their oatcakes, in recent years. Walls is a great sailing centre
with events and activities almost all year round. Sadly, the
community has, like many others in Shetland, lost members to
accidents at sea. The shop, garage, surgery, care centre and
health centre add to the convenience for locals, but country
shops in Shetland suffer increasingly from the effects of big
supermarkets in Lerwick and their futures are far from certain.

The road forks in Walls, the left branch crossing a bridge
and leading south past the shop to Saltness, Grunnavoe and
Vadlure to Whites Ness. The Whites Ness peninsula reaches
south, almost touching Vaila. It divides Vaila Sound from
Gruting Voe and is an excellent walking area. To the east lies
the Ward of Culswick, high above its skirting fringe of moors
and cliffs. You may be able to make out the broch on the right
against the skyline. Look out for the tiny, enchanting house at

Point, set like a gem into a curve of the shoreline at the Stead of Whitesness.

Returning to Walls and turning left, there is a small loop road which branches right past the Loch of Kirkigarth and links the branching settlements of Bardister, Stennestwatt and Brunatwatt, curving finally north and connecting with the A971 again. Continuing through Walls, a road leads left past old council houses and a church, to the pier from which the boat to Foula leaves. An old manse near the junction has been converted into a camping booth and has an interesting garden. Stapness is signed left just beyond the village as you rise up the hill and houses here enjoy the finest views of Walls spread out below. Further out of Walls still, Burrastow is signed left leading past Riskaness, Lera Voe and the shore base for Vaila with its tiny broch-style oil store. This branch has a short loop back through Greenland and Burraland and a longer loop via Vesquoy, both of which rejoin the Walls road to Mid Walls and Dale of Walls. A new road was cut through the Dale of Walls, to Upper Dale and out to the Sandness road. The Guide now returns to Bridge of Walls.

From Bridge of Walls the road forks right for Sandness. The area to the north is full of large lochs, and at one time a hotel for anglers was built here. You can walk for miles along the silent loch shores and across the hills between them. This part of Shetland has many prehistoric sites and the Scord of Brouster, signed to the right just north of the fork to Sandness, has been excavated and interpreted for visitors with an information board explaining the features of the Neolithic village and the local vegetation and habitats from the period.

The road from Lerwick to Sandness still feels very long and tortuous. But compared with the journey only a few years ago, it is splendid. After you pass the junction to Dale of Walls, it is only a few miles to the green pastures and lovely coastline of this fertile and attractive corner of Shetland. A scatter of single houses, crofthouses and clusters of dwellings fills the landscape,

Haa House, Sand.

all lying in the lee of the massive bulk of Sandness Hill to the south. There is a school at Sandness, and the ferry to Papa Stour formerly plied from the pier at Melby just below the site of old Melby House, the seat of power in times long gone by.

The remarkable history of pure Shetland wool took a leap forward in recent years when the spinning mill was set up. The story of Shetland Woollen Mill is something of a recent legend. Peter Jamieson from Sandness conceived the idea of buying the machinery from a closed-down mill in England. He found one, dismantled and packed all the parts, took them back and re-constructed them in Sandness. The products now made here go straight to the top of the market and are sold in Harrods and other exclusive shops abroad. Staff at the mill welcome visitors.

Visit the glorious sandy beach at Norby and walk around the cliffs to Little Bousta, past rocky, sheltered coves and dramatic headlands. There are many prehistoric sites and some of Shetland's bonniest crofting landscapes. This is the approach to the old route to Kellister and Snarraness.

Huxter, at the far end of the road past Sandness, is the furthest settlement west in Mainland Shetland and has many features worth exploring. A broch site and several other prehistoric, smaller sites are found nearby, as well as a freshwater loch with marshy fringes rich in wild flowers each summer. The burn runs westwards into the sea, through a gulley where several old click mills once turned to grind the grain harvested from local fields. A great deal of restoration work has been done on the mills in recent years. This has halted the decay which would otherwise have rendered them little more than heaps of stone, like most of these mills. Fossil fish scales have been found in places along the rocky coast in this area.

Huxter is also a starting point for one of the loveliest and most dramatic walks in Shetland, along the cliff tops right round to the Dale of Walls. It passes above the magnificent Bay of Deepdale and is only a short way from the summit of Sandness Hill, from which views stretch almost the full length of the isles. Foula, when the sky is clear, dominates the seascape westwards and is seen from here at its most powerful and brooding. Seen from Foula, the rise of Sandness Hill is one of the clearest features along the Shetland profile. Once you get to the Dale of Walls, you will find one of the most beautiful burns in Shetland. The crofthouses here are trim and well tended, with a continuous flow of colour from garden

Cley Stacks across
Coppa Wick near Dale
on the far west coast
of the Mainland, with
Papa Stour beyond.

flowers to wild flowers along the burnside.

There is magnificent coastal walking all the way from
Dale of Walls right round the coast to the south and east to
Watsness, along the cliffs through some of the West side's most
beautiful coastal scenery around Mid Walls. A number of lochs
and crofting townships, some more recent houses and a string of
ancient sites can be seen. Foula dominates the seascape to the
west all the way along the coast here.

More dramatic sea- and landscapes and wildlife feature as
the coast curves round towards Footabrough, at the head of
Footabrough Voe, with its broch site overlooked by a number
of houses and crofts. Springtime here is especially rich in wild
flowers and bird life, as the land has been little changed and a
number of deserted settlements in the area bear witness to a
larger local population in earlier times. The coastal route leads
along the southern shore of the voe, round wave-battered
Braga Ness, across rock-strewn cliff tops to the south-east.
Overlooked by the Hill of Scarvister, the scenery is craggy and
exposed. A singularly lovely corner is the deserted township of
Littleure nestling into the lee of The Peak, a protective arm of

159

rock jutting out across a tiny natural harbour.

The island of Vaila to the east soon comes into view. A watch tower, hunched onto the cliff top of a precipitous headland, stands looking out to sea. Eventually the shoreline swings north hugging Vaila Sound, the higher mass of hill and moor above giving increasing shelter from westerly winds and soon Burrastow comes into view. Burrastow House dates from 1759 and was once a highly rated hotel, with a reputation for wonderful local food.

Vaila was inhabited from ancient times and a large number of prehistoric sites have been identified in the island. It is privately owned and can only be visited by arrangement. Vaila Hall stands today in a magnificent setting. From the 1580s its history is well documented, with the ownership changing roughly every hundred years. Cheyne, Mitchell and Scott, all key Shetland figures in their day, added in turn to its buildings and features. In the 1890s the island was bought by Yorkshire mill-owner Herbert Anderton. His descendant, Henry Anderton, laid on expensive but very popular banquets in the great hall in the 1970s. It was sold to Dorotta Rychlik in the 1990s. Vaila forms a particularly important link in the chain of events which have shaped Shetland's fishing history. It was here that Arthur Anderson first devised a scheme to revolutionise Shetland fishing management and the livelihoods and wellbeing of fishermen and their families. A painting by an unknown contemporary artist depicts Anderson's fishing business and the beach in Vaila.

There are prehistoric sites in the island and sections of ancient boundary walls. Magnificent natural arches, sea cliffs, sea caves and stacks around the shores draw many a sailing boat in for a closer look during the summer. Wild flowers are prolific, especially since Vaila has become an organic farm, with reduced pressure on grazing. The great house and its gardens have been restored along with the reservoir, road and other buildings on the island. Vaila, like much of remote Shetland until recent times, has no mains electricity and uses generators. The oil tanks which hold the fuel for generators and boats are stored in a remarkable new building in the form of a small, perfectly built stone broch by the new service pier for Vaila, which screens beautifully the lurid but functional tanks from view. A second building, for use when rough sea delays crossings, has been constructed to resemble a small lighthouse.

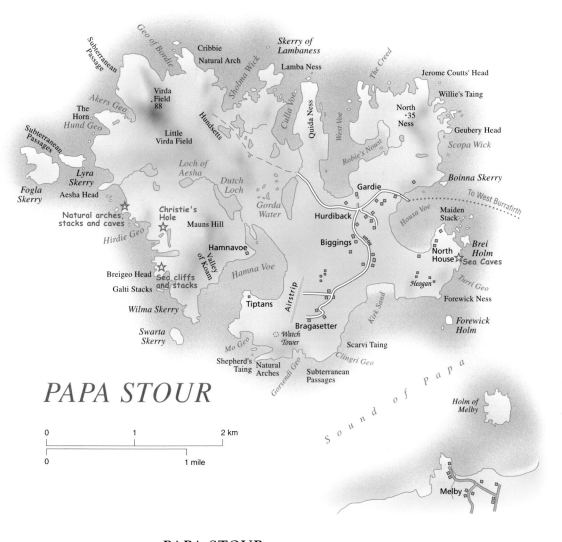

PAPA STOUR

Papa Stour, which means 'Great Island of the Priests', is one of the most magical of Shetland's smaller islands. Around the coast, the volcanic tuffs and lavas have been carved by the sea into a spectacular series of cliffs, stacks, blow holes and geos. Sea caves around and even under the island are among the finest in Europe and attract canoeists from all over the world. Many people have experienced particular feelings of peace and calm here, when walking through the island, whose scale accounts for some of its charm.

Here, more than perhaps anywhere else in Shetland, you can see the contrast between the inby (enclosed) and outby land. Generations of folk have taken turfs for animal bedding, soil improvement and roofing. The stripped ground to the west of the hill dykes has bright-green mounds remaining at intervals, created by the piling up of turfs for collecting and transporting back to the crofts. Each heap once belonged to a particular family or individual. To the east, just over the boundary wall, there is contrasting lush pasture and deep soil with fields knee-deep in flowers. The flowers in spring and summer have become well known as a result of their scent; a scent so strong that during summer fogs, or darkness, as the old fishermen's stories tell, men far out at sea, way out of sight of land, were able to guide themselves home by following the effects of both the drifting waves of perfume and the 'Möder Dy', a subtle current, almost a pulse of movement in the water, indicating the approach of land.

Tales that survive of Vikings, elopements and shipwrecks have enthralled listeners for generations. In the early 1800s, islander Gideon Henderson was paid to keep a young man in the island, ostensibly because he was 'insane'. His well-to-do family apparently found his eccentric temperament a major embarrassment. The Hon Edward Lindsay was a prisoner in the island for 26 years. After several attempts, he was finally helped to escape by a Quaker, Catherine Watson, who was convinced of his sanity; a conviction upheld by the subsequent declaration by the Vice Chancellor's Court in London. There is a spring in the island called 'Lindsay's Well' to this day.

Stack alongside Lyra Skerry from Stourhund, to the far west of Papa Stour.

The Papa Stour sword dance, a curious, traditional dance, with its medieval overtones was almost lost but is now saved for posterity. Archaeological sites abound all over the island. The most famous is Da Biggins, excavated by Dr Barbara Crawford during the 1970s and '80s, thought to be the site of the house of a Norseman of considerable importance. An interpretive panel has been erected on the site.

A modern day saga could be written about the 'hippies' of Papa Stour. As a result of population decline in the 1960s and 1970s, the school closed and some islanders feared that Papa

Looking west from
a croft at Biggings,
Papa Stour, towards
Mauns Hill.

Stour would become yet another uninhabited island. One local
man took the controversial step of advertising for new members
of the community and a colourful procession of folk arrived
over several years. Some stayed and others left, yet more stayed
a short while and 'flit' or removed to other parts of Shetland.
Several decades later many families still remain, some of whom
have set up thriving businesses and contributed greatly to
island life. There are still people who, hearing tales of wealth
and housing, freedom and excitement, arrive in Shetland
hoping for instant satisfaction of all their needs and finding life
far harder than they expected.

To the north of Papa Stour lie a cluster of tiny islands
called the Ve Skerries. In calm weather they are havens of
tranquillity, where the silent sea rises and falls only inches, but
in a storm, nowhere could be more dangerous. For centuries
these were a menace to shipping and many lives were lost when
wrecks struck the low, sea-obliterated rocks in bad weather.
Particularly heartbreaking was the loss of the crew of the *Ben
Doran* in 1930. A lighthouse was eventually erected in the
1980s. No lives have been lost here since. A memorial to the
crew of the *Ben Doran* stands in Sandness churchyard.

163

Gaada
Stack *Sheepie*
Arva Skerry The Ness *Hellibaas*
Logat Head Strem Ness
East Hoevdi Freyars Skeld
Mucklegrind
Soberlie Skiodar Ruscar Head
Hill
Bloberg Ruyhedlar
North Bank Codlafield Head
Swaa
The Burns Head
Kame *Flick Lochs* Gossumeador Taing
Rokna Bark Hill *Overfandal* Head
Skerries Loch Sloag
Nebbifield The Hamnafield Pier
Sneug, *To Walls*
418 Ham *Ham Voe*
Hornalie Mires Baa Head
Hamar
Wester Tounafield *Mill Loch* Little Ham
Hoevdi Durga
Mucklaberg Ness
Wick of Smallie *Shoabill*
Mucklaberg *South*
The Daal *Wick*
Broadfoot
The Noup Naggards Airstrip Mid Hoevdi
Punds
Skirnawilse
Biggings
Helliberg's
Wick

FOULA

Boat Harbour

South Ness Hord Rippack Stack
Head
Doalie *Boniberg*

0   1   2 km
0   1 mile

Foula

Curved aedge o da wirld
a conductor staands, makkin
symphonies o licht

From *Sunset Trowe Da Gaada Stack: A Response to a Photographic Image by Colin Baxter*, by Christine De Luca.

Foula is a massive natural fortress of Old Red Sandstone which guards Shetland's approaches from the west. The full power of its natural forms can only be experienced by walking among the peaks, or standing at their feet. The Sneug, the highest point, is some 1377 feet (420 m) high and the cliffs at the Kame are sheer, towering 1246 feet (380 m) above sea level, second only in the UK to those of St Kilda. The nearest Shetland coastline is 14 miles (22 km) away and is often barely visible.

Foula's sandstones are relieved by a metamorphic band on the east side. Tiny plant fossils can be found in a few places and rare trace fossils from early creatures. Many wild plants survive here, but the birds are Foula's most impressive wildlife and give the island its name: *Fugl-oy*, or 'bird island'. A large colony of great skuas or Bonxies breeds here, as well as Arctic skuas, kittiwakes, guillemots, puffins and fulmars. Islanders used to scale the cliffs to harvest eggs in spring. Shetland's most attractively coloured and patterned sheep are found here.

From Ristie in the north, with the dramatic natural arch of Gaada Stack offshore, south through Ham to South Ness is a walk of almost four miles, but on a fine day you can wander three times as far. From Shetland the striking profile of Foula dominates the scene to the west with the great hills of Hamnafield, the Sneug, the Kame, Soberlie, the wide glacial valley of the Daal and the lower hill of the Noup to the south. The locally famous 'Sneck o' da Smaalie' is a wickedly slippery scramble down a cleft to a cliff foot, not recommended without local guides and climbing equipment.

Often weather-bound, Foula demands extraordinary

qualities of toughness and independence among its human population. Lack of natural harbours puts fishermen at a disadvantage but few crofting communities have withstood the temptation to leave for softer, easier lives with such resilience. Families who have had to leave spend much of their spare time back 'in the isle', coming by ferry from Walls or by plane from Tingwall. Foula school, one of the smallest, but best-equipped in Britain, is used by the whole community. There is a unique multi-sourced electricity generating scheme. Wind, when it blows, generates power and surplus energy is used to pump water to a high loch, providing water power when the wind drops.

Archaeological and historical features exist, but many have been destroyed or lost. A broch was said to have

The Noup, Smallie and Wick of Mucklabrek from Hamar, Foula.

stood at the north end, and a 'Picts' house at Crougar. These, plus a cairn at Harrier, have disappeared but traces of Neolithic houses, an ancient chapel and burial ground at Harrier remain, where, legend says, a monastery formerly existed. A possible Viking boat burial, a few burnt mounds and burial cists have been recorded and a 'bog' body was reportedly uncovered and immediately reburied during peat digging in 1883. Records of Norse history and folklore survive, including the legend of Queen Katherine of Foula and a ruin still bears her name. The old Norn speech survived longer here than in the rest of Shetland, as did the old Julian calendar, officially ended in 1752 in Britain. Old Yule is celebrated on 6 January and new year on the 13th.

A number of ships came to grief on Foula's shores in bad weather before the lighthouse was built. In 1948 a schooner

Gaada Stack just
north of Ristie, Foula,
at sunset.

struck Da Heed o da Hurd and her cargo of timber was lost. *The Oceanic*, sister ship to *The Titanic*, ran aground and sank off Foula during the First World War. There were other war-time casualties. A Whitley bomber crash-landed and despite a dramatic impact, all the crew climbed out alive. Carrier pigeons survived the crash too, and they were fitted with messages and released to summon aid. Foula folk recall the tragedy of a Canadian Catalina which crashed into Hamnafield in thick fog in the early 1940s. Seven men died but one survived, allegedly because he had been sitting in the look-out tower when the plane hit the ground. Foula folk erected a particularly fine war memorial here.

You can get no further west in Shetland. But, if you have the stamina and the weather is kind, climb the great hills and when you reach the top of the Sneug, gaze west and south, scanning the far horizon for the faint mark of Orkney which is just visible if the conditions are right. You may even see the mast on North Ronaldsay. During the era of the Haaf fishing, men, according to local stories, would 'row Foula doon' – row so far west that even Foula sank completely below the eastern horizon.

167

North-East and Central Mainland

Will you come oot fae da toon da-day
An we'll hear da laverick sing,
An waatch da stenshakker dart owerda broos
O da hills a Lunnasting.

From *Macarism* by Rhoda Bulter.

The Guide now returns to Brae in Delting and completes the route around the North-East Mainland before continuing south. One of Shetland's largest villages, Brae has grown rapidly during the past 20 years. It makes a good base to stay while exploring the North Mainland and Muckle Roe. The village's setting is very attractive, a scatter of buildings clustered around the head of Busta Voe where only a narrow strip of land divides it from the head of Sullom Voe to the north. Streams flow down from the high moorland to the east and there is rumoured to be gold among the fine shingle sand of the beach. But little shelters the village from bitter northerly winds in winter. Ancient prehistoric sites are found in the hills all round Brae and there must have been many more along the shoreline, long-since lost under more recent building, but a broch site still survives at nearby Burravoe.

The oldest buildings are around the old pier, looking across the water to Busta House, one of Shetland's oldest buildings, now a fine hotel. There are legends and stories galore about this lovely old house and there are few more pleasant places to spend an evening in Shetland. A number of traditional crofthouses stand among more recently built houses along the main road and several housing estates present a rich variety of architectural styles. Brae is well served by its two garages, large shop, hotel, building centre, leisure centre, boating club and post office. There is a printing business,

community office
and a health centre
with doctor and
dental practice
nearby and a
residential care
centre for the
elderly. Near the
Mid Brae Inn there is
one of Shetland's rare
older tree plantations.

Busta House, Brae.

   A junior high school
has been built near the modern
swimming pool, replacing an older
one which has been imaginatively
converted into the community hall. The former hall now
looks incredibly small and inadequate, standing below the
present-day road surface opposite the shop and the junction
with the Sullom Voe turnoff. The tendency in Shetland to
repair roads by simply adding layer upon layer of road-surfacing
materials has resulted in many properties ending up below road
level, and is only now beginning to be addressed. You can
explore several small roads leading away from the main road
through Brae, south to Burravoe, west to the white-painted,
airy Church of Scotland or north for Northbrae and the chapel
and east up into the hills, past the graveyard and the new all-
weather sports pitch behind the school.

   Brae had a lively role to play during the Second World
War, with a sea plane base only a few miles up the road.
Sullom Voe reaches right down to Northbrae and a small arm
extends east into Voxter Voe just to the north. Here the
Valayre Burn pours into the sea from its source in the hills
above. The gorge that the burn flows through is one of the
best of its kind, with relict trees, roses and honeysuckle
growing in places along its lower reaches. Voxter Outdoor
Centre, a former manse, used during the last war as a small
field hospital, stands at the voehead. It offers excellent
residential and environmental study facilities to groups. There
is a walled garden with apple and cherry trees. Trondavoe, a
little to the north, once had an old smuggling hole, but it was
filled in many years ago. Scatsta airport, a little further on, was
constructed to service the sea plane base during the war and

now serves the oil terminal, said to be the largest in Europe. There is a weather station here too, which contributes regular forecasts to Radio Shetland.

When T.M.Y. Manson wrote his *Guide to Shetland* in 1932, he said of this area, 'the principal feature of the panorama is the remarkable Sullom Voe, which winds for eight miles...its suitability for boating may here be emphasized and visitors at Brae will be able to enjoy it to the full'. What a contrast today! The oil terminal site dominates the area, especially at night, when it twinkles like a distant city, but by day little is seen that doesn't nestle into the low hills behind. The only real intrusion is the small cluster of flare stacks which burn by day and dominate the sky by night. A lurid, pulsing glow can often be seen over the area from quite distant parts of Shetland. But critics are often accused of ignoring the flares out in the oilfields beyond the horizon, where many more times the amount of gas is flared off and the energy waste is far higher.

It is hard to believe, coming fresh to Sullom Voe, what a remarkable alteration to the land and sea here was effected by the building of the terminal. Half of Orka Voe, a colossal area of sea, was filled in and built over, with enormous technical and engineering difficulties, subsidence, saturation, drainage and slippage. One oil worker told me that he left a lorry parked on a section of infilled land one night and that the next day it had sunk and vanished completely into the waterlogged depths. Yet the terminal stands and functions as if it was built entirely on terra firma. The seashore and seabed nearby are monitored regularly for pollution and so far, the results published have revealed remarkably clean beaches, compared with other oil terminals. Otters frequent the area and the road to the terminal has a hazard sign at one point which warns about otters crossing; and they frequently do.

East of the head of Garth's Voe, a small crofting settlement once flourished, but in the Second World War it was selected as the site for an RAF base. The picturesque township of Graven was 'swamped in a sea of concrete' as one local man put it. Sixty years later, much of the concrete is still there. The sizeable Burn of Laxobigging flows out to sea here, swollen by water drained from an immense area of hills and moorlands which stretch up as far as Crawsiller Knowe (*crawsiller* is the Shetland dialect word for mica) overlooking Dales Voe to the east.

From Sullom Voe the road crosses north of Graven to

Firths Voe on the east side of Shetland and meets the A968 road from Voe to Toft and the ferry to the Northern Isles. A huge construction camp was built here for the building of the terminal, now all demolished bar a sports centre. The village of Mossbank, beyond, was an important business centre in the north, visited every fortnight until the 1970s by the ferry, *Earl of Zetland* from Lerwick, and it was formerly the crossing point for the ferry to Yell. Several large, uninhabited islands lie in Yell Sound not far away. This community perhaps more than any other suffered from the 'oil invasion' as it came to be known. Masses of extra housing and facilities were built for the incoming oil workers and a huge new school replaced the older one. But as the oil pace slowed, employment was strategically reduced and the population fell, leaving empty dwellings, an altered landscape and an uneasy community which is slowly picking up the threads and gearing into a new identity and dynamism.

An interesting story is told of an old woman who lived in a crofthouse on the south side of the hill overlooking Firths Voe. Many years ago she began to behave in a very strange way, coming out of her house and shouting and screaming at some sort of invisible intruders. She railed at them for bringing their machines onto her land and ordered them off. Frantic with rage and wretchedness she bewailed the mess that they were making of her beautiful fields. It was assumed that she was losing her mind, and few paid any attention. But many years later, when an oil pipe was laid across that stretch of ground, with diggers churning up the ground for months as the work progressed, a few folk remembered her anguish and wondered whether the invisible machines she had 'seen' and screamed at, were some kind of premonition. The crofthouse where she lived became a ruin and the fields overgrown.

The new ferry service goes to Yell from Toft, another mile or two round to the north, and the road continues north to Brough beyond. Toft was once an old port for Leith traders and whalers; now a fine carpark, a waiting room with toilets and a telephone stand above the beach and queues form and manoeuvre into line for each ferry crossing. The hill to the west is oddly green; evidence of massive reseeding after the huge construction camp was demolished. Three disused sports centres were not demolished, however, and it may be some time before their unsightly bulk vanishes from the scene.

Looking north-east
along Dales Voe
towards Fora Ness.

Cars returning from Yell take the A968 south to Voe. The
road follows Shetland's east coast here, climbs up the north face
of the Hill of Swinister, then turns south at a sharp, dangerous
bend overlooking dramatic Foraness, joined to the shore by a
double tombolo. It runs under the steep shadowing bulk of
Dales Lees to the west, alongside Dales Voe with its saltmarsh
at the head and salmon cages offshore, sheltered from easterly
storms by the narrow barrier of Easter Hill of Dale. From here it
is only a few miles to Voe, past a scattered community of crofts,
small farms and houses. Until the late 1990s the scene was
dominated by the marvellous white blades of the Sussetter Hill
aero generator. Technical problems curtailed its useful life
however and after it was sold, despite rumours of it being
shipped to the third world, in the end it was blown up.

The narrow road which leaves the A968 and leads north-
east up Gardie Hill carries on and drops over into Collafirth, a
tiny community still holding a marvellous air of old Shetland.
Separated by the long heather-covered ridge of Garda Ness
from the wide road through Dale, with the broad valley and
expansive views, the area is like another world. The old croft of

173

Quhamm is now derelict, but until not long ago still bore the old thatched, or 'tek', roof, with its moulded chimney pot, and a well-tended kale yard. From just beyond the cluster of houses by the shingly and rocky shore you can walk right round the coastline into Swinning on the east side of the ness. The cliffs are steep in places but the seascapes and seabirds make for breathtaking views. Look out for otters and seals.

Having detoured north from Brae via Sullom Voe and Mossbank and down to Collafirth, the Guide now returns to Brae and describes the route to Voe from there. These routes, the A968 and the A970, meet at Tagon, just north of Voe.

A mile south of Brae on the way to Voe, a small road leads off west to Wethersta. Here farms and crofthouses stand looking out across Olnafirth and south-west towards Swarbacks Minn. A small industrial site here has seen many an enterprising business get started. A number of houses have been built in recent years and there are many fine gardens with some splendid newly constructed dry stone walls. Sadly not a trace remains of the old house built here in the 1600s, contemporary with the one at Jarlshof. There can be good walking around the coast here on a fine day, with wide sea views over to Muckle Roe and East Burrafirth.

The hills slope up steeply to the north and the ground to the south drops away from the road to Olna Firth. On the shore, below the road, is the site of one of Shetland's four whaling stations. A cluster of buildings remains where once there was a hive of activity; smoke, steam, smells and noise now only dim memories among a dwindling number of older Shetlanders. But you can still pick up the odd piece of whalebone washed up along the beaches nearby. In spring, the roadsides between Brae and Voe in places are golden with daffodils. Here and there short stretches of the former single-track road can still be seen. One loop near Voe has been signposted as a parking area and is a good place to stop so that you can admire the marvellous views. But exercise caution entering and leaving this lay-by, as traffic often roars past at dangerously high speeds.

The head of Olnafirth supports two settlements, Tagon on the northern slopes and Voe itself around the southern shore. Tagon has a pub in addition to the shop and church and there is a large house, set among trees, which was once a doctor's surgery. The A968 to Mossbank and the North Isles ferries branches off here. A short way north along it stand the local primary school and village hall. Here every August the Voe Agricultural Show is held. Marquees and stalls, cattle and produce competitions and a full programme of events, well supported by refreshments, make this a day worth planning for. Check the date in advance at the Shetland Tourist Office.

Heading south from Tagon, a right turn off the main road leads to Voe, one of Shetland's most attractive villages. The setting is very photogenic and the old buildings a delight, and full of history. The old weaving sheds, the truck system and trade are not so very long gone and the present bakery flourishes. The old post office and shop were altered into a restaurant in the 1990s and one of the weaving sheds was converted into a splendid and spacious camping böd. A number of new houses have been built, some with sizeable trees suggesting a favourable micro-climate. The big house stands squarely above the village among its own large trees, indicating the benefit of good shelter from the south-west.

The route from Voe through to Aith and Bixter, with many smaller settlements, has already been described more fully in the West Mainland chapter.

The Loch of Voe, which flows out into Olnafirth here, is thought to have been the site of Shetland's own ice cap during the last Ice Age. Many glacial features survive in the area and are well worth looking out for. Notice the very large glacial erratic behind the war memorial on the main road, just south of Tagon. There are more around the loch itself, especially on the north and eastern slopes above. A tree-planting project near the loch met with some success and is likely to be added to, so the appearance of the surroundings may alter considerably over the next few years.

The road to Laxo and Vidlin and to the ferry to Whalsay joins the main road just south of the Loch of Voe. There is often a cluster of cars parked near the junction. People frequently car-share, or make use of the main route buses, leaving cars at the nearest point for the drive home. You pass a couple of lochs on the south of the road, which from time to time have been visited by migrant birds. So if you are interested, pull off the road and scan the water and the marshy margins for waders. I once saw a purple heron here. Peat banks can be seen here and big, covered peat stacks are often built nearby and visited regularly by their owners for fresh stocks of fuel.

Heading east towards Laxo, just before you come to the sea, the road to North Nesting turns off south. You can take this route as a fascinating, though slower, alternative to the main road to Lerwick. Massive moorland expanses separate the communities of North and South Nesting. Kirkabister is well worth exploring and has some excellent coastal walking. The view south from almost any point on the Kirkabister road offers fine panoramas of the South Nesting skyline, with the Ward of Bressay and the Noup of Noss rearing dramatically up far behind to the south. A ruined manse dominates the skyline at Kirkabister and one of Shetland's Iron Age promontory forts is found nearer the cliff edge, facing a small island which was once joined to the mainland. Sturdy walkers can take to the coast here and walk right round to Billister. Beware of collapsing cliff edges here; keep well back.

Returning to the North Nesting junction at Laxo, the head of Laxo Voe is interesting, with a wide shingle bar almost sealing it off from the open sea; a stretch of muddy estuary and a prehistoric mound on the overlooking slope to the west. The wide road to the ferry continues past the hamlet here and the

Looking north from near Neap, Kirkabister, towards Valla Ness and Stava Ness.

Whalsay ferry pier, a carpark and toilets are off to the right. Watch out if you carry on towards Vidlin, as the new wide road ends abruptly, reverting to a narrow ribbon of single track. In spring and summer the verges of the old road are dazzling with wild flowers, especially orchids. The new roadsides boast little more than gravel and grass.

There is a peaceful quality about this corner of Shetland. The poet Rhoda Bulter was born in a crofthouse near the south-facing shore and gleaned much of her inspiration from the life and spirit of the area. There are a number of famous wreck stories from the wild coastline around it and tales too of smuggling. A road leads off to the hamlet of Skelberry to the right, but the main Vidlin road curves north and passes the loch of Kirkhouse, another good place to scan for birds, but avoid stopping in passing places, as it can disrupt local traffic. The roads to Lunna, Lunning, Swinning and Vidlin meet at a crossroads next to the shop and across the road stands the recently refurbished Vidlin Hall.

Going west past the shop at the crossroads, the road to Swinning climbs gently up and over a hill, dropping down into a broad, peaceful valley full of signs of former cultivation and settlement. Today only a handful of original houses remain, with a few recent additions and conversions. Salmon farming became a major new industry in the 1990s and this voe was ideal for cages. At the end of the road, well-established gardens have managed to support some sizeable trees, including fern elder, oak and beech, unusual species for Shetland. Here too can be seen glacial deposition features and a number of prehistoric sites have been identified nearby. For those with good heads for heights and sure feet, a fine walk can take you north round the coast from here to Collafirth. The slopes are steep and slippery and there are some awkward crossing places where streams cut deep channels as they run over the edge into the sea. A beautiful but deserted steading still stands forlornly in a small valley about a mile north of Swinning. The old couple who lived here until recent years, were great local historians and welcomed visitors.

From the Vidlin crossroads continue north if you intend to explore the Lunna Ness road. The road is single-track all the way, with some blind bends and plenty of unrestricted sheep access, so be warned. At first you can see well out across Vidlin Voe, then the route deflects to the west and crosses the

watershed, dropping
down to a sheltered
sea, where otters are
frequently seen. You
get wide views here
right across Yell
Sound to Ronas Hill
and Northmavine.
Even the Ramna
Stacks can be seen
briefly against the sea
and sky. As the road curves
round into West Lunna Voe, you
see a small tombolo and several houses and other buildings.

Lunna Kirk, Vidlin.

Lunna House, built in the 1660s, dominates the scene and its
windows stare out towards Lunna Kirk and the beautiful,
sheltered area around it, with its curious scatter of historic
ruins. Lunna House was the first base for the 'Shetland Bus', a
secret resistance operation run by Shetland and Norway during
the Second World War, before it moved to Scalloway, the
headquarters being then at Kergord.

Two roads once ran down from Lunna House and both can
still just be traced by the rise of an embankment and some
stonework on the grassy slope to the north. One went down to
the seashore and the other levelled out and followed the
contour of the hill round to the east, where almost two
centuries ago a beautiful garden was laid out. The terrain is
ideally formed for a garden, with a gently sheltering curve of
the hill enclosing an arena protected from all the worst angles
of wind and facing a splendid view out to the islands across the
sound. Now only grass, moss and heather survive.

Lunna Kirk is one of Shetland's oldest and most
attractive, with many interesting features. A walled enclosure
behind the kirk has some puzzling remains in it, consisting of
mounds and banks, thought by some to have been an ancient
ecclesiastical site. On the skyline to the south, there is a
continuation of the wall, with a small folly at its highest point.
Slightly to the north and down at the seashore is a one-time
booth, or shop and trading station, above what would once
have been a drying beach.

The Stanes of Stofast are worth a special visit by anyone
with an interest in geology. High on a peat moor, east of the

road a mile or so north of Lunna House, they stand where they once fell, released from the crushing grip of a vast glacier. From a distance they could be a ruined castle; close to, especially if viewed from the south, they resemble a giant sphinx, with a strangely beautiful profile, gazing sternly out to the eastern ocean.

Vidlin is the largest village in this corner of Shetland, with evidence of human settlement here going back many thousands of years. There is a considerable area of level land and the head of Vidlin Voe provides a good, sheltered harbour for boats. The community is a thriving and industrious one, with many successful entrepreneurs among its members. There is a newly built school and village hall and a well-stocked shop and garage. Salmon farming developed on a large scale in the late 1990s here and there are some sizeable farms and crofts. The ferry to Whalsay uses the ferry terminal in Vidlin when wind and sea conditions render the Laxo terminal unsafe.

To reach the tiny, very attractive settlement of Lunning, go right through Vidlin, bearing north where the road to Leveneap turns to the south, then, where the road follows parallel with the shore out to Kirkhouse, look for the sign to Lunning. The steep, single-track road winds up and over the heights here, past the loch of Gerda Water; the views from the top are marvellous, but if you are visiting by car, it makes more sense to stop on your return, when you will be facing the view as you descend. The terrain here is craggy and wild. Make sure you are safely off the road and not blocking entrances or passing places should you stop. A wide pull-off at the summit overlooks the dramatic loch of Longa Water which lies below, with Little Water beyond it, stretching out towards the south, surrounded by a kind of moon landscape of rocks and cliff faces, with the Noup of Noss seen far away in the distance across the sea. There is rough, but excellent walking in this area, which is full of prehistoric remains and ancient place names. The delights of the secret Fora Dale and the remote house of Bonidale are well worth exploring, particularly in good weather.

The road continues eastwards, dipping and twisting, past Gelins Water down into Lunning itself. There is only a small area of level land here and it has been cultivated for centuries. Two ruined mills can be found on the north-facing slopes of the hills to the south, leading up to Mill Loch. Here only a handful of houses and outbuildings stand today, looking east, out towards the west coastline of Whalsay spread out across a stretch of wide, exposed sea. Only a few decades ago, virtually every house here had a thatched roof. A standing stone can be seen here. There is a lovely panorama across the mass of small skerries and larger, uninhabited islands in Lunning Sound. Drivers should note that there is limited parking space. Ask, if you wish to go walking and leave a vehicle, and avoid obstructing local activity. There is no straightforward access to the sea and the coastline is wild and rocky.

This is as far as you can go to the east, so the text now returns to the point where the Vidlin road turned off the main road at the Loch of Voe and heads south through the 'Kames'.

The Kames, a series of long ridges and broad valleys, run almost due north-south down the central mass of Shetland. The main road between Lerwick and Voe runs for much of its length down the easternmost valley, with Mid Kame to the west and East Kame to the east. Wide, peat-covered slopes rise up each side to high moors beyond. These heathery, peaty hills have been heavily glaciated and the massive ridges are smooth and steep. Their alignment reflects the underlying geology, revealing the heavily faulted bands of contrasting rock types lying close together like knives in a drawer. Each type has eroded differently, the most resistant remaining as high ridges, while the more easily worn rocks became the valleys in between. The Kames form the continuation of Shetland's 'backbone' of high ridges and moors. It is possible that prehistoric islanders may have retreated from seashore locations and survived in settlements in some of the deeper valleys when the first Norsemen arrived in Shetland. Evidence may lie in the place names such as Pettawater, or 'Loch of the Picts' in Norse terms.

The road into South Nesting turns east off the main A970 and branches south again at the Nesting shop. A small island just offshore to the south-west is connected to the mainland at low tide. This stretch of very sheltered sea is Catfirth and it provided a safe location for a number of naval bases during both world wars. Some of the remains of buildings, bunkers and other features can still be found nearby. There are beautiful sea- and island-scapes off Gletness, on Nesting's southernmost coastline. There is a seemingly unending variety of prehistoric sites and in spring and summer, wonderful wild flowers, especially in May, when primroses blanket the lime-rich fields and banks. The area has several

Looking south-east from near Gletness, South Nesting, towards Score Head and Score Hill on Bressay with Noss beyond.

lochs where unusual waterfowl often feed and a wonderful winding, enchanting coastline much frequented by otters.

South Nesting, with its limestone bands beneath the ground surface, is full of tiny valleys, gorges, peaks and hollows. Vivid green, fertile fields tuck themselves in between knolls and hummocks of limestone outcrops and a wealth of wild flowers gild the roadside verges in summer. Try to visit both South and North Nesting, which are quite different in character, but equally rewarding to the courteous explorer. The best visits can be made to coincide with days when local halls are open for teas and homebakes. As well as crofters and craftsmen, Nesting men were expert seafarers, voyaging around the world in fishing, whaling, trading, naval and merchant navy ventures throughout the centuries. Look out for local history exhibitions featuring some of the more famous characters while you are here.

Nesting is sheltered from the west by miles of high, wild moors and valleys, full of Shetland's marvellous moorland birdlife. But the eastern fringe is more populated and the ground more cultivated. There are some particularly dramatic corners, such as the Quoys Burn, a gorge and tiny melt-water channel which runs almost due north into the hills; Flamister in its high, remote hollow overlooking Catfirth; Gletness, with its dainty narrow headland and multitude of prehistoric sites, just peeping above ground level and Ling Ness, tantalisingly beautiful but often inaccessible because of private access problems. The nature of the coastal territory is very special, but here more than in many other parts of the islands, private land ownership controls access. Most landowners are pleased to be asked for permission to walk across their areas, but there can be exceptions. Lambing time is the most likely to be awkward, so be considerate.

The road which links North and South Nesting hugs the low cliffs and skirts the hills to the west, passing beside many old and new dwellings, as well as prehistoric sites of various kinds. Stone walls, old signs of cultivation and drainage indicate times of much higher local populations and more intensive working of the land. At Skellister a side road cuts off to the east and threads through South Nesting. The eastern slopes of the Hill of Skellister overlook the wide, sandy and pebbly Muckle Ayre at the head of the West Voe of Skellister. Much of the story of local geology can be told on this beach, where mica crystals sparkle in the edge of the sea and pegmatite, tourmaline and enormous felspar crystals flash among the schist and gneiss pebbles.

A series of headlands reaches out to the north: Tur Ness, Ness of Skellister, Ling Ness and the Moul of Eswick. On a fine day, away across a turquoise sea to the north, the Neap is visible, a headland in North Nesting. The clustered settlements of Housabister, Kirkabister and the Neap itself are clearly seen, with the higher Ward of Symbister in Whalsay rising behind them in the distance. In wild weather, the seas that hammer onto the beach can be enormous, as can be imagined from the smooth roundness of the pebbles. The beach at Housabister to the north is not as exposed and the pebbles there are far rougher by comparison.

Return to the junction with the main road in order to follow the guide south towards the Tingwall Valley. The Loch of Girlsta to the east is said to have been named after a Viking maiden who drowned in the loch. It is Shetland's deepest loch, and home to the extremely rare Arctic char, which are thought to have become established here as the ice retreated, over

10,000 years ago. At the southern end of the loch a narrow road forks east, signed for Brunt Hamarsland, 'brunt' meaning burnt, place-name evidence of the early practice of clearing woodland for use. The hamlet here lies out of sight over the skyline and commands marvellous views over Catfirth. Residents have had splendid sightings of killer whales in recent years.

Just south of the Brunt Hamarsland junction is the settlement of Girlsta with a number of houses scattered on either side of a crossroads. Here one road winds uphill to the west and drops down into Stromfirth and leads finally to Whiteness. To the east, a narrow road leads down towards the sea. The main road carries on south to Tingwall, with the tiny, picturesque croft of Linkster set like an ivory jewel in a green crown to the west, just before the airport runway comes into view. Tingwall airport serves the whole of Shetland as the base for the air ambulance. Scheduled flights also serve the Out Skerries, Fair Isle and Foula, and until 2001, Unst as well. The main road connects here at a large junction, with the road to Walls and the West Side, then curves east, past the Tingwall crossroad and rises up a long hill before descending to Dale and the golf course a mile to the south.

Returning to Girlsta, a short stretch of road leads to where a limestone kiln once operated; part of it can still be seen. Quantities of broken limestone would have been spread, alternating with layers of peat until the kiln was full. It would then have been fired and the resulting ash slaked with water and stored in barrels, ready for use. There are fine views east here across to Wadbister on the far shore, a scene which gradually filled with salmon farming activity in the 1990s. A well-established garden with trees lies at the end of the Wadbister road, which turns off east just past Girlsta. For many years, the owner allowed visits by wedding parties, who wished to be photographed in a colourful, gracious garden setting, a rarity at that time.

Another road turns east after the Wadbister junction. This is the northernmost access to the Tingwall valley and leads over the hill, past one of Shetland's biggest quarries. Laxfirth lies over the far side and as the narrow road bends south towards Strand, it passes by a curious little building with three pointed windows. This was once a school. The road now meets up with the other access road into Strand which left the main road just opposite the Linkster access. As you pass the

northern end of the Strand Loch, look out for otters and
seabirds in the shallow sea inlet to the left.

The road forks at Strand Loch and a branch runs between
a large number of houses which have been built recently and
also passes an interesting building with a large car park. After
the grounding of the *Braer* and subsequent oil spill, large sums
of money were sent to Shetland by concerned people all over
Britain and elsewhere. One initiative which followed was the
setting up of an oiled bird unit which was built in Tingwall.
The centre is run by an SSPCA officer and injured or oiled
birds are taken here and treated. If they recover they are
released into suitable habitats and in certain cases flown south
to reserves or centres where their future recovery can be
monitored in more suitable environments.

The road continues over the hill to the south-east, and
down to a T junction with Breiwick signed left and Califf to
the right. There are small hamlets and some large farms here
overlooking the sea and the oil rig servicing base opposite.
An archaeological dig on a sizeable prehistoric settlement to
the west of the service base here uncovered valuable
information about an early archdeacon of Shetland whose *teind*,
or tithe barn, once stood here at Kebister.

Retracing your route, follow south along the road which
passes between the loch and Tingwall school and hall. There
are many lovely gardens in the area and you can often watch
Shetland ponies in the fields near the farm, before you reach
the junction with the main road to Lerwick. To enjoy the full
length of the Tingwall Valley, cross over the main road and
continue south towards Veensgarth and Herrislee. The Tingwall
Agricultural Museum was established by Jean Sandison in the
1980s in her farm buildings at Veensgarth. The collection
includes Shetland traditional furniture, household items,
crofting and blacksmith tools, a forge, coopering and
wheelwright tools and agricultural implements and machinery.
The development of the museum saw a revival of interest in old
ways and traditions, leading to a series of folklore evenings
which became very popular. These in turn led to interest in
reviving Shetland's traditional dances and their links with
other Northern and Scandinavian traditions.

The old Tingwall primary school has been modernised and
a new village hall built close by. In medieval times, Tingwall
Church was the head church for the whole of Shetland. The

Weisdale Voe from
Scord of Sound in
April snow.

original church was built on a splendid site, on top of a rise in
the land. It is thought to have been built around 1136 and
dedicated to St Magnus. Like the churches at Ireland near
Bigton and Papil in West Burra, it had a tall round tower. This
church was replaced in about 1790 by the modern one. The
churchyard has some elaborate old gravestones in a mausoleum
and a stone sarcophagus. Just past the church there is a recently
constructed garden and memorial to a pilot who was killed
when an ambulance plane crashed a few years ago.

In Viking times, the Lawting, or parliament, met in
Tingwall, giving it its name. The site still exists, though much
altered in appearance from the original structure, at the
northern end of Tingwall Loch. An excellent interpretive
display stands in the nearby car park. A modern entertaining
version of the Ting, the 'Althing Debate', occurs regularly in
winter, with a programme of topics debated before large,
enthusiastic audiences in the local school.

From this point the Guide describes the route north to
Weisdale and Kergord, before returning to Tingwall and
proceeding to Scalloway and Lerwick.

From Tingwall, the road west passes the small airport and the Planticrub nursery. It rises and crosses a watershed before dropping past the Westing Hotel down into Wormadale with Nesbister below. A viewpoint here allows you to pull off and enjoy stunning views down Whiteness Voe and west across the White Ness and Strom Ness peninsulas, as far as Foula in the distance. Shortly after the Nesbister road turns off to the left, another road leads down into South Whiteness, which is one of the best otter-watching places in Shetland. There is a shop and an old schoolhouse near the junction. Some excellent walks can be enjoyed in the area and superb views can be found from the ridge tops, especially the Hill of Hellister, from which you can see the whole of the Whiteness peninsula.

Just past Whiteness Primary School, the road turns north into Stromfirth, a hidden valley, discreetly guarding many beautiful secrets. There is a route through to Girlsta and Wadbister from this point, skirting one of Shetland's most beautiful lochs, Strom, which is fed by a substantial stream. At the seaward end, it flows with such force out to sea at low tide and the sea enters with such power at high tide, that there has been talk of a tidal energy facility being built here. During the last World War, eggs were sent from Stromfirth, as they were from many other places, to the troops in Europe. One local lass wrote her name and address and a message on one egg. The soldier who received it came to Shetland after the war and met and eventually married her; a story still told and loved by her descendants.

There are lovely views south down the voes before the winding road arrives at Weisdale, with its shop, garage and fine jewellery workshop and showroom nearby.

The Weisdale valley is one of Shetland's longest and most magnificent, lying between two sheltering ridges, 800 feet (240 m) high to the west and 500 feet (150 m) to the east. The east-facing hill is scored by water channels and a small corrie can be seen; an unusual glacial feature in Shetland. The Weisdale Burn is almost a small river and it flows to the sea, which here reaches deep inland. You can watch seabirds or even otters, and small whales have been known to enter the shallows. At the head of the voe, the main road west crosses a bridge and continues up the hill. The guide detours here and takes a side road north along the valley floor past the church and manse towards Kergord.

A thriving community once lived along the valley; families tending their crofts, sharing labour and resources as demand dictated. Then the sheep invasion struck. Exceptionally grim accounts of evictions and cruelty in the Weisdale Clearances were described by John Graham, in his well-loved novel *Shadowed Valley*. Many people left the area, some walking over the ridge towards Aith. Bitter tales describe men being forced to demolish their own homes in 1855 and build the Weisdale Mill out of the stone. This building has been converted into the Bonhoga art gallery. The road carries on north past some large tree plantations, known loosely as Kergord Forest. One ruined cottage still stands, deep inside the Lindsay Lee plantation, with a tree growing out of the old hearth; a haunting sight. Originally a house called North House stood here. A new house, built for an incoming farm manager, was named Flemington after the Fleming family who lived there. This was changed to Kergord House later. In 1940, it was used as the headquarters of the Shetland Bus, the name given to the secret operation which ran supplies, agents and resistance workers between Norway and Britain during the Second World War. Guides and Scouts have a camp here and there is a tree nursery at Kergord where rare native species have been propagated with increasing success.

The Guide returns now to Tingwall and takes the road through the Tingwall valley, which runs south from the Herrislee crossroads to Scalloway, winding between broad fields and metamorphosed limestone outcrops to Asta. The narrow road has passing places and entrance ways. The Loch of Tingwall, beloved of anglers, is skirted by acres of marsh flowers in the spring and summer. Waterfowl and waders frequent the loch in spring and summer. Gardens attract migrants and birdwatchers saw an exceptionally rare blue-cheeked bee eater here one year. Tingwall Loch has an interpretive panel in the car park depicting a scene from the Norse parliament which is visible on a short promontory across the water. Loch of Asta, much used by Shetland model yacht racers, is partially bordered by the Asta Golf Course. The road emerges at the Scalloway junction, after passing a bus depot. Scalloway Scord quarry gapes wide to the left.

The limestone-rich, fertile valley of Tingwall has been settled since the earliest times. Ancient lands have been successively farmed and old house sites used for newer ones, each new structure obliterating the former one. On the site of one new house, built over the site where an earlier, traditional crofthouse stood, over 200 prehistoric artefacts were found. These consisted largely of stone tools, bone and pottery. An ancient standing stone, its origins long since lost and forgotten, stands close beside the road; a burial cist, uncovered by accident in a quarry, can be found not far away. Several ancient structures border Tingwall and Asta lochs and a large burnt mound stands opposite the bus depot close to the Scalloway junction. A broch was discovered relatively recently during house construction work in Scalloway itself.

Some think of Scalloway as the jewel in Shetland's crown. There can be few finer settings to any settlement than the marvellous backdrop of harbour and islands. The traditional approach to this large village, or small town as some prefer to see it, is from Lerwick, and down the Scord, the steep, winding descent from the ridge of hills between Shetland's east and west coasts. Buses and cars stop here so frequently for the stunning views that a layby and interpretive panel were eventually installed to accommodate them. Scalloway fringes the heads of two adjacent bays and the balance of land and water, influenced by the ever-changing skyscapes, is mesmerising. Islands lie scattered across a silvery expanse of water, boats and harbour features, buildings and farmland combine to set a splendid scene, crowned with the gaunt remains of its old castle.

Scalloway Castle was built by forced labour in 1600, and stories abound concerning Earl Patrick Stewart who lived here for a few turbulent years. The *Court Book of Shetland 1615-29* has survived four centuries, recording civil and criminal trials which took place here. Theft, murder, assault and even alleged witchcraft featured among the crimes of the day. The Castle, though ruined, is accessible and has an excellent interpretive display on the ground floor. Originally four-storeyed, the castle has fine turrets with chequered corbelling, vaulted kitchens, sturdy cellars and a great hall which can all be explored. Fine views over Scalloway and the islands can be seen from the upper-storey windows.

A large, modern secondary school has been built beside the earlier one and the primary school shares the same site. The swimming pool and leisure facility alongside is open to the public at regular times and is a good place to repair to should the weather turn unfriendly. There are several shops, including the two main stores which open from early morning

Scalloway Castle.

until late at night and on Sundays too. There is what locals claim is Britain's best fish and chip shop as well as pubs, a hotel and several eating places. The recently built North Atlantic Fisheries College stands prominently across the bay at Port Arthur and apart from the study and training facilities, offers an accommodation block, restaurant and evening film and lecture facilities throughout the year. There is a knitwear factory with a sales shop situated conveniently next to the castle, where you can easily spend a couple of hours.

Scalloway Museum, established and run by volunteers, is well worth visiting. There is a range of interesting displays and exhibits, which are constantly being revised and improved. Most significant is the feature on the 'Shetland Bus'. Scalloway played a key role in the running of the operation. A total of 206 missions were carried out during the early 1940s, landing ammunition and secret agents by night in Norwegian fjords and bringing back refugees and resistance workers. Prince Olaf's slipway, not far from the Museum, commemorates this link between Shetland and Norway.

Spend time too, simply walking through Scalloway,

189

exploring the streets and houses. The Bulwark is a beautifully restored former booth hugging the very edge of the waterfront near the harbour. The old Scalloway Haa, built around 1750 for the Scott family, still stands imposingly within its walled and stepped surrounds. Stop to read the curious plaque on a house wall along the street nearby.

It is only seven miles from here across the hills east to the present-day capital, Lerwick.

Da Bulwark House, Scalloway.

TRONDRA AND BURRA ISLES

A slash of metamorphosed limestone slices right through the north-eastern corner of Trondra and outcrops here and there in other parts of the island. This creates fertile soils in some places, and a remarkable variety of wild flowers in spring and summer. The bridge from the Mainland to Trondra was built 30 years ago, close to the north-eastern corner of the isle. The population had begun to decline seriously and though there was divided opinion about the wisdom of a bridge, there is no going back now and the island is seeing an increase in housebuilding and people moving back again. There are some important local prehistoric sites and a vast heritage of local stories and memories from harder, more self-sufficient times gone by. A new public hall helped restore island confidence and many a fine night of music, dance and feasting has taken place there since it was built. Burland, with its imaginative and popular Crofting Trail, is one of Trondra's treasures. Shetland cattle, ponies and sheep graze close at hand and various poultry species including Shetland ducks, geese and hens range freely around the outbuildings. There is a fine traditional Shetland boat-building workshop and a restored mill here.

The twin islands of East and West Burra lie to the south of Trondra. The rocks of the islands are heavily metamorphosed. Pebble beaches abound and here you may find examples of most of the local rock types, broken into small pieces and polished by the sea. Summer reveals the island in its most flamboyant flowering beauty; many birds nest along the shores and on the open ground, so watch where you walk and try not to disturb them. Shetland's oldest swimming pool, a natural rock pool extended years ago by concrete walling, still remains, where Shetland's first lifeguard kept watch in the summer and fishermen and their children learned to swim in safety; a skill which may have saved many lives over the succeeding years. Shetlanders love Burra especially for its wonderful beaches; Meal Sands and Minn at Papil attract large numbers of local people on hot, summer days and the swimming is exhilarating!

These islands were intensively settled over thousands of years. They have a strong fishing tradition and a large proportion of local families still live by fishing, salmon farming or fish processing. The islands are thought to have been chosen for early Christian settlements, judging by the number of early Christian carved stones which have been found. The most famous is the Monks' Stone, found in the churchyard in Papil. The original stone is now displayed in the Shetland Museum. There is a fish factory and several salmon farms, a garage, repair workshop and petrol station, as well as a large number of crofts.

Burra is gradually becoming a dormitory for Lerwick workers. Since the coming of the bridge in 1971, new waves of house building have swept through the scene. It is a place to walk, rather than drive, round. The Viking name of 'Hamnavoe', meaning sheltered harbour, makes it virtually certain that there was once a Norse farm, or more than one, nearby. But the remains of these probably lie buried beneath the walls of present-day crofthouses such as Branchiclett and Mail. The old fishing cottages of Roadside are especially attractive, with their wrought-iron fences and geranium- and begonia-filled porches. One tiny workshop is beautifully decorated with symmetrically arranged sea shells.

The old and new schools overlook the village. Hamnavoe itself has only made relatively recent concessions to cars and roads. Sheep ruled up to virtually every doorstep (they still sleep on some, as is evident on the morning after by the scatter of droppings, or 'sheep's pirls'!) and some houses still have no gardens at all; standing white-walled and trim surrounded on all four sides by grass right up to all four walls, like toy houses on green velvet cloth. A maze of tiny paths threads among the houses to this day and are still in regular use. Sadly the big new shops in Lerwick have taken their toll on local services and Hamnavoe has lost three shops in recent years, including an excellent local butcher's shop. The remaining shop and post office is well stocked and welcoming.

The village harbour is protected by a promontory terminating in Fugla Ness with its lighthouse. Walk out here on a summer's day, when the turf is blanketed with sea pinks, and imagine the same scene in winter when white seas rise like mountains and smash against this sheltering barrier, tossing huge rocks about like matchboxes. As you gaze back across the harbour at the clusters of houses old and new that glint in the sunlight, imagine the scene a hundred years ago, when no fewer than three fishing stations operated from here. There are traces of prehistoric settlements, several burnt mounds and also the site of a souterrain.

If you have time, explore more of Burra and contrast the bleak, windswept moors with the other settlements to the south of the island. There is a wide, open stretch of rocky moorland between Broch and Toogs, where Arctic terns nest in spring, so please give the birds a wide berth if you are here at nesting time. Broch, Toogs, Houss, Bridge End and Papil display a variety of houses, old and new, ranging from traditional crofthouses and small bungalows to ostentatious villas, scattered across a truly beautiful landscape. Perfect views from here take in small hills, tiny valleys and hollows; a maze of islands and headlands, the massive bulk of the Clift Hills to the east and the open sea with Foula set like a gem in the centre of the western horizon. Fine walks can be had round Kettlaness and Symbister to the south and Brunaness to the north. Many a tiny track leads over to isolated dwellings and most of the shoreline is walkable, affording access to some of Burra's wilder, dramatic corners.

The Monks' Stone of Papil.

On a fine day, take the track south uphill from the road to Heogaland and stand by the underground reservoir on the summit. From here there are uninterrupted views across the tapering headlands of East and West Burra, over a pattern of islands as far as Fair Isle in the south, right round to Foula in the west and the whole face of West Mainland to Scalloway and the hills beyond to the north. To the east lies the

Fugla Stack and
The Heugg to the
south of West Burra.

massive southern backbone of Shetland, the Clift Hills, with
the sheltered Clift Sound at their feet. The great steep slopes
are uninhabited and raw in their wildness, only the wide
Quarff valley breaking through their bulk a little to the north.

All the smaller islands are sadly no longer lived in.
Hildasay, Oxna, South Havra, Linga, Langa and Papa – their
names ring like faint bells, tolling the passing of a distant age,
with all the history of centuries of family life and struggle, the
fishing, the croft work and knowledge that went with it.

Retracing our steps to cross the Trondra bridge, we return
to East Voe and the Shetland Mainland. A small side turning
to the right leads to Uradale and the beautiful natural gorge
and Burn of Sundibanks, immortalised in a lovely Shetland
song and clad in a mass of primroses every spring. A fine walk
begins from the shore here and leads along the ridge to the
south into Wester Quarff, a route tramped regularly by the
Quarff folk many years ago. High up on the horizon to the
east, are the gaunt outlines of two buildings. These were built
in 1938 to carry Shetland's first ultra short-wave telephone
link with mainland Scotland.

LERWICK

The route from Scalloway to Lerwick offers you two choices.
You can go the 'north route', turning right onto the main road
at the Brig of Fitch, passing Dale golf course and Gremista farm.
Or, after leaving Scalloway and passing the Scord Quarry, you
can fork right just over the hill and take the old 'Black Gaet'
route, the B9073, turning left for Lerwick at the 'sooth road'
junction. The north route is about a mile longer, but if you
enjoy golf, then a few hours on this course offers a real
challenge. The green hillside here is sheltered from the
prevailing southwesterlies, at least a little, and if you look
closely, you can see the route of Lerwick's first 'meal road' north,
faintly visible crossing the greens and rising to the brow of the
hill to the left. But there are eyes watching you as you play.
Birds, especially crows and occasionally seagulls, have taken to
swooping down and snatching up golf balls, flying off with them
and dropping them far away in the heather moors around!

Lerwick, Shetland's capital, grew because of the shelter
provided by the island of Bressay against the wild winter seas
and storm waves which lash the east coast during the year.
Bressay Sound is a perfect natural harbour, valued by sailors for
centuries for its shelter and accessibility from both north and
south. To this day, incomers arriving to live in Shetland are
called 'sooth moothers' in reference to their having arrived via
the south mouth of the harbour.

Trading posts grew up where visiting ships could do
business and as more and more buildings followed, the
development towards a town became inevitable. Today giant
cruise ships lie at anchor in Bressay Sound, where Viking
adventurers, Dutch and German trading vessels and French
men of war sheltered hundreds of years ago. Today, small
boatloads of tourists are ferried ashore from the visiting floating
hotels of cruise ships to sample the delights of the town and the
best of Shetland's produce, contributing greatly to the islands'
economy. The town is constantly evolving as businesses come,
change and go, buildings are altered, and streets and harbours
are transformed by modern facilities and features.

The town of Lerwick dominates life in Shetland,
(according to many country folk, far more than it should!) and
the steady 'drift to the toon' has swelled both the population
and the proportion of resources which have to be spent on it.
Yet the town is barely 300 years old, Scalloway, the historic

Lerwick and
Bressay Sound from
Ward of Bressay.

capital, having been gradually eclipsed as Lerwick's trade and
population grew. Here, the Shetland Islands Council have their
meetings and departments; the hospital, Shetland's largest
secondary school, two large primary schools and Shetland
College of Further Education all serve the island community.

If your time is limited, try to see the older parts of the
town if you can. Visit the beautiful sea front with its wharves
and slipways and tiny stone warehouses, known as 'the
Lodberries'. Walk through the lanes with their stone houses,
winding steps and alleyways. Some lucky folk live here, but
others think them not so lucky, fearing damp and salt water
seepage, battering from the east during storms and even, it is
claimed, fish down the chimneys in exceptionally savage
storms! The Lerwick lanes still hold echoes of the past and you
can wander all day through the tiny narrow stone-bound ways
between some of Lerwick's oldest houses, up and down the face
of the once-long-ago sea cliff and hillside, from 'Hillhead' as it
is still called, to the sea and back.

Explore Fort Charlotte, the Cromwellian star-shaped fort
built in 1665 to subdue the Dutch, who burned it down in

1673. The fort was built on a high sea cliff, and would have dominated the whole area as the tiny settlement of Lerwick clustered below and to the south, along the shore. The fort lay in ruins until 1782 when it was rebuilt and equipped with guns, parade ground and barracks. Shetland's first-ever 'proper' road, built as part of the fort's requirements, led from the fort up to the Knab overlooking the sea.

The Shetland Museum is a must for those who have several days to spend in Shetland. Here you can see items from every era of the islands' history and get a clear idea of where you can go and what you might find. The Shetland Library too is worth visiting. It has a wide section of books on Shetland, and for the visitor with a special interest, the Shetland Room holds a veritable treasure trove of books old and new on the islands. Here too, back numbers of the *Shetland Times* newspaper are kept bound or on microfiche. Staff are knowledgeable and keen to help with research. For those with a hunger for research, the Shetland Archives are well worth a visit and there is a Shetland Family History Society centre where descendants of former Shetland families can spend time searching for information about their own family's story.

There is a beautifully restored and laid-out interpretive facility in the Böd of Gremista, birthplace of one of Shetland's famous sons, Arthur Anderson, founder of the P&O shipping

Lerwick Town Hall, waterfront and the Bressay ferry from Victoria Pier.

Bressay Sound and
The Lodberries,
Lerwick, at dusk.

company. The adjacent beach was once used for drying fish.
Don't miss Lerwick's Clickimin Broch, a ruined prehistoric
fort, at the seaward end of the loch, which you can get right
inside. There is a footpath all round the loch, from which you
can observe a remarkable range of visiting waterfowl and
waders each year. Otters feed and play here too and, though
shy, sightings are frequent, especially in the early morning and
late evening. You can enjoy a swim if you feel inclined, or a
fitness session at the Clickimin Leisure Centre and
refreshments afterwards.

Shetland gears up for its visitors with a crammed
programme of events, exhibitions and special displays in the
summer months. The local museums open new displays and in
Lerwick the Islesburgh Exhibition, held in the community
centre, celebrates a glorified, simple, happy past. It features old
open hearths, or the later 'Modern Mistress' or 'Victoress' iron
ranges, the framed pictures of the *Gospel Ship* and wooden
glove- and sock- stretchers. It was a life of few possessions, a
life ruled by weather, seasons and animals, dependent on family
members and good neighbours to cope with peak croftwork
periods, help in emergencies and join in celebrations. The
reality was probably considerably harder and more gruelling,
but nevertheless many former crofters admit to missing many
aspects of their previous lifestyles. Here you can watch spinning

197

and Fair Isle and lace knitting, listen to local fiddlers and learn Shetland dances. Look for the spinning wheels with their different styles; the 'tushkar' which was used to cut peats and the 'kollie' lamp whose light illuminated the interiors of Shetland homes before electricity arrived.

In the summer there are often guided tours of the town which are very informative and often entertaining as well as interesting. Maps and guides to walks in Lerwick, plus advice on routes, are available from the Tourist Office. Always check here to find out what performances, local shows or special events are on during your stay. Free leaflets are produced about the different areas and island topics of interest.

Armed with the latest information on eating places and watering holes (for the refreshment scene in Shetland can change from year to year), explore passageways and arches, stopping now and then to refresh yourself in a café, coffee house or bar. Some of the latter, *The Lounge* in particular, are famed for their live, spontaneous music-making. You might hear an Irish whistle, a guitar, a Shetland fiddler or a visiting musician from far away, come to sample the magic of local music-making.

Shoppers can wander from the sublime to the ridiculous in terms of novelties, warm woollen underwear of the old style and wonderful hand knits. Shops selling Shetland lace scarves, fingerless gloves, locally made pottery and jewellery rub shoulders with others selling plain, practical supplies for all four seasons. Ships' chandlers, excellent charity shops and hardware stores make for even more exciting exploration.

Detail of fishing boat, Lerwick Harbour.

The town was established during the days of fish trading and the industry is as alive today as it has ever been, but the technology has changed beyond all recognition. The seafront itself can be a wonderful place to walk, investigate or just sit and soak up the atmosphere. A marvellous variety of vessels passes through Lerwick during any one year and the Esplanade is a great place from which to observe and enjoy them. There are boats from every corner of the globe, whether oil-related, survey vessels, cruise ships or cargo ships. Fishing boats all bear the registration codes of their ports of origin: L.K. is Lerwick, B.F. is Banff in Scotland

and any passing fisherman will cheerfully tell you the home port of other vessels. Look out for marine protection vessels in their pale grey-green paint; even the Greenpeace ship *Rainbow Warrior* visits occasionally. Yachts, speedboats, rowing boats and, grandest of all, the Bergen three-masted schooner *Statsraad Lehmkul*, are frequent sights.

There are few greater pleasures in Shetland's capital than an exploration of the waterfront, both old and new; from the small boat harbour where the splendid replica Viking galley *Dim Riv* and the beautiful *Swan*, a restored zulu fishing boat, as well as the lifeboat and a score of other craft are moored, to Holmsgarth where the big Aberdeen ferries anchor. For the uninitiated, fishing boats and boats of all kinds are an immensely exciting spectacle, not only by day, but at night as well. The traditional darkness of the sea at night is a thing of the past; now you look out not over the pitch black, moonlit or starlit sea, but over a dark expanse filled with shimmering reflections and a dazzling array of lights, warning buoys and coloured navigation lights, some flashing at different speeds.

Lerwick has expanded so far from its original seafront settlement that a number of crofting townships and farms have been engulfed with houses and other buildings. Sound, once a peaceful crofting settlement, where smoke drifted from a handful of small houses and cattle grazed between rigs of corn and kale, is now home to thousands of people who live in the housing estates of Nederdale, Sandveien and Ackrigarth and the private estates of Fogralea, Murrayston and Westerloch and the large villas crammed into the steeper slopes above. Shops, a garage, community centre and a large primary school cater for growing local needs. More expansion is likely in the years ahead. A glorious sandy beach, the Sands of Sound, still soaks up the sun to the east here and the flower-strewn grassy approaches are well used and much loved.

There is an enjoyable walk along the sea road here from the roundabout out to the Ness of Sound with good birdwatching and fine views across to Bressay. At the ness itself there are extensive wartime remains; old bunkers and crumbling concrete foundations can make for some hazardous but interesting exploration. The wide, sweeping fields and attractive tree-clustered farmhouse of Seafield add greatly to the graceful proportions of the scene but the threat of more housing developments is ever present.

ISLE OF NOSS

Noss National
Nature Reserve

The Cletters
Point of
Heogatoug
The Rump
Noss Head
Noup of Noss
Geordie's Holes
Rumble Wick
Hill of
Pundsgeo
North Croo
Cradle
Holm of Ness
Hill of
Setter
Barn Stane
Feadda
Ness
Point of
Hovie
180
Mansie's
Berg
Visitor
Centre
Gungstie
Geos of Hovie

Cullingsburgh Geo
Geo of Vatsie
Hellia Cluve

2 km
1 mile
1
0
0

Score Head
Outer Score
Inner Score
Score Minni
Bars Geo
Blue Geo
66
Aith
Ness
Globa
Hill of
Aith

Loder Head
Rules Ness

Minni of Aith

To Old Skerries

Holm of
Beosetter
Ness of
Beosetter
Sweyn
Ness

Holm of
Gunnista
Gunnista

Bay of
Cullingsburgh
Voe of

Ander
Hill
Setter
Bruntland
Brough

Setter
Everby
Loch of
Setter

Loch of
Brough

Loch of
Grimsetter
Seli Geo
Grut Wick

Green Head

Round Point
Hamar

Mid Dublin
Bard Head
Natural Arch

The Bard
Giants Leg
Orkneyman's Cave

Maatrut
Geos of the Vere

Millburn Geo
Huster Roo
Wadbister
Loch of
Seligeo
Mossy
Hill

Kebister Ness
Stacks of Vatsland
Holms of
Vatsland
Easter Rova
Head

Kirkabister

Daal
165
The Ord

BRESSAY

Ward of
Bressay
226

Ward Hill

Clodisdale
Hoyersta
Hoove
Pettyfirth
Wart

Ham

Hevdi
Ovuss
Lourie's Stane
Kirkabister Ness

33
White Hill
Baa
Berg
Heogan

Hill of
Gunnista
Maryfield
Gardie
Ho.
Bressay
History
Centre
The
Glebe

Grey Head
Dalnaberg

To Bergen, Torshaven and Reykjavik (seasonal)
To Aberdeen and Kirkwall

Fora Ness

116
Hill of
Grimista

Bód of
Gremista
Gremista

Voe of Leiraness
Sound

Fort
Charlotte
LERWICK
The Knab
Bret Wick
Taing
of Ham

Seafield
Ness of
Sound
Voe of Sound
The Nizz

Clickimin Broch
Loch of
Clickimin
83

Sound

Ness
of
Trebister

Ness of
Setter
Loch of
Trebister
Gulber Wick

Milla Geo

Dales Voe

Loch of
Kebister

Giossa
Water
Hill of Shurton
Sandy
Loch
175
A970

Hill of
Brindister
75
Brindister
Foulageo
East Voe
of Quarff
A970

Oiled Bird
Unit
Houster
Hill of
Herrislee
135
Veensgarth

Laxfirth

Swinster

Catwalls

Brig o'
Fitch
Hill of Fitch

Mossy
Hill
Loch of
Run Wick
Hill
Garths of
Sand
Gulberwick
B9073
Lang Lochs

Setter

Easter
Quarff

Wester
Quarff

Wormadale
A971

Nesbister

Hoove

Brugarth

Point of
Nebister
Voe of
Whiteness
Whiteness Ness

Hill of Tingwall
Law
Ting Holm
Loch
of
Tingwall

Neigles
Water
128
Loch
of
Asta

Grista
North Setter
South
Setter

Asta
Outhabreck
The Scord

Grostane
Bersa Hill
Flossy
Loch
Sundibanks
Loch of
Brindister

Scrae
Field

Loch of
Couster

Hill of
Grista
Setter
Hill
Loch of
Ustaness
Brüo
Loch
Loch of
Garth
107

Loch of
Houlland
Loch of
Burwick
Houlland

Berry
Scalloway
North Atlantic
Fisheries College
Scalloway

Easterhoull
Ufradale

East Voe
of Scalloway
Bür Wick

Strom Ness
Stromness Voe
White Ness

Hogaland
Burland
Crofting
Trails
B9074

TRONDA
Cliff Sound

Bressay and Noss

BRESSAY

Without the island's sheltering bulk to the east, Lerwick and its excellent harbour would never have become established. The haven of Bressay Sound has seen ships drop anchor for several thousand years. Bressay should be experienced, if at all possible, from the sea as well as from the land. Enquire about local boat trips which enable you to appreciate the superb cliffs, underwater wildlife, deep sea caves and natural arches for which the island is famous.

Like much of Noss, Bressay is composed of ancient sandstones, with a small but spectacular volcanic vent and related geological intrusions and alterations nearby on its eastern face. Bressay sandstone made first-class building stone and quarries were worked until relatively recently. The stone dykes in Bressay reflect this and many a fine house in Lerwick was built from Bressay sandstone. Very fertile soils have formed over the sandstone, allowing for some crofts and a large farm to become well established. These are connected by attractive but very narrow roads, which require careful negotiating.

From Lerwick, a roll-on, roll-off ferry takes you to Bressay in just ten minutes. Once on the island, the road leads from the ferry point past the Bressay History Centre and Maryfield House (once home to an infamous factor, John Walker, and now run as a hotel) and then comes to a T-junction. A left turn takes you past the large farm and laird's house at Gardie, first built in 1724 and altered a number of times since. You can enjoy clear views of Lerwick's seafront as you approach the north-west corner, with its fishmeal factory, scattered settlements and beautiful coastline. To the right the road heads south, following the shore as far as the church, then it turns inland to the east. A side road leads north past the shop and the primary school and reaches a number of small crofting townships. You can walk out to Bressay's northern seashore here, and explore a number of good beaches with fine views out to sea.

A road runs south opposite the shop, and winds between the higher and lower pastures with their crofts. The highest

point in Bressay is the 'Waart', or the Ward, a hill topped with
TV and radio masts accessed by a track leading up opposite the
Glebe. The views from the top are quite unbelievable. You can,
on a clear day, see Foula to the west, Fair Isle to the south and
Unst to the north, as well as many smaller islands and much of
the Shetland Mainland besides. Closer to lie the streets and
features of Lerwick, laid out like a map below you.

The road continues past Ham, one of the best sites for the
tussock grass, or 'tushie girse', which was planted in the 1890s,
and ends a mile or so further on at the Bressay Lighthouse. This
was built by David and Thomas Stevenson in 1858 but it is no
longer manned, and like all the other Shetland lighthouses, has
been made automatic.

The remaining lighthouse buildings are to be used for
tourist accommodation and the lighthouse interpretive display.
On a fine day you can follow the cliff tops east from the
lighthouse along as far as the Bard, where a massive First World
War gun still stands on its mounting, pointing out to sea. Watch
out for the steep cliffs and the collapsing dug-out shelters and
bunkers nearby. Bressay had an important role during the

Gardie House, Bressay,
across Bressay Sound
in the last light of a
mid-winter afternoon.

Everby and Ander Hill on the east side of Bressay.

Second World War, with anti-aircraft guns, heavy and light, operating. From here you can see Mousa and the whole east side of the South Mainland stretching away towards Sumburgh.

From the shop crossroads, a road heads due east across the island to Broch and the Noss ferry point. At various points along this narrow single track, access roads lead off to other small settlements. Marvellous walks can be enjoyed all round the island. Ander Hill in the east rises up like a bastion against the bitter easterlies that sometimes blast Shetland. A look-out tower, built by the Admiralty and now ruined, stands at the highest point. From the ridge you can look down on to Cullinsbroch with its collapsed broch, site of an ancient church and graveyard with a tombstone to a Dutch skipper erected in 1636.

It was here that the famous Bressay Stone, mentioned earlier, was found and its replica stands today where the original stood for centuries. The whole surrounding area is full of ancient remains and the ruined crofthouses may well have originally been built from stone taken from the broch and other prehistoric structures nearby.

Shortly before the road terminates at the Noss ferry car park, a track to the right leads to the deserted townships of Grimsetter and Gorie, the latter the site of one of Shetland's first exotic greenhouses, famous for its peaches, plums and grapes; and beyond, south to the ruined settlement of Wadbister. A prehistoric souterrain, or earth house, was discovered here. Excellent walking can be enjoyed among the old settlements and along the cliff approaches.

Look out for displays by the thriving Bressay history group which researches into local history and provides talks and holds exhibitions during the year in their small museum near the ferry pier.

NOSS

Noss, a small uninhabited island just east of Bressay, has some of the most spectacular seabird breeding colonies in Britain and is an essential place to visit. The whole island is now a designated National Nature Reserve and two wardens live here, and research and interpret the island for visitors every summer. There is a small interpretive centre in the restored pony pund behind the former farmhouse of Gungstie. The island is accessed by a small boat which you hail from the Bressay shore. Toilets are provided. Check before you visit, to make sure that you avoid the one day each week when the island is closed.

Composed largely of ancient sandstones and mudstone deposits, the strata is exposed along cliff faces. Weathering has eaten into the exposed rock, creating marvellous ledges and crevices for seabirds to nest in. From the rocks just above sea level, to the thick grassy sward at the top of the cliffs, a range of birds raise their young from spring to summer in a very special hierarchy of nest sites. In the basement of this ornithological 'high-rise block' are the shags and guillemots. Next, on first-floor level, come the razorbills. Higher still, fulmars have set up colonies and here and there are some kittiwakes. Going further up, gannets dominate, creating not only the bulk of the noise but the smell as well. At the top, nearest the edges, come puffins. Further back from the edge and right across the top of the grassy summits of the stacks are the greater and lesser black-backed gulls.

Today's seas break against high sandstone cliffs which were formed as sediments, settling on seabeds themselves beneath the ancient seas of 300 million years ago. Some layers in the

Noss Head
across Rumble Wick,
Isle of Noss.

sandstones are said to contain minute fossils of primitive
creatures living at that time. The Noup of Noss, the highest
point of the sheer eastern cliffs, stands 600 feet (180 m) above
the sea below and is a landmark on the horizon from far away
to the north, south and east. Over the whole island, a thick
growth of grass, heather and wild flowers provides grazing for
sheep, shelter for ground-nesting skuas, pipits, skylarks and
other birds, as well as a wonderful backdrop for visitors. The
ruins of long-derelict crofthouses can be seen on the south-
facing levels above many acres of former runrigs.

There are ancient remains here too, albeit well buried by
time, in particular those of one of Shetland's early Christian
churches. There is usually one special open day each year with
activities and refreshments. Allow at least three hours for a walk
round the whole island, and four if you want to take time to draw,
gaze out to sea or rest and enjoy the atmosphere. If you want to
enjoy the seabird cliffs but not a long walk, opt for a short boat
trip from Lerwick (weather permitting). The close-up spectacle
of birds, caves and sealife makes these trips unforgettable.
Tickets can be booked and times are posted in the tourist office.

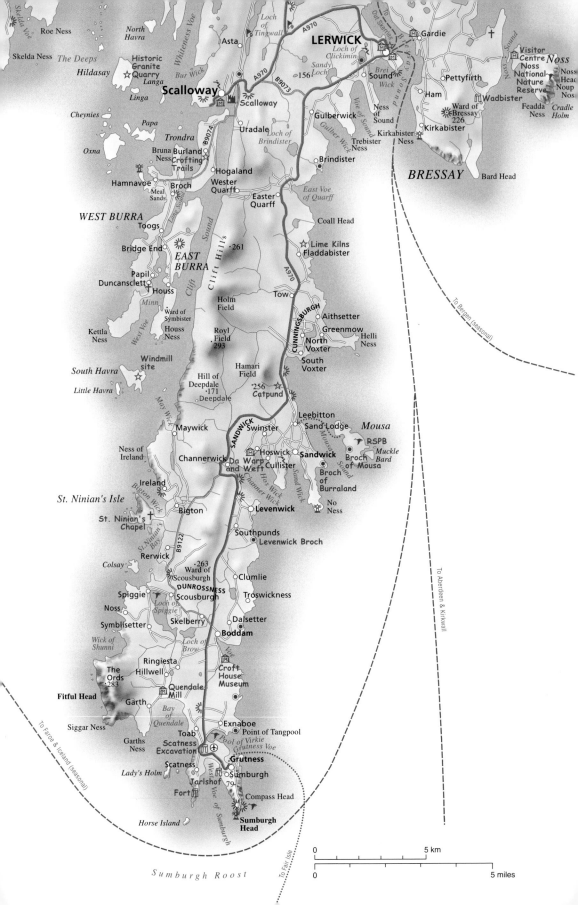

South Mainland

tawny-gold in Autumn sun, they lie
Like lions asleep.

From *The Clift Hills* by Christian Tait.

From Lerwick, the main road to the south leads to Quarff, Cunningsburgh and Sumburgh, and a host of beautiful places, large and small, on the way. Outside Lerwick you pass the reservoir of Sandy Loch on the right and the residential blocks of the Lerwick Observatory on the left, where weather data is gathered on every day of the year. You may even be lucky and see a weather balloon being released. Just south of the Observatory a narrow road branches left and crosses a stretch of moorland past small lochs. The road drops down towards Gulberwick, and there are marvellous views to the south along Shetland's eastern coastline.

Gulberwick is a scattered community that has grown relatively recently. Much of the scale of the old hamlet has been lost, but a new, more modern effect is now emerging as houses are built and changes made. Often in winter the waves funnel in so furiously that water breaks white far out to sea, giving the bay a wild, white splendour. In 1148, Earl Rognvald and his crew are said to have been driven ashore at Gullbervik and the *Orkneyinga Saga* records the hospitality he enjoyed at a local house and how he teased his hostess. Canoeists enjoy exploring the coastline round here and on calm summer evenings venture out round the headlands, which are full of sea caves and dramatic clefts and arches.

Quarff is the next village to the south after Gulberwick. Something strange has happened to the land here at some point far back in time. Where most of the valleys in Shetland cut north-south, the Quarff valley, or 'Quarff Gap' as it is often termed, cuts straight across the ridge east-west in a deep U shape. Some experts have suggested that the valley may be all that now remains of an ancient river which ran east towards long-vanished inland lakes draining some of the long-lost

mountain ranges to the far west. A growing community here
enjoys some fine views and particularly fine displays of wild
flowers in summer. Some houses face the sea to the east at
Easter Quarff, some, at the far end of the Quarff turn-off, face
west at Wester Quarff and there is a scattering of dwellings
alongside the road right through the valley between the two.

There is a fine walk from Wester Quarff north along the
high ridge to Scalloway, a route much frequented in days gone
by, when Scalloway was the capital and roads did not exist.

Fladdabister is one of Shetland's gems and deserves a
special visit. Among a tangle of old cottages, many now
derelict, down near the east-facing shore a few miles south of
Quarff, wild flowers swarm each spring and summer. There are
meadows between the road and the sea worthy of a visit in
their own right. Drifts of primroses, celandine and king cups
bloom in profusion and a tangle of ferns, bilberries and wild
shrubs festoon the steep sides of a beautiful gorge which has
been cut by a lively stream running east from the high slopes
behind. The flowers are only part of the pride of Fladdabister
though. Near to the shore, perched on a jutting rocky outcrop,

The dawn silhouette
of Noss and Bressay
beyond Ward of
Greenmow on the
east coast of the
South Mainland.

are the remains of some lime kilns, witness to a thriving limestone-processing business which operated until the 1930s.

The beach here is renowned for the attractive calcite pebbles worn smooth by the sea from rocks torn from the cliffs nearby. In places the rock face by the beach has been smoothed into hollowed curves where the calcite banding is strikingly clear and bright. They lie among strands and bales of seaweed in a lovely curve, facing north-east towards Bressay and Noss. Seals often gather just offshore, watching your every move. You can enjoy coastal walks from here along the shore, both to the north and south. From Fladdabister you can continue south towards Cunningsburgh.

Just before you reach Cunningsburgh, a road turns left signed for Aithsetter. This is the first of several small, single-track roads which wind among the tangle of crofting communities between Cunningsburgh and the sea to the east. They are full of interest and character, as are the local folk, about whom George Lowe, writing in 1774, said, 'The people of this small spot, a stout, hardy race by all accounts the wildest in Shetland.' There is a primary school, garage and shop, and a splendid new village hall which hosts a series of teas and attractions through the summer. Try to find out what is on during your visit and if possible, aim to visit Cunningsburgh on its annual show day in August. Produce of all kinds, livestock, crafts and plants, refreshments and entertainment make the Cunningsburgh Show a great day out.

You could if you have the time spend several peaceful hours following the twists and turns of road and shore here exploring the hamlets of Aith, Gord, North and South Voxter, Aness and Greenmow. Old and new buildings, ancient and modern agricultural methods and techniques stand side by side. Electric cables swing from post to post over new gardens and

Lime kilns, Fladdabister.

rigs of Shetland oats and kale. Hybrid hens scratch alongside Shetland ducks and fast cars glide quietly past a field where you might see an old Ferguson tractor hard at work, its well-maintained engine belying its 60 years of age. But do explore here with consideration and courtesy, as folk are busy, proud of their traditions and wary in case people park their vehicles across passing places, field accesses and driveways.

On a fine day you could walk out to Helliness, a peninsula which reaches far out into the sea to the east. From the trig point on the hill at its tip there are magnificent views back to Shetland's east-facing coastline both to the north and south. A deserted nineteenth-century farm, along with some sturdy stone walls, stands among lush grazing below you to the west of the summit. Excellent views out to sea here cover everything appoaching Shetland from the east and south and Helliness would have been an important look-out point over the centuries.

To continue exploring the South Mainland, leave Cunningsburgh and head south along the A970. The road passes close to a shingle beach as you leave the village and the cliffs, hills rise steeply to the right. One of Shetland's most important

Looking south-east from Setter across Wick of Sandsayre towards Sand Lodge and Ward of Burraland.

archaeological sites lies here. The burn of Catpund courses
through a narrow valley here and in its steatite bed lie the marks
of ancient quarrying. Bowls and troughs were carved *in situ* and
chipped out whole as finished vessels here in prehistoric and
Norse times. You can still see the outlines of vessels cut into the
rock. Large stone vessels, troughs and bowls of Catpund steatite
have been found on archaeological sites far from Shetland.

The road to Sandwick turns left just south of Catpund.
The land here sweeps down and opens out to the east below the
broad moorland hills to the west. Sandwick itself is a tiny
seashore-hugging hamlet of little more than half a dozen
houses, but it has lent its name to a much bigger area,
consisting of a series of hamlets and settlements, forming a
sizeable community between the main road to Sumburgh here
and the sea. Look out for the booklet *Footsteps through Sandwick*
which was produced by local children and guides visitors
through the area. There is a bakery, a shop and garage and a
modern junior high school with public swimming pool nearby.

The ferry to Mousa leaves from a pier in north-facing
Leebitton. The scatter of houses here is a picture to see in the
summer, their gardens overflowing with colour. A new pier has
been built just below these cottages on the left, and at low tide
the sea draws back to expose rocks on which seals often haul
out. The scene is picturesque at all times but especially so at
sunrise when the low-angled early light intensifies the colours
of walls, roofs and gardens and the rich shades in the backdrop
of hills behind.

Just beyond the Mousa pier stands the sombre bulk of
Sandlodge, one of the larger and longer-lasting lairds' houses,
with outbuildings and a sizeable walled garden attached.
Sandlodge is still lived in and its lovely garden is tended. Once
a year it is opened to the public. The house and grounds are
enclosed by splendid dry stone walls or 'dykes'. Beyond that
again, is the site of the Sandlodge mine, opened in 1798, with a
series of tunnels which ran out a considerable distance into the
sea. A vein of rich copper-bearing rock runs close to the shore
and under the sea here. Insufficient ore was found to make the
mine financially viable, though the quality was said to be very
good. A number of companies succeeded each other in attempts
to make a decent profit from the ore. But extraction was tricky,
costs proved too high and the mine closed. There were various
attempts to reopen the mine between 1920 and 1922.

Try not to miss a visit to the island of
Mousa, now managed by the RSPB, famous for
its Broch which is cared for by Historic
Scotland. The boat crosses daily whenever the
weather permits, during the summer tourist
season. Fast walkers can cover the whole island
in a couple of hours, but I prefer four in order to
explore in comfort. There is marvellous scenery, a
mass of seabirds and a carpet of wild flowers. On the
east side there is a wide, shallow bay where seals and
their pups often come in close and stare at you for hours.

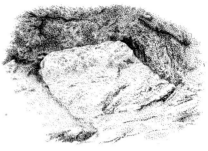

Norse steatite bowl carved into the rockface, Catpund.

Mousa Broch is not only one of the seven wonders of
Shetland, but probably of Scotland too, if not Britain. It is the
biggest and the best-preserved broch in Britain and the
drystone-walled, fortified tower house, built during the Iron Age,
is still standing after 2000 years! The scale doesn't really hit you
until you are inside it and it has to be seen and, if possible,
climbed, in order to be believed. The entrance is narrow and the
walls thick. Only one person could ever have entered at a time,
allowing the inhabitants plenty of scope for vetting and dealing
with intruders. Sit on a stone ledge inside and meditate for a
while on the extraordinary skill of the folk who must have built
the broch. Peer into the recessed rooms and the stone-lined
wells and store chambers. If you do climb up the internal stairs,
built between the outer wall layers, watch your step and take
your time. This is definitely not an experience to be rushed.

The *Orkneyinga Saga* tells of Erlend the Young, who one
spring abducted Earl Harald's mother Margaret from Orkney
and fled to Mousa with her. They were there for several
months, so there must have been reasonable comfort and
provision at that time.

The most exciting time to visit Mousa is in the middle of
the night in July. Storm petrels nest inside the stonework of the
broch. During the day, the parent birds are out at sea, but they
come ashore after dark to feed their young. Shetland summer
nights are very light, so the best darkness falls after midnight.
The experience of sitting huddled silently inside the broch in
twilight and hearing the walls suddenly come alive with sounds
is unforgettable. The tiny petrels skim past at high speeds and
despite the darkness, and the watching strangers, find their way
instantly to the right crack between two stones to locate their
own chicks.

Mousa today is uninhabited, the last family having left in the nineteenth century. But when George Lowe visited in 1771 he found 11 families there and reported it as being 'tolerably well cultivated' and 'producing well'. Outside the broch little can be seen of the structures and defensive walls which once formed a crucial part of the whole complex. In Low's time, house foundations and the remains of a big wall were still standing. Today, only ruins remain of once well-kept farm buildings and grass covers the once productive acres. Beware the 'maalies', or fulmar petrels though, as they nest among the tumble of rocks along old stone walls and in old planticrubs. The fluffy chicks look adorable, but if you come too close, you are likely to get spat on and sprayed with foul-smelling, unwashoutable oil. This defence mechanism has been a factor in the successful spread of these birds. The oil, when sprayed onto other seabird species, clogs their feathers and they can suffer as a result. Look out for seals and seabirds on your way back to the Mainland.

If you wish to visit the Broch of Burraland, follow the cliff tops past Sandlodge and south along the cliffs. This broch stands opposite Mousa Broch and formed part of a network of Shetland brochs around 2000 years ago. If you have time, follow the cliffs round and walk out along the No Ness peninsula. There is a spectacular, cliff-hugging, narrow road which terminates at a small turning area. Here are marvellous views of the whole of Sandwick from the sea. A good time to see it is late on a summer's evening, when the hills stand out dark against a luminous sky, turning slowly through a soft version of all the colours in the rainbow as the light fades. Don't leave your car in any passing or turning places here; you could cause considerable inconvenience to farmers and crofters.

From the south-western corner of Sandwick a single-track road winds into the hamlet of Hoswick, clustered tightly above the sea. There is a pub, a knitwear factory and opposite, the Warp and Weft Museum with its excellent café and sales corner. This is a splendid place for a wet as well as a fine day out. The displays give you a real insight into local life in times past, especially about the weaving industry and also the history of the harvesting, or Caain, of pilot whales which stranded from time to time on local beaches. Read some of the copies of proceedings from the famous court case of 1890 where for the first time in Shetland's history, local people won the right to keep what they salvaged and not forfeit it to the laird. There are many old-fashioned machines on display and a large collection of old radios and signalling transmitters from fishing boats and local communications bases.

The great sweeping curve of sand and shingle here forms a popular beach in the summer. This beach was the site of a great 'whale caa' in September 1888, mentioned above. At one point outcropping rocks can be examined to find fool's gold, or iron pyrites, glinting out of them. From Hoswick you can see back across to Sandwick with the old and new schools, swimming pool and the spread of houses of many styles and sizes.

Shortly before the Sandwick road out of Hoswick rejoins the main road to Sumburgh, another small road leads left signed for Rompa. It winds up and over a broad hill and drops down to a tiny handful of houses, strung out along a south-facing slope immediately above Channerwick. The lines of scores of old rigs are clearly visible on the hillside, but none are now in cultivation. The bay here is exceptionally attractive with its massive shingle beach, burns and beautiful meadows. These are packed to the rims with a wealth of wild flowers in late spring and summer. Two burns run into the bay from the hills to the east, west and south, sometimes through narrow gorges with waterfalls. There is no room for parking along the Rompa road, but there is a turning place above the houses and the return journey takes you over the hill facing across the whole of Sandwick, with magnificent views north across the headlands of No Ness and Cumlewick, right to Noss in the distance to the north.

Three separate ways lead down into Channerwick, or Chandrick, as local people call it, but they are narrow, steep and do not make for sensible turning or parking. The view is so splendid that it is tempting to stop, and there is a short section of old road where you can park and enjoy the view. The shingle beach is worth exploring for small specimens of local rock types and the whole area is of interest to geologists. As little as 50 years ago, there was a considerable population at Channerwick. Now many of the older houses are empty. Two particularly fine gorges have been cut by streams flowing down into the bay from the hills of Midfield and Roylfield to the west and north. The road goes south above Channerwick, takes a wide curve to the left in the crook of the valley, then straightens out for a short while. If you look across the bay to the north, the stark

slash of a deep geo makes for a striking cliff scene.

From here there are two routes to Sumburgh. This book follows the western route south first, then returns to this point to follow the eastern route south via Levenwick, through Clumlie, Dalsetter and Dunrossness to Sumburgh.

CHANNERWICK TO SUMBURGH VIA BIGTON

The main A970 swings round to the south above Channerwick in a wide bend. At its mid point, take the single-track road which branches off to the west. Passing places have been constructed at various points where road visibility is bad. The road winds and dips across moorland, descending along the side of a narrow valley where picturesque crofthouse ruins bear witness to a past age where every available acre of productive ground was worked. The road bends to the south and Bigton, St Ninian's Isle and the sea to the west come into view. Prepare to branch off into the village, as the road southwards continues well above the village down the 'long straight mile', a section of road as straight as a ruler which is bordered by marvellous flowers in summer.

Bigton is a large village, with a heart of traditional cottages and more recent buildings. The narrow lanes which twist and turn between the buildings are very attractive, each turn revealing a new angle of backdrop scenery: hills, islands and seascapes. Look out for local events advertised in the shop. Bigton has a shop, café and a lively and creative community and there is rarely a weekend without something 'on' in the village hall.

At the northern end of Bigton, a narrow lane runs out of the village and across to the straggle of houses on the south-facing hill ahead. This hamlet is Ireland, and boasts one of the most magnificent views in Shetland, out across St Ninian's Isle and the scatter of islets to the south, with Fitful Head as a stark and sheltering backdrop. There was once a towered church here, one of only three in Shetland. Today nothing remains of the site, and even the precise location of the building has been lost. Some moulded stones of Orkney Old Red Sandstone were found locally, which are thought to have originated as part of the fabric of the ancient church. One is in the Shetland Museum collection, which bears traces of carving and shaping; possibly as part of pillars or other elaborate features.

Maywick lies a mile or two north of Bigton and is beautifully situated and full of charm. A handful of houses cluster together above a north-facing beach, sheltered from the worst of the south-westerlies by higher ground. You can walk along the cliff tops all the way round to Bigton in fine weather, enjoying views which take in both the west side of Shetland and the whole of Clift Sound up to Scalloway. South Havra lies a few miles out to sea to the north-west, with its windmill tower silhouetted against the skyline. A new business started up in Maywick in 2000, producing fine oak-smoked fish. But as with all small, compact settlements, space, especially for parking, is at a premium and local people, their work and animals should come first. So once again, if you have a car ask locally for a suitable place to park, and make it clear you are aware of the problems. Your thoughtfulness will be much appreciated.

The beach itself is very attractive, with both sand and shingle, and is sheltered from the east, west and south, affording calm, peaceful beachcombing during weather in most of the prevailing wind directions. But it is not an ideal place to go during a good northerly blast! The cliff faces are loose and there are frequent small rockfalls. At first you may not see the access to the beach. Turn left between the cottages and look out for a 'sneck', a small gap between the first cottage on the right and the barn to its left. This narrow track leads to a series of boulder steps and the beach below. The access is not a good one for the less mobile and agile. If you are a long-distance walker and have a liking for longer, rougher routes, a beauty begins here and leads you north along the Clift Hills to

Brooch, St Ninian's Isle Treasure.

Quarff, some 15 miles away as the crow flies. It is not advisable to tackle this route alone, or if there is any risk of bad weather.

ST NINIAN'S ISLE

At the south-west corner of Bigton, a road to a large farm turns off at a right angle and crosses a cattle grid, where signs direct you right for St Ninian's Isle along a tiny single-track road. A picnic area and interpretive sign have been provided just behind the beach and there are good views of the island even if you are unable to walk to it. The exquisite sandy ayre with the island and its superb cliff scenery is one of the most famous Shetland scenes. Occasionally breached in winter, the narrow 'sand road' stretching out across the sea is a stunning spectacle. Tides and currents sweeping round the back of the island meet on either side of the ayre, constantly washing sand from the seabed up to form what is technically termed a 'tombolo'. Tombolos are a feature of sinking coastlines.

You should allow at least 15 minutes to cross the ayre in reasonable comfort and a little longer back again. Soft sand makes for heavy going, but apart from that, the flat, gleaming silver pebbles of phyllitic schist are so exquisite that you may well lose time gathering them and skimming them over the sea. Turn the pebbles this way and that to see the crystal faces reflecting light differently at different angles, just like the silken weave of a damask table cloth. Allow longer if you wish to climb the sandy track up into the island to see the ancient, ruined chapel site of St Ninian. This lies on the east side of the isle, overlooking the beach, a short way to the north.

The hoard of elaborately chased bowls, spoons and other items since known as the St Ninian's Isle Treasure was found here. Replica pieces are on display in the Shetland Museum and islanders hope to see them restored to the islands, instead of being kept in Edinburgh.

Rabbits have drilled the island thoroughly with their burrows and sheep graze alongside them quite happily. Starlings nest among the chapel walls and all kinds of seabirds frequent the wilder, western cliffs. A walk right round the island would take a good two hours or more, but beware dangerous cliff tops, especially in wet, misty or windy conditions.

Back on the mainland, the small township of Rerwick (not to be confused with Reawick on the West Mainland) is a real treasure, set amid some of the best-preserved and best-tended rigs in the whole of Shetland. A small sandy beach lies to the south and although (or maybe because) access is far from easy, the beach is one of the quietest and most peaceful in the South Mainland. Take your time as you pass along the road here, as the wild flowers can be particularly dazzling in summer.

Scousburgh with its cluster of dwellings and hotel, lies a few miles south of Rerwick and enjoys wide panoramas across Spiggie Loch and Dunrossness to the North Sea to the east and the Atlantic Ocean to the west. The former post office with its red telephone box stands virtually on top of a large broch site. Vanlop is signed left and the road rises up the hillside and skirts the rising moorland to the east. Fabulous views down over the whole of St Ninian's Isle from here are really worth seeing, especially during a fine sunset.

The road divides at Scousburgh, one branch heading east to Robin's Brae and the A970 to Sumburgh, while the western route goes steeply down towards the sea. A burn flows out from the north through a narrow valley and five ruined water-mills still stand in sequence along its course. A tangle of tiny hamlets lies between the west and east coasts here, connected by narrow lanes. Among them nestle traditional buildings, beautiful gardens and fine fields, concealing countless ancient sites beneath them. This area was densely populated in prehistoric times. The whole area is sheltered from the north by Ward of Scousburgh, a hill where a wonderful bronze Viking brooch was found, now on display in Shetland Museum.

Spiggie is a gem of a loch, well known for the many waterfowl which rest and feed here during the migration season. Swans overwinter on the loch, which has formed in relatively recent times. It is extensive and lies in a north-south curve across the floor of a shallow valley, surrounded by crofting settlements. Formerly it was an arm of the sea, but the waves built up such heaps of sand that eventually the dunes sealed the area off and it became a fresh-water body. The Peerie Voe, west-facing and petite, has been the subject of many a prize-winning picture in local photographic competitions. The view out to sea is exceptionally fine, framed either side by sea cliffs, with islands and stacks between. Here a large burn flows briskly out to sea from the loch. Look for the noosts in the

Loch of Spiggie from
the north.

banks to the north of the beach here. You can gather a wealth
of different seaweeds and you might be lucky enough to find a
sea bean – a tropical drift seed from the West Indies, round,
dark brown and polished – lying stranded by the tide after
crossing half way round the world!

Noss cliffs can be seen stark and dramatic against the
skyline to the south-west and they are almost too beautiful to
be missed. The tiny hamlet of Noss itself lies at the end of a
narrow road which cuts up west from the road around the south
side of Spiggie Loch. Here you can walk for half an hour in a
loop back round to Spiggie, taking in a section of some of
Shetland's finest cliff scenery. Fulmars glide within feet of your
head, making the best use of thermals. Puffins nest here too, as
they do at Sumburgh Head, and the view across the sea to
Foula makes it even more worth while.

Rising almost sheer from the sea, the massive bulk of
Fitful Head can be seen from a considerable distance out at sea
both from the south and the west. At night a warning light
flashes rapidly from the summit.

If you have time, explore East Longland and Brow Loch
and the many lanes and paths which criss-cross this corner of
Shetland. Archaeological sites occur in many places and the
local sandy soil produces wonderful fields of carrots and
potatoes, while gardens are brimming with flowers and
vegetables. As well as sheep, ponies and cattle graze here, and
some real mixed farming can be found. There is excellent

219

walking in the hills which rise to the north of the whole area.

Quendale has had a turbulent history and is well worth a visit. Local farmers grow more crops than in much of the rest of Shetland, which can be vulnerable to damage, so be careful where you walk and ask permission before crossing fields and fences. Unimaginably violent storms lash the coast here from time to time and over the centuries sand has been driven further and further inland. Now a hummocky, grass-covered expanse of ground behind the sand dunes covers the sites of many buildings, including a church. The beach was once quarried for sand, but this was thankfully stopped before further damage was caused to the machair, as this habitat is called. The settlement of Brake lies nearby, famous for its Pictish symbol stone, the Brake Stone, found in 1998.

Quendale Mill.

A large, restored water-mill at Quendale Farm is a must for visitors, with its shop, imaginatively designed interpretive displays and extensive range of old machinery. Garths Ness, where the *Braer* struck in 1993, was a place of disaster long ago. This area, together with much of the land to the south and west, was once home to many Shetlanders who, during the infamous Clearances, were deprived of their homes and crofts in singularly violent and objectionable fashion by the agents of the big landowners of the day. Ask at the mill for more information about this period.

The road from Quendale leads back to the main A970 beside a garage and several shops.

CHANNERWICK TO SUMBURGH VIA LEVENWICK

The road swings round a curve to the south, with Levenwick below to the left. There are two roads into this settlement, the first one turns off the main road soon after the bend, but if you can, stop for a while above the village to take in the whole panorama. Where the lower houses almost meet the sea, just above the beach, with its band of glowing sand and tiny sand dune fringe above, there is a graveyard built onto a large, symmetrical green mound. There are theories that beneath the

mound may lie the remains of a Viking ship burial. A telephone
box stands at the junction and you can walk or drive into the
village from here. Once off the fast main road, you are back in a
quieter Shetland again, with small, fenced fields, a scatter of old
and less old houses and a curve of cliffs descending to a superb
white sandy beach. Turn left again off the side road opposite a
bus stop, following the sign for Netherton, a tiny cluster of
houses near the shore. In summer verge sides and gardens down
here are brilliant with red-hot pokers and meadow cranesbill,
many of which have spilled over into ditches and banks. The
road splits, one short leg carrying on to a turning point and the
gated track to the cemetery, the other turning left for the beach.
Here the tiny parking area with its picnic site is often packed
with cars in the summer. This beach is glorious in all weathers,
but is especially appreciated in days of southerly and westerly
winds, when it is more sheltered than many.

Whales and dolphins can sometimes swim into the wide,
sheltered bay and occasionally have difficulty getting out again.
A minke whale stranded here in July 1997. There is a good
walk around the cliffs from the eastern end of the beach. A
little scrambling skill is required, but the views from the top are
fabulous. A herring station once operated from the shore here
and remains of old piers and an artificial drying beach can still
be seen. Watch your feet as you pass by the extreme north-
western corner of the cliff, as the 'beach' stones lie thick among
the grass. The cliff scenery and wild flowers and birds in spring
and summer can be breathtaking.

Levenwick hall is often open for Sunday teas in the
summer and there is a very modern care centre not far from the
famous Levenwick shop, which for many years opened at any
time of day or night, barring Sundays. For Clumlie, the next
settlement along to the south, rejoin the main A970 and turn
left as soon as you see the sign at the next turn-off.

Clumlie has some good, level acres of land and a large farm
with a few other scattered crofts, many long since empty. One
has within its boundary wall a sizeable broch, out of which much
of the croft buildings were probably built. Above and behind to
the west, the skyline was dominated for almost half a century by
an early-warning station during the cold war. Communication
masts and transmitter dishes, which transmitted and received
signals and later directed messages across the sea to the oil rigs,
stand silent and slightly menacing high up on the ridge. By the

turn of the new century, mobile telephone masts were being
constructed as yet another wave of technology began to rise
alongside the older one. Arctic and common terns nested in the
rocky wildness around them in their thousands until the later
1980s. Now only a handful of those numbers remains. From the
Loch of Clumlie a burn pours down towards the shore at
Trosswickness, passing the ruined remains of a long string of mills.

The lowermost of these mills, at Trosswick, is still in
perfect working order and come February, if the loch is full
enough, a sack of corn, oats or bere dried over many weeks
beforehand in the farm kiln may be hefted to the mill and
poured into the hopper. The stream may then be diverted
through the mill lade to turn the horizontal wooden blades, or
'feathers', on the vertical tirl, or shaft, below the mill floor.
The grindstone above is a hand-cut masterpiece of
craftsmanship. Few sounds are more evocative of the hardier,
simpler way of life in old Shetland than the sound of the water
racing and roaring below your feet, the rapid, rhythmic
clattering rattle of the mill gear, the clapper and shoe as they
spin the stone and crush the grains. Flour and bran hiss softly

Netherton and
Leven Wick early
in the morning on
a calm spring day.

as they spill into the circular well and mount up in a soft, pale, circular mound around the edges. The meal is raked into a heap, shovelled into a tray, sieved and bagged ready for baking. Remaining coarse fragments are set aside for the cows.

The Clumlie and Trosswick road leads south over the hill and drops towards Dalsetter. In a stone dyke or wall alongside the road here, there is a huge, round boulder with a special history. It is a glacial erratic, of what has been identified as Tonsbergite (an unmistakable dark-pink crystalline rock from near Tonsberg in Norway). The exact course and sequence of glacial movement across Shetland during the ice age has been confusing and difficult to establish. The evidence provided by the Dalsetter Stone gave very precise indications of movements towards the end of the last ice age. The stone has, sadly, lost some of its grandeur because of the selfish hackings of greedy rock collectors, in their futile attempts to secure themselves a piece of the stone as a souvenir.

Dalsetter has a massive ruined broch site with defensive earthworks around it. Foundations of other buildings almost certainly lie beneath the ground. There is access through fields nearby, from the road, but take care to close all gates behind you if you find them closed and try not to damage stone walls. The precipitous cliff edge here comes quite close to the broch, so be very careful if you decide to explore the coastline. Four other broch sites can be seen from this point, some clearer than others, and a fine afternoon's walk can take in all of them.

A fish-curing station operated from Boddam in days long gone by and an old fishing booth still stands down by the shore. A little further south, a road turns left and winds between stone walls and flower-crammed verges and passes Boddam's star attraction, the Crofthouse Museum. The old crofthouse of Southvoe with its barn and byre, kiln and mill here were fully restored and equipped with all the tools, furniture and fittings typical of a traditional Shetland crofthouse of around 1870. Don't miss this experience, in particular because of the immensely knowledgeable and friendly local guides, who bring the place to life. There is always a fire burning in the hearth and sometimes the fiddle is brought down from the wall for an old Shetland tune. Ask to see the home-made mouse trap or 'moose faa'. The wooden box beds are of interest too; how on earth did so many folk sleep so crammed together and with so little room to stretch out?

The name 'Dunrossness' means 'headland of the roaring tideway' and refers to the almost constant din from the 'roost' or tidal currents just to the south. Here, currents from both sides of Shetland meet and tangle into some of Shetland's most feared seas. There has been considerable development in the area and many new houses and housing estates were built as oil- and airport-related employment rose. As the oil phase began to wind down the local population level dropped. The large modern Dunrossness primary school takes its name from the whole area, as the children come here from all around.

Exnaboe stands opposite the airport with yet another broch at Eastshore at the end of the road, which is now actually slowly falling into the sea. A modern boating club stands nearby and on a rise of ground behind it are the ruins of some old croft buildings almost certainly partially built from the stones of the broch. Here the cottages overlooking the Pool of Virkie have some of the best birdwatching in Shetland, as many migrant waterfowl, seabirds and waders first alight in the shallows below them. Hot on the heels of the birds come the birdwatchers and locals can watch both!

Toab, to the right of the main road, has seen huge changes in the landscape, especially during the Second World War. There is a mixture of housing, old and new, as well as a shop, a hall and a broch site too. You can walk along the shore here to the wonderful Quendale Sands, where massive dunes have been known to lose thousands of tons of sand during gales and hurricane-force winds, burying fields and buildings behind them. The humps and hollows to the north of the beach cover landscapes of the past, home now to interesting grasses, sedges and rushes which enjoy the sandy habitat.

There are warning lights on the roadside as you approach the line of the airport's main east-west runway, which are red during landings and take-offs. A little beyond the lights lies the Scatness excavation. Here, many years ago, a broch site was breached during road building. In the last decade of the twentieth century, an archaeological dig began, which soon proved to be one of the most exciting in the country, revealing extensive Iron Age, Pictish and Viking remains. If you visit Shetland during July, you may be able to join guided tours around the site and examine the reconstructed Pictish and Iron Age buildings which have been built nearby. The team from the Living History TV programme came up for several

224

Puffin with a beak full
of sandeels.

summers and researched the technology and craft skills of the different periods.

Sumburgh Head with its stark white lighthouse, built in 1820 by Robert Stevenson, stands guard high on the wild, tilted rock faces of Sumburgh Head, Shetland Mainland's southernmost tip. No longer manned, the lighthouse tower works automatically; the gleaming prisms still revolve and sweep their vital beams of light far out across the lethal currents of the roost to the south. Today the offices and rooms are home to the Shetland branch of the RSPB, a fabulous vantage-point for birdwatching headquarters, and SOTEAG, the Shetland Oil Terminal Environmental Advisory Group. There is also self-catering accommodation for visitors.

If you are lucky, you may glimpse humpback whales breaching in the sea around Sumburgh Head, especially in June. Every year now 'whale-watching' weekends are held and increasing numbers of locals and visitors flock to try their skill with telescopes and binoculars, summer sea-fog permitting. A massive prehistoric promontory fort stood here until it was largely destroyed by the lighthouse construction work, only a short section of rampart now remaining. But it is not human interest which draws hordes of people to this exposed site, but bird life. There are several interpretive panels and a sizeable car park provides a safe stopping point for thousands of visitors every year.

Some of the most spectacular island seabird colonies in Britain are found along these cliffs and the access and viewing points are constantly being improved. Puffins may potter and mutter within a few feet of you; gannets dive and bonxies harrass; guillemots whistle and eider ducks croon; kittiwakes cackle and the sea seldom ceases its assault and battery at the feet of the shelving rock faces. Sea pinks carpet the turf in spring and other wild flowers cram every nook and cranny of the cliff faces from May to September. At times the scent is almost overwhelming. Fine views can be enjoyed from the top of Sumburgh Head. Fair Isle lies away to the south, Noss is just visible to the north and east and below you to the west lie Sumburgh Hotel, the archaeological site of Jarlshof, Sumburgh Airport and the fertile fields of Dunrossness. The underlying beds of sandstone here provide wide, gentle slopes and fertile, even soils; as a result, farms are larger than in many other parts of Shetland.

The coastline today probably follows a very different course from that reached by the first settlers, allowing for a sinkage of about 16 feet (5 m) of vertical land during 6000 years. The original landfalls may lie beneath the present shallows of the surrounding sea, which batters the coast and in winter sends clouds of spray washing over the ancient ruins, which are now protected by tough sea defences. Only half of Jarlshof stands today, the rest having been swept away by several thousand years of storm seas, which still occasionally cast sea-worn artefacts onto the local beaches. It was just such a storm which revealed Jarlshof in the first place, in the early 1900s, uncovering masses of stonework and debris. The discovery led to the excavation and the present world-famous site becoming established as one of Shetland's major attractions; a layer-cake of cultures – Bronze Age, Iron Age, Viking, Medieval – all preserved one above the other. Take time to go round at your leisure, as the site is overwhelmingly complex.

The beaches are among Shetland's most splendid; long, wide stretches of pure white sand, deserted for much of the year and on sunny summer days, they come close to perfection. From whichever direction the wind comes, at least one sandy beach remains sheltered. You can walk north from Sumburgh Head, following the eastern cliff tops and drop down to the shore at the Lawards, where a massive storm beach was hurled up in the famous storm of 1900. Fish and plant fossils have been found among the rocks here and the boulders are a patchwork of beautiful patterns of lichens. You can also follow the west-facing cliffs and the shore along to Jarlshof as long as you can negotiate a few walls and fences with safety and without damaging them. Beware scattered rocks hidden among long grass as you approach Jarlshof itself. Keep an eye open for migrant birds among the bushes of the Sumburgh Hotel garden, one of the best places to spot newly arrived rarities.

Scatness to the west lies parallel with Sumburgh Head. The road into Scatness becomes a track as you head south beyond the houses. There are a number of small lochs and it is worth looking out for smaller migrant birds here, sheltering among the grassy hollows. The ness narrows towards its southern tip and to reach the prehistoric blockhouse fort of Ness of Burgi, you need to be able to scramble and clamber

Fitful Head, Scatness
and West Voe
of Sumburgh, from
Sumburgh Head.

with some confidence. An excavation of the site in 1935 found traces of fireplaces and small amounts of bone and pottery. The fort has a central entrance door and thick-walled cells to either side and a third to the west, greatly damaged by erosion. A second fort site exists not far from this one, but with much less of its structure still visible.

This headland takes a ferocious battering from the full force of winter Atlantic rollers and the south-westerly gales which can assault Shetland at any time of year. But the best time to visit is in late May and early June, when the sea pinks or thrift blanket every square inch of ground space across the ness and right onto the rocks at the sea's edge. It is a very different place today, from the scene which would have met your eyes during the last war. Bunkers, many of which can still be found, were constructed all over the area and thousands of servicemen with their camps, huts, gun emplacements and guard posts dominated Dunrossness for many years. Local people had to present passes to enter the Scatness area unless they were under 16, and the rattle of anti-aircraft fire shook the windows in local houses whenever enemy aircraft were sighted.

Stacks of
Skroo

The Nizz
The North Light
Lighthouse
Cristal Kame

Dronga

•67

Skroo

Mopul

SuaversteIn

Millins-houllan

North Fellsi Geo

Ward
Hill
217

Wirrvie
Brecks

Tower of Ward Hill

Stacks of Wirrvie

Heads of Peitron

Ler Ness

•Mast

Brae of
Restingsged

North Naaversgill

Furse

North Gavel

Burrista

North Haven

To Grutness

Breiti Stack

Pier

Bird Observatory

Bu Ness

•145

Eas
Brecks

Colsta

South Haven

Airstrip

•68

South Gavel

•118

Huni

Kista

Goorn

Hundi Stack

Vaasetter
Pund

South Ramni Geo

110

110

Hunds Hillie

•51

Field

Sheep Craig

Reeva

Stonybreck

Haswalls

Claver's Geo

The Hilliers

Fogli Stack

Malcolm's
Head

•108

North Whaleback

The Crivy

Leogh

South Whaleback

Swartz Geo

Mathers Head

Haa

George
Waterston
Memorial Centre

The Fless

The South Light

Pier

South Harbour

The Burrian

Head of Tind

Meo Ness

The Keels

The Skerry

FAIR ISLE

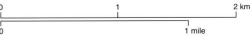

0   1   2 km

0   1 mile

Fair Isle

Whether you arrive in Fair Isle by air from Tingwall on Mainland Shetland, or by boat from Grutness near Sumburgh, the approaches are dramatic in the extreme. It is easy to see why so many people have been drawn to visit the island throughout the centuries. Fair Isle, which is now owned by the National Trust for Scotland, appears at first glance to be bare and exposed. But as you explore, it opens up into an endless delight of hidden corners, spectacular geos and cliffscapes.

A large number of archaeological sites have been identified here and several from different periods have been excavated in recent years. The present occupied buildings have been sensitively preserved and modernised, new ones built and old ones altered with great attention to overall impact and scale. Two graceful aero generators provide the electricity needs. But perhaps the most striking visual feature throughout the spring and summer are the wild flowers which grow from one end of the island to the other in glorious profusion. Orchids over a foot high can sometimes be found growing in the marshy areas in good years.

There is a thriving community in Fair Isle, the southernmost of the Shetland Islands. Its location in the sea makes it a frequent first landfall for exhausted migrant birds blown off course by storm winds on their annual flights between Scandinavia and southern Europe and beyond. An astonishing variety of species turns up each year, making it one of the best places in the world for seeing large numbers of different species of birds, including many rarities.

Migrant Bluethroat.

Facilities for visitors are well developed and there are few Shetland communities more welcoming, a quality for which the islanders have been well known throughout several centuries. The world-famous bird observatory and hostel are well worth a visit. Equipped for guest comfort as well as scientific study, the observatory plays an important part in monitoring and analysing migrant bird movement within a global network throughout the world.

Heligoland traps are set in key locations around the island and checked at regular intervals. Any birds caught are weighed, recorded and released. Storm petrels breed here in the summer. They are caught, weighed and ringed at night, attracted to the nets by spotlights, though it seldom gets very dark.

Fair Isle lies in the middle of the fairway between Northern Europe and America and despite its relatively small size, many vessels have been wrecked here. On 23 May 1868 the 1800 ton *Lessing* from Bremen struck Clavers Geo in thick fog and by a miraculous combination of luck and skill, all the crew and the 465 German emigrants and crew, *en route* for New York, were rescued. In 1877 the full-rigged *Black Watch* from Nova Scotia, only four months old, was wrecked at Shalstane and 23 crew and passengers were saved. On 12 March 1915, the 4323 ton Danish steamer *Canadia* ran aground at Helli Stack.

Fair Isle's most famous wreck, the Spanish ship *El Gran Grifon*, went aground here in 1588. The crew were sheltered and fed by the islanders who were massively outnumbered. The famous patterned knitwear to which the island gives its name is believed to have been introduced by the Spaniards and is still

The western cliffs of Fair Isle – looking south from Ward Hill to the headlands of Ler Ness, Colsta, Kista and Reeva with Malcolm's Head in the distance.

230

Looking across South
Harbour from the sea
towards Springfield,
Vaasetter and Sheep
Rock.

hand-knitted here; locally hand-made garments resting
comfortably at the top end of the market for such goods. By the
end of the 1990s, a number of other local crafts and skills had
developed including traditional Shetland boat-building, fiddle-
and spinning-wheel making, stained glass and hand-felting.

An excellent local museum is a must for every visitor and
tells in more detail the history and traditions of this unique
island community. The museum commemorates George
Waterston, whose passion for birdwatching and love for the
island helped keep him sane during long imprisonment in
Germany during the Second World War. He spent his hours
planning a birdwatching observatory for the island. After his
release, at the first opportunity he bought the island and
eventually realised the dream.

Island history is often sung here too and *Fridarey*, the
Norse name for the island, is also the name of a local folk
group. Two places of worship, the kirk and the Methodist
Chapel, are used alternately on Sundays and visitors are made
very welcome at both. In the kirk, a beautiful new stained-glass
window is worth a visit in its own right.

231

Travel & Holiday Information

Every year the Shetland holiday-maker scene changes a little. Shetlanders are creative and enterprising, always coming up with new ideas, a new craft, eating place or interpretive facility, but the main attractions – the scenery, wildlife, traditions and welcome – never change. For up-to-the-minute information, make the Shetland Tourist Office your first port of call, or better still, write to or telephone them in advance. They will send you details of all the latest prices, travel options, transport within the islands, accommodation and activity possibilities, together with extra items to suit your own needs and interests. There will be leaflets on many Shetland topics and individual leaflets for each area of Shetland. Their telephone number is 01595 693434, or you can write to them at Market Cross, Lerwick, Shetland Islands.

During your stay, buy the local newspapers which have excellent advertisements for local events, auctions, sales etc. The islands have their own broadcasting station and Radio Shetland (92.7 FM) presents half an hour of news every weekday from 5.30 pm, as well as additional programmes with features and interviews.

The *Shetland Times* comes out every Friday morning and the entertainments pages are well worth scanning for ideas. In addition there is a free magazine, *The Shetland Visitor*, published every year, which is packed with information for visitors and most shops and venues have stacks for the taking, so get hold of one as soon as you can and peruse it at your leisure. They also have a web site. Increasingly these days, local communities produce their own visitor information in the form of booklets or leaflets. Try to gather a selection of those you are likely to get to, as they will add greatly to your enjoyment.

Visitors are welcomed at all times of year. Every season has its own merits. Spring can be cool, but tends to have clearer weather than the summer, when heat is often followed by days of sea fogs. Autumn skies are stunning, with glorious sunsets and magnificent cloudscapes. Both autumn and winter can provide marvellous opportunities to watch the northern lights (aurora borealis, or 'Merrie Dancers' as they are called in Shetland). Winter is the time for the famous fire festivals; the Up Helly Aa of Viking guisers with their flaming torches. But summer is the most popular time, when nesting birds, young lambs and ponies and acres of wild flowers enrich the landscapes.

CULTURE & LANGUAGE

Shetland's culture and language are constant sources of interest and study. Newcomers to Shetland will notice the Shetland dialect immediately, but some districts have stronger forms than others and Shetlanders could be said to be virtually bilingual. Islanders have a natural courtesy which requires them to modify their own way of speaking in order to be understood by strangers. But a chance hearing of two local folk chatting away can be a revelation. Whalsay retains the richest and strongest form of Shetland dialect still to survive. Many years ago attempts were made in schools to stamp out dialect in children, 'for their own good'; the idea then prevailing that only English, spoken well, would secure them a good job and future prospects. Sadly this attitude, together with the arrival of television, resulted in the overall reduction and dilution of daily use of the dialect and the local education authority is now promoting dialect as an important element in the curriculum.

Food as a luxury item, or eating out as a leisure activity, are recent innovations. Traditional eating patterns remained much the same for years, as food was home grown or caught. But changes came in with supplies brought up during the War and even more so during the later oil 'invasion' when construction workers were fed like lords. Certain Shetland dishes retain their popularity, however, and no village function or wedding would be complete without cured and dried or 'reestit mutton', 'tattie soup' and 'bannocks' . Older generations speak wistfully of 'stap and crappin' a fish-liver and oatmeal dish, 'kirn milk', a unique curd made with untreated milk and 'sharp blaand', a tangy drink derived from the liquid remaining after butter is made. A number of traditional soups are now produced on a commercial scale and, through skilful marketing, are now on sale in a number of prestigious outlets in the UK and abroad. Tea and homebakes accompany many an entertainment and you can surprise your host by asking for a 'peerie scar' of milk or a 'peerie corn' of sugar; the dialect terms for 'a little bit' of liquid or food.

MUSEUMS, EXHIBITIONS & ARCHIVAL INFORMATION

Shetland gears up for its visitors with a crammed programme of events, exhibitions and special displays. The local museums open new displays and in Lerwick the Islesburgh Exhibition, held in the community, celebrates a slightly glorified, simple, happy past; a life of few possessions, a life ruled by weather, seasons and animals. The reality was probably considerably harder and more gruelling, but nevertheless, many former crofters admit to missing many aspects of their old lifestyles. Here you can watch spinning and Fair Isle and lace knitting, listen to local fiddlers and learn Shetland dances.

Visitors are welcome at the Shetland Library in Lerwick. After several decades in its purpose-built Hillhead home, it has moved to newly converted premises in an old church. The library service reaches every corner of Shetland with its two mobile library vans. Schools are well served through school libraries. Much of the published work on Shetland can be accessed through the Shetland Room. A large collection of literature is housed here, including many old and wonderful volumes, as well as microfiche records of newspapers and other literature. A number of well-known Shetlanders gifted their own collections of Shetland books to the library, so that they could be enjoyed by islanders in the future, and the collection is steadily added to as new works are published. Several computers add to the research and information facilities.

A priceless store of original texts, letters, diaries, articles and documents and a number of old books, reprints and recent anthologies are kept in the Shetland Archives. On a rainy afternoon, an hour spent here, reading some of the vivid accounts of life in Shetland several hundred years ago, can enrich a visit immensely. Whether visiting sea captains, travelling preachers or scientific researchers, all record memories and evidence of an island life long since vanished and forgotten. Some of the works of past writers on Shetland have become collectors' items and are eagerly sought after at the local Shetland book auctions. From time to time, new treasures turn up and it is tantalising to imagine what fresh revelations still survive, as yet undiscovered.

A growing number of visitors come to the islands to trace their ancestors who left Shetland during the past few centuries. The Shetland Family History Society has an office in and is eager to help with research.

Arts in Shetland are also well catered for, with an Arts Trust which supports travelling exhibitions, resident artists and sculptors, writers and drama and dance teachers. Concerts and theatre shows, a film club and bursaries for exhibitions and study trips all receive funds. Village halls and local hostelries host evenings of singing or musical entertainment, locally written plays and poetry readings. Traditional tales, legends and rich local folklore are enjoyed at story-telling evenings.

RELIGION

There is a remarkable variety of spiritual and religious groups in Shetland, with a wide range of places of worship. These include Salvation Army, Plymouth Brethren, Quakers, Buddhists, Baptists, Bahais, Mormons and Jehovas Witnesses amongst others every week. Catholic, Episcopalian, Church of Scotland, Unitarian and Evangelical Christian denominations keep in touch through an active ecumenical trust and share in a number of joint events every year.

LEISURE & RECREATION

Leisure and recreation in Shetland is incredibly well provided for, with sports, swimming and fitness-suite facilities now available in all the main islands. There was a time, not long ago, when football was virtually the only competitive sport. Some badminton would be played in the halls, especially over the autumn and winter months, and Shetland model yacht racing had a great following.

Subsistence farming left little time for leisure. Now, not only is the range of sports and leisure pursuits astonishingly wide, but the standard of play has improved to the point where Shetland teams go to all the Inter-Island Games, returning with steadily increasing numbers of medals, and Shetland is planning to host the Games in 2005. It is not unusual to find Shetlanders playing in national teams. Youngsters are doing well too, with many sports including table tennis being played to a high standard in junior teams.

A recently revived sport is yoal racing, when special hand-built wooden boats of a traditional Norse design are raced by teams of men and women. The rowing clubs are very popular and membership is growing. Rowers practise hard every fine night around Burra, Scalloway, Aith and other villages where there are clubs. Few sights are more lovely than the slim profile of a beautiful yoal in stark outline against the glare of the setting sun reflected in a silver-pink sea. A number of Shetland craftsmen have kept yoal-building skills alive and their workshops can sometimes be visited. A race on a different scale is the Bergen to Lerwick yacht race which creates excitement every summer, with concerts and parties to welcome the Scandinavian contestants.

Boat trips, which have facilities for the disabled, are available for visits around Noss and Bressay, and Foula, or out on sea-angling trips.

Cycling in Shetland can be wonderful, with good roads, minimal traffic and few serious gradients but on occasions the wind makes up for that! Bicycle-hire facilities are widely available.

Walking in Shetland is a liberating experience. Traditionally Shetlanders have walked the 'banks' of the shoreline, the hills and cliff tops and in most places walkers are welcome. It is always sensible to prepare for a change in the weather, though, and there are many ways in which you can increase the pleasure of your trip. The most important tip is to speak to local people. You can learn more in five minutes' conversation with a local resident than you can in weeks of reading guidebooks!

Enjoy walking in Shetland, while ensuring that your visit is welcomed by those who live and work there by following this advice:

SHETLAND WAY OF WALKING
CONSIDERATION FOR YOURSELF:

- If possible, walk with a companion and let someone know your intended route and anticipated time of return.
- Good maps of Shetland enhance every walk. The 1-25,000 Ordnance Survey maps are ideal for walkers. A compass is essential on moorlands if fog descends.
- Warm clothing and footwear with good gripping soles. Waterproof or breatheable outer clothing, an extra jumper, gloves and a hat, some food and drink; a basic first-aid kit.
- A camera, spare film and extra lenses. Take a plastic bag to protect them from salt-laden wind.

- Avoid cliff edges, boggy ground and slippery rocks.
- Keep away from aggressive nesting birds.

CONSIDERATION FOR OTHERS:

- Ask for permission before crossing fenced crofting areas or farmland and for advice about parking a vehicle if you have one.
- Avoid walking near sheep with lambs. Walk along the edges of fields of grass, or other crops, not across the middle. Never take dogs anywhere near livestock.
- Don't try to climb stone walls or barbed-wire fences. Use stiles wherever possible, but if you have to open a gate, always close it securely behind you.
- Never close a gate which has been secured in an open position.
- Keep water supplies clean, take all litter home and avoid risk of fire.
- Photograph wild flowers, don't pick them. Keep well away from nesting birds.

MUSIC & FESTIVALS

Shetland is extraordinarily rich in music. Traditional tunes are as popular today as they ever were. Traditional songs are less of a feature, though there are plenty of new songs written and annual competitions and events keep song-writing alive. The legendary Tom Anderson made Shetland fiddle music famous. He held annual summer schools in Stirling and spent much of his life saving and gathering old tunes and teaching them to young Shetland children; his 'Peerie Angels'. An annual music festival brings in hundreds of entrants and scores of performers, with great competition for the titles of Young Fiddler of the Year and Young Musician of the Year. The Shetland Folk Festival has become world famous and several other major musical events punctuate the calendar.

Shetland's most famous festival is Up Helly Aa, which takes place on the last Tuesday of January each year. Often assumed to be a relic of the Viking Ages, it is in fact a Victorian spectacular, based loosely round the ancient Viking ship burial tradition, but with a practical purpose at its heart. At one time, the ancient tradition of winter fire celebrations in Lerwick began to get a little out of hand. The streets were extremely narrow and the once popular local custom of tar-barrelling, common to many northern Scottish towns (and still celebrated in a few) left a trail of damage after the uproarious barrellers had passed by, scorching the doors of wealthy or powerful local individuals with their fiercely burning barrel as they passed by. A series of meetings and discussions in Lerwick led to the evolution of a new, colourful ceremony, redolent of Victorian Viking splendour, and with social order carefully observed.

The festival is designed to take place with proper attention to safety and little of the original wild abandon survives. All is strictly controlled by a committee and office bearers. A man has to serve for many years on the committee before being eligible for inclusion on the list of future Jarls. Men only are allowed to take part and the day itself is led by the Guizer Jarl and his henchmen, the Jarl Squad, consisting of male members of his family, relations and friends all dressed in Viking costume.

This group leads the processions during the day, making pre-arranged visits to schools and hospitals, and reading the elaborately designed, painted proclamation or 'Bill'. This text is erected in a central place and contains humorous, hidden references to individuals or incidents, which amuse passers-by.

Other squads follow the Jarl Squad, dressed in their own sets of costumes, which are hand made for the occasion, with much secrecy, until the night of the event itself, as the exact nature of the dress and the acts are revealed only to those taking part. The Jarl Squad escorts the dragon ship to the burning site, where the Guizer Jarl makes traditional speeches. Then, after the mass singing of three special songs and

'The Bill' – Up Helly Aa proclamation at Market Cross, Lerwick.

some rousing cheers, the torches fly through the darkness into the galley and flames rise into the sky. Fireworks often accompany the burning. The crowd stays to watch until the dragon head on the prow collapses, then the streets begin to empty as people make their way to the many halls where acts will be performed all night long.

After the burning, hundreds of strangely dressed men in teams, or 'squads', travel from hall to hall, performing at each venue a short dramatic presentation complete with costume and music, which usually features a topical incident or controversial item from local recent history. Performance quality varies a great

The Guizer Jarl and burning galley, Up Helly Aa festival.

deal from squad to squad, especially towards the end of the night! Each squad follows the others in carefully arranged succession, so that all halls see all acts. Each hall is organised by a group of Shetland ladies who provide food and soft drinks all through the night. Guests eat, drink, watch the acts and dance the night away. There is always a local holiday on the Wednesday, so that those who took part can sleep and recover from the after-effects! Each year hordes of visitors and foreign media flock to watch, film and report the spectacle.

Lerwick's Up Helly Aa has been lighting up the streets of the town every year (except for a brief interruption during the war) for well over a hundred years. Many other villages and communities have their own, less formal versions where women and girls take part in the procession, a few lucky lasses are seen, dressed as Viking princesses, in the jarl squad and men help to host and serve guests. In Hillswick, Scalloway and Brae the Viking ship burns as it sails in the sea, creating some wonderful images. Visitors can choose from many Up Helly Aas spanning some of the darkest months from January through to March.

Agricultural shows take place in the height of summer in Walls, Cunningsburgh, Voe and the North Isles, all hoping for better weather and more vistors than each other. The North Isles have shows too and there are few better times to visit than on their show days. They are well spaced out, so everyone in the islands who wishes can get to all of them. Look out for the programmes in the *Shetland Times* and in local shops. Traditional produce can be admired, such as Shetland tatties, Shetland kale and green eggs laid by the old variety of Shetland hens, the finest hand-knitting, Fair Isle patterns, Shetland lace, hand-spun wool and home baking. Superb displays of pot plants, exotic, greenhouse-grown fruit and local vegetables and arts and crafts compete for your attention with a programme of livestock parades, sports events and sheepdog handling.

Every Shetland district has its Community hall with a hall committee who programme each year with an astonishing variety of events, from wedding receptions, jumble sales and fund-raising functions to concerts and political meetings. There are a few tiny halls still in existence from the days 'before oil', which look impossibly small by comparison with the large, well-equipped buildings used today. Look out for posters and advertisments in the *Shetland Times* for hall teas, which are served in a selection of villages in rotation, on Sunday afternoons during the summer months. There are often craft stalls, exhibitions and sometimes music to enjoy, as well as teas with homebakes.

Entertainment comes in many forms and an unusual one to look out for is an auction; the sale rooms in Lerwick attract a colourful following. Displenishing sales are held to sell entire house contents, often at the house in question, or just outside it. Shetland pony sales are held in October, cattle marts are seasonal and fish markets take place regularly. For some, the regular book sales in Lerwick are a 'must' and books about Shetland sometimes fetch enormous prices.

Regattas feature regularly throughout the summer and local people attend in good numbers. There are races for different age groups, including children, teenagers and men and women. Fishing competitions, or Eelas, involve dozens of small boats heading out to sea at a given time and returning *en masse* to count and compare their catches. In the evenings the prizes are awarded in the local hall, and a Shetland supper of bannocks, tattie soup and reestit mutton, or maybe some fish, is served and a band plays for dancing.

Brae has its carnival day, with a grand parade of floats onto which money is thrown by the crowd, to be caught in buckets and given to charities afterwards. Aith has its Lifeboat Day and Scalloway has a Gala Week, with activities on every night. The Children in Need event has taken off in Shetland and each year fund-raising ideas vie with each other.

The Simmer Dim Rally was established in recent years as the national midsummer motorcylists' festival. Hundreds of black-leather-clad bikers arrive on the ferry from Aberdeen for an increasingly popular and extremely well-behaved gathering and enjoy themselves greatly.

Festivals and celebrations, often with local variations, took place all year round until relatively recent times in Shetland. Special days, dates for certain tasks, some very ancient in origin, spanned the whole calendar. Bonfires at Christmas and New Year were common in Shetland and other Nordic countries at one time and some communities still carry this on today. Midsummer bonfires were also a great feature at one time, as they still are in many other Scandinavian countries, where the festivities follow patterns that go back over a thousand years. Those who are interested in this aspect of island history should read James R Nicolson's *Shetland Folklore* for a fuller account. A simplified calendar of traditional and ancient festivals follows.

The Old Shetland Year

A calendar of traditional celebrations in a simplified, chronological order. A brief account of what took place is included, where it is known. Few are still remembered and sadly fewer still kept up.

5 Jan	Yule E'en	Old Christmas Eve. Guizers, or 'Skekklers', dressed in elaborate straw costumes, went round entertaining friends and neighbours. Dancing, music and a dram or two followed the guizers' arrival and much fun was had by all.
6 Jan	'Old' Yule	Old Christmas, still celebrated in Foula.
13 Jan	Old Ne'erday	Old New Year.
Late Jan	Uphalliday	Norse festival to celebrate the ending of winter. The original name for Up Helly Aa, the last day, or end of the Yule holiday period.
29 Jan	St Antony Day	
2 Feb	Candlemas day	Pre Reformation festival.
		Pigs said to be killed at this time and prepared for use later.
		Weather lore: 'If Candlemass day be bright and fair,
		Half of the winter's to come and mair
		If Candlemass day be wet and foul,
		The half of the year be gone at yule'.
22 Feb	Petermas Day	Feast of St Peter.
24 Feb	Løbers-mas	From Old Norse Leap Day. An old rhyme says: 'The lark will be greet as long after Løbers-mas as it sang afore Candlemas'.
17 Mar	Bogel's Day or Marimass	Feast of St Mary. Start of a spell of bad weather. A tiny patch of corn was sown on this day, carefully monitored as the year went by and harvested to make Buggle cakes, which were eaten on the next year's Bogel's Day. The weather on the last three days of March was often wild. This spell was called the Bogel Ree.
25 Mar	Lady Day	Start of the crofting year. Last three days of March were called the 'Borrowing days'. Various versions; in one, the weather for the three summer months was predicted from these three days. 'The first of them was wind and wet, the second of them was snow and sleet, the third of them was such a freeze, it freezed the birds nebs to the trees.'
14 Apr	The 'Feast of Perpetua and Felicity'	Mentioned in a conveyance from Sandwick dated 1360.
16 Apr	Simmermill Day	Start of the summer half year. An old crofter commented: 'Certain things had to be planted by then, Shetland kale and corn as well. Tatties didn't matter so much'.
1 May	Maunsmas (St Magnus) and also Beltane	Bonfires were lit and danced around. Young folk competed to leap across the fires. This date marked the start of the Haaf fishing season. Beltane Ree was a three-day fishing festival, or foy, a surviving relic of sun-worship of the god Bael, with many rituals and ceremonies.

24 Jun	Johnsmas Simmermill Foy, or midsummer festival	Young girls would pluck Johnsmas (plantain) heads, pull out the stamens and bury, or hide, them. The next day they were examined and if more stamens had grown, a wedding was likely to follow. Some accounts refer to sleeping with them under their pillows to dream of future husbands. Dutch fishermen arrived and celebrated with festivities marking the start of their summer herring fishing season. More bonfires were lit.
4 Jul	Martin o' Bulliamas Day	If it rained that day, it would rain for 40 days. Likewise if fine, 40 fine days would follow.
1 Aug	Lammas	End of the year's Haaf fishing. 'Lammas speets' (heavy rain)
23 Aug	Laurencemas	Feast of St Lawrence.
21 Sept	Matjomas	Feast of St Matthew.
29 Sept	Michaelmas	Feast of St Michael. The end of the growing season.
14 Oct	Winter Day	Cattle brought in and tied in their stalls (and the first Saturday after Winter Day was called Winter Sunday Saturday).
1 Nov	The feist of Hallamas	A time for roofs to be repaired.
3 Nov	Soloman's E'en (originally Samhuinn)	
11 Nov	Martinmas	Feast of St Martin. Shetland leases traditionally began and ended on this date.
30 Nov	Andersmas	Feast of St Andrew.
4 Dec	Barbarasmas	Feast of St Barbara.
17 Dec	Sow Day	Seven nights before Christmas.
	Tulyas E'en	On Tulya's E'en two straws were laid in a cross shape at the entrance to the corn and hay yard, a hair from the tail of each cow was plaited and hung above the byre door and a glowing peat was carried through all outhouses to guard against Trows.
18 Dec	Helya's E'en	The night after Tulyas E'en. 'Milk-an-mell' was eaten and this rhyme was said, to protect children: Mary Midder, had de haund Roond aboot for sleepin' bound. Had the lass, and had the wife, Had the bairns au der life. Mary Midder, had de haund Roond da inants o' wir laund.
19 Dec	Byana's Sunday	Sunday before Christmas. Half a cow's head was boiled and eaten for supper. A candle was set into the eye socket of the cleaned skull and it was lit and carried through the house on Yule morning.
20 Dec	Tammasmas	Feast of St Thomas. No work or amusements were allowed after dusk. A rhyme says: 'The very babe unborn cries 'O dül, dül', For the brakkin o' Tammasmas Nicht Five Nichts afore Yule! Some records refer to Tunderman's nicht, possibly a relic of Norse worship of Thor.
25 Dec	Yule	

Chronology

Dates BC are approximate   * = indicated from 20th century finds

BC

40,000	Mediterranean plant and tree species growing in Shetland. (See Fugla Ness, Uyea)
10,000	The last Ice Age ends.
8000	Shetland hit by world's largest tidal wave from NE, triggered by vast submarine landslide.
4000	First traces of Neolithic settlers in Shetland.*
3500	Scord of Brouster first settled.. Jarlshof first settled.. Stanydale 'temple' built.
2500	Cache of barley laid down in a house at Ness of Gruting. *
2000	Blanket bog begins to form. Bronze smith working at Jarlshof.*
1500	Scord of Brouster abandoned.*
1000	Clickimin Broch settled.
500	Beginning of the Iron Age.*
100	Probable establishment of Picts as a distinct political grouping.
40	Probable date of manufacture of a Roman pottery shard in Clickimin Broch excavation.

AD

80	Tacitus, the Roman historian, writes of maritime tribes in Northern Europe.
100	Mousa Broch built. * Clickimin abandoned.
98	(Nennius records) a Saxon attack on the Picts, which 'laid waste the Orkneys'.
300	Roughly the end of the Iron Age.
400	Approximate start of a colder, wetter period of weather lasting until about 800 AD.
500	Iona Christian centre founded. Monks begin to venture northwards to Orkney, Shetland, Faroe and Iceland.
550	Roughly agreed as the start of Pictish Shetland. Brake Stone carved.
563	First Christian missionaries thought to have arrived in Shetland.

600	Brude MacBile laid waste the Orkneys.
682	(Nennius states that) Vikings have overrun all the islands of Britain.
749	Christianity established in Shetland.
750	Bressay Stone erected.
800	First Viking settlements established in Shetland. St Ninian's Isle Treasure probably buried at about this time.
843	Kenneth Mac Alpine united the Scots and Picts in Scotland.
900	Roughly the start of the 'Little Climatic Optimum', a period of warmer, dryer weather lasting for 300 years.
910	Jarl 'Turf' Einar dies after a peaceful reign.
950	Rough date of an English coin found at Scatness.
995	Norway becomes officially Christian.
1000	Silver thistle-headed brooch lost in Gulberwick, found almost a thousand years later by a schoolboy.
1065	Approximate date of death of Earl Thorfinn the Mighty. Earldom split between sons Paul and Erlend.
1117	Magnus Erlendsson killed at Easter in Orkney. Cult of St Magnus begins.
1190	Document in which Earl Harald Maddadarson refers to himself as the Earl of Orkney.
1195	Shetland confiscated from Earls of Orkney by King of Norway.
1200	Serious deterioration in climate begins about now.
1231	Earl of Angus succeeds to Earldom and the Norse line becomes extinct.
1263	King Haakon with 200 war galleys, shelters in Bressay Sound, *en route* to try to defend the Hebrides.
1300	Poor climatic period comes to an end.
1302	Apostles Church built in Bergen, funded largely by rents from Shetland and Faroe.

1312	Raids by Scots on Shetland.	1640	Dutch warship and three armed vessels of the Dutch East India Company attacked by Spanish warship.
1321	Angus line ends and Strathearne line succeeds to Earldom.		
1350	Black death.	1653	English fleet of 94 ships capture 50 Dutch herring 'busses' in Bressay Sound.
1369	More Scottish raids on Shetland.		
1379	Earldom of Orkney and Lordship of Shetland passed by marriage to St Clair of Roslin, until 1468.	1665	Fort construction begun, Lerwick.
		1667	Commissioners of Supply established.
		1670s	French and Dutch at war.
1391	Probable date of the murder of Malise Sperra during a struggle for control of Shetland.	1673	Dutch burn Fort and part of Lerwick.
		1677	More Dutch fishing boats burned.
1397	Norway united with Denmark under Queen Margrethe, and ceases to exist as a separate kingdom.	1680s	Fisheries begin to decline.
		1688	'9 years war' begins. Token storming of Scalloway Castle by Lerwick gentry.
1418	A Scot, William Tulloch, appointed Bishop of Orkney (and Shetland).	1690s	Bad harvests and famine.
		1696	Act passed for the Settling of Schools, to reinforce the legislation of 1616.
1469	On 28 May Shetland was pledged in pawn to Scotland for 8000 florins, to be redeemed in due course.	1700	Smallpox. John Brand visits Shetland.
		1702	'3rd war of containment' of France begins.
1471	The Lordship of Shetland was annexed to Scotland, with the Earldom of Orkney.	1703	French burn 100 Dutch herring 'busses' in Lerwick harbour.
1500	Approx. beginning of a period of climatic deterioration lasting well over a century.	1707	Act of Union between Scotland and England. Shetland becomes politically part of Great Britain.
1560	Scottish Reformation. 'Kirkmen' began to arrive in the islands.	1713	Shetland's first official SSPCK school opens in Walls.
1562	Earl of Bothwell fled to Shetland after defeat of Mary Queen of Scots at Carberry Hill.	1721	John Buchan, minister of Northmavine, gets four schools established in his parish.
1565	Queen Mary gave Robert Stewart a grant of her lands of Orkney and Shetland.	1730s	Greenland whaling begins. Potatoes introduced to Shetland.
1577	Evidence taken of complaints about Laurence Bruce of Unst.	1736	*Isabella* takes mail and general cargo to Aberdeen once a year.
1588	Spanish transport ship wrecked on Fair Isle.	1738	Charter granted initiating educational changes; allowing agriculture, trades, knitting etc. to be taught.
1598	Muness Castle built in Unst for Lawrence Bruce.		
1600	Scalloway Castle built for Earl Patrick.	1740	Revd John Mill, minister of Dunrossness, starts his diary.
1611	Privy Council Act abolishes Norse law in Scotland.	1750s	Greenland whaling peaks. Far haaf fish production increases greatly. Smallpox vaccinations reduce deaths.
1615	Earl Patrick and son hanged in Edinburgh.		
1616	Privy Council Act passed for the establishment of schools in every parish in Scotland.	1752	Gregorian calendar officially replaces Julian calendar. Many parts of Shetland continued to use the old one.
1628	Date on Bressay tombstone of Agnes Gifferd 'ane vertuous and discreit gentlewoman.'	1755	Population at 15,000.
1629	Outbreak of plague.	1760	Govt. subsidy awarded to a trading consortium in Leith to deliver mail to Lerwick five times a year.
1630s	Famine. Some lairds support Covenanters' cause.		
1636	Captain Claes Jansen Bruyn of Durgendam dies after his ship reached Bressay Sound from Mozambique.	1763	Bruce of Symbister pioneers new fish curing and drying methods.

A P P E N D I X

1770	Smallpox contained, allowing birth rate to rise and population level to increase. Lerwick grows rapidly.
1774	George Lowe visits Shetland. Happyhansel School opens in Walls.
1776	Flax spinning factory built at Catfirth.
1780s	Industrial Revolution begins in Shetland. Kelp production begins and Sandlodge copper mine opens.
1790s	The first *Statistical Account of Shetland* compiled by Sir John Sinclair. The start of 20 years of Press Gang operating round Shetland. There were 1100 Shetland men serving in the Navy in 1793 and 3000 in 1808.
1797	A road was built from Lerwick to Tingwall.
1803	Education Act passed, enabling teachers' salaries to be increased.
1809	Arthur Edmondston writes *View of ancient and present state of Zetland Islands*.
1813	*Doris* lost with all hands *en route* for Shetland.
1814	Several lodberries now in Lerwick.
1815	Greenland whaling in full swing.
1816	Lerwick's first Parochial School opens.
1820s	'Hay & Ogilvy' ship builders established. First big farms laid out at Sumburgh and Sandlodge. Faroe fishing starts.
1821	Shetland Bank starts; own notes printed.
1825	First steamer service to Shetland. Paddle steamer *Sovereign* runs between Aberdeen and Lerwick.
1830	Tingwall farms laid out. Tenants moved and runrigs ploughed over.
1832	Fishing disaster on east side of Shetland; over 100 men lost. Reform Bill passed, giving landowners and tenants the right to vote.
1834	Herring boom.
1836	Shetland's first newspaper, *The Shetland Journal*, is launched.
1839	Edward Standen visited Shetland; began to promote Shetland hosiery.
1841	*The New Statistical Account of Shetland* produced.
1842	Great herring crash; biggest ever financial disaster for Shetland.
1843	Poor Law enquiry commission.

1847	Arthur Anderson returned as MP for Orkney and Shetland.
1848	Potato blight strikes.
1849-51	Meal roads being constructed in various parts of Shetland.
1850	A road was blasted through Mavis Grind connecting Northmavine with the rest of Mainland.
1850s-70s	Weisdale Clearances.
1856	Gas lighting installed in Lerwick.
1859	50 Greenland whaling ships in Lerwick harbour on 9 March.
1861	Population at 31,670. Emigration increases.
1862	Anderson Education Institute gifted to Shetland by Arthur Anderson.
1867	*Diana* enters Ronas Voe after 6 months trapped in ice; 14 months at sea.
1868	First steamship service to N. Isles; *Chieftain's Bride*.
1871	First *St Magnus* sailed. Emigration surge; 4640 Shetlanders leave during next 10 years.
1872	Landmark Education Scotland Act passed to set up state schools. *Shetland Times* newspaper founded.
1874	Tar barrelling banned in Lerwick. John Brown installs steam-driven hammer in Freefield engineering shop.
1875	Herring fishing begins and Faroe fishing declines.
1877	Lerwick Harbour Trust founded and the *Earl of Zetland* begins her 68-year service.
1885	The *Shetland News* founded.
1886	Crofters' Holdings Act introduced. Victoria Pier opened in Lerwick. Betty Mouat, shipwreck survivor, drifts to Norway.
1888	Lerwick Fever Hospital built.
1889	Local Government (Scotland) Act. Zetland County Council set up.
1893	Dr Jakobsen begins his studies of Scandinavian words in use in Shetland.
1900	The 'Great Gale' strikes Shetland from the south-east.
1904	27 July German fleet anchored off the Knab.
1905	First motor boat, the *Napier Major*, visits Shetland.
1913	First cinema, the North Star, opens in Lerwick.

1914	First World War begins. Sea plane base at Catfirth. 10th Cruiser Squadron based at Swarbacks Minn.	1974	Ninian oil field discovered. Zetland County Council Act passed. Shetland Bird Club launched.
1917	Lerwick becomes a convoy port.	1975	Zetland County Council is replaced by the Shetland Islands Council.
1926	First seine nets introduced for inshore flatfish catching.		In a referendum in the same year Shetland votes 'No' (56% against 'yes' 43%) to membership of the EEC.
1932	Mains water and sewerage system and electricity supply connections begin in Lerwick.		*Earl of Zetland* ferry replaced by inter-island car ferries.
1933	The first civil aeroplane lands in Shetland.	1976	Fishing Limits Act established securing 200 mile fishing zone.
1934	Epidemic of typhoid; 243 cases recorded during the year.	1977	Radio Shetland first broadcast. Herring fishing ban imposed.
1936	First scheduled air service established.	1978	*Esso Bernicia* spills 1100 tonnes of heavy bunker oil.
1939	Second World War begins. Sullom Voe becomes an RAF base. Over 20,000 military personnel arrive.	1979	Drilling licences for oil are renewed.
1943	America lends three submarine chaser boats to the 'Shetland Bus' operation.	1980	The first plans are debated by Trinity House which lead eventually to the automating of all Shetland's lighthouses and the loss of all remaining lighthouse keepers and their families from the communities.
1947	Town and Country Planning Act passed. The *New Shetlander* is launched.		
1950	Echo sounders and Decca navigation technology increase fishing efficiency.	1981	H.M. Queen Elizabeth and King Olaf of Norway open the Sullom Voe Oil Terminal. First Shetland Folk Festival held. Shetland Field Studies Group established.
1953	New power station opens at Gremista.		
1955	Noss officially becomes a National Nature Reserve.		
1960	Shetland's first fish-processing factory opens in Scalloway.	1983	Shetland Knitwear Trades Association set up.
1961	The new Gilbert Bain Hospital opens.	1985	Hamefarin in Shetland.
1963	*Shetland News* ceases to be published.	1991	HIDB restructured into Highlands and Islands Enterprise by Conservative Govt. Shetland Enterprise formed.
1964	First oil-exploration licences released in Britain. Television arrives in Shetland.		
1965	Highlands and Islands Development Board established. First Norwegian purse seiners arrive.	1993	*Braer* oil tanker wrecked off Garth's Ness; 86,238 tonnes of oil spilled.
1966	Shetland Museum and Library open. Highlands and Islands Development Board (HIDB) set up by Labour Govt.	1995	Bonhoga Gallery opens. Clickimin Centre opens.
1967	Snowy owls arrive in Shetland and breed in Fetlar.	1997	Scatness sees beginning of Viking/Pictish excavations.
1968	Shetland Archeological & Historical Society formed.	1999	Lerwick and Shetland host the Cutty Sark Tall Ships Race.
1970	Air service between Sumburgh and Baltasound, Unst, begins.	2000	Waste to Energy plant comes on stream. A new *Shetland News* periodical appears in colour.
1971	Oil discovered in the 'Brent' field to the east of Shetland. Trondra and Burra sea bridges built.	2001	Shetland Aerogenerators install three wind turbines between Scalloway and Lerwick.
1973	Oil rig servicing begins in Shetland. Sandy Loch reservoir constructed near Lerwick.	2002	P&O Ferries era ends. North Link takes over. 'Sting Ray' trial tidal generation project commences in Yell Sound.

Historic Sites and Artefacts Checklist

Böd of Gremista, Lerwick

Böd of Nesbister, Wormadale

Booth of Ollaberry

Catpund Quarry, Cunningsburgh

Chancel arch, Sand

Clickimin Broch, Lerwick

Cullinsburgh cross slab, Bressay

Fladdabister kilns

Fort Charlotte, Lerwick

Haa of Burravoe, Yell

Haa of Sand

Hanseatic Booth, Symbister

Hjaltadans stone circle

Jarlshof, Sumburgh

Lerwick Lodberries

Loch of Huxter, Whalsay

Lunna Church

Lund Graveyard

Mousa

Muness Castle, Unst

Pier House, Whalsay

Quendale Mill, Dunrossness

Scalloway Castle

Scalloway eclipse stone

Scatness, Sumburgh

Scord of Brouster, Walls

St Ninian's Isle, Bigton

Standing stones, Busta

Stanydale, Gruting

Stenness fishing station, Eshaness

Strom Castle

Sumburgh Lighthouse

Tingwall Law, Ting Holm

Underhoull Broch, Unst

Uyeasound

Vementry chambered cairn

Vementry guns

White Lady of Queyon, Yell

Yoxie, Whalsay

MUSEUM ARTEFACT HIGHLIGHTS

Viking comb

Gulberwick brooch

Dutch coins

Kebister armorial plate

Shetland knives

St Ninian's Isle Treasure; (replicas only in Shetland)

Papil Stone

Bellarmine jar

Model ships

Best Landscape Guide

BEST BEACH GUIDE

Shetland has over 200 sandy beaches at various points around its 3000 miles of coastline, many small and inaccessible, but all beautiful in different ways. Winter storms can often alter the appearance of a beach and the quantity of sand may vary from year to year. A small selection of my favourites is given here, with some notes for additional information. Details about sea shells are not included, because collection of shells is not recommended as it damages the habitat. Some beaches can provide shelter at both ends, hence several wind directions are listed in some cases. Bear in mind that strong winds can be turbulent and the degree of shelter in some conditions will be variable.

The symbols following each place name give rough indications of beach quality, accessibility, degree of shelter from the wind, provision of toilet, car parking facilities, etc., and other features as follows:

Star rating for sheer loveliness:
*good, **very good, ***beautiful, ****exquisite

N,S,W,E, and NE, NW, SE, SW; sheltered from the north, south, west and east, and from the north east, north west, south east, south west, etc.

    A1 = easy access
    A2 = access possible
    A3 = some walking required
    A4 = access more difficult
    T   = Toilets provided
    CP = Car parking available
    IP = improved facilities planned

Norwick, Unst ** S, SE,SW, A1, CP, IP.
Burrafirth, Unst ** W, E, S, SW, SE, A2.
Skaw, Unst ** SW, W, A1, CP.
Sandwick, Unst *** W, SW, NW, A3, IP (Prehistoric and historic sites nearby).
Tresta, Fetlar *** N, NE, NW, E, A1, CP, IP.
Lunda Wick ** S, SW, E, NE, A1, CP, IP.
Breckon, Yell *** S, SE, SW, W, E, A4, IP.
West Sandwick, Yell *** E, SE, NE, N, A2, CP, IP.
Gossabrough, Yell ** S, SW, W, A1, CP.
Norby, West Mainland ** S, SW, SE, E, A2, CP.
Melby, West Mainland ** S, SW, SE, A1, T, CP, IP.
Sandvoe, West Mainland *** E, W, A1, CP, IP,

(Ancient chapel nearby. Old Haa house not far away).
Reawick, West Mainland ** N, NW, W, A2.
Banna Minn, Burra Isle ** E, SE, NE, A3, IP.
Sands of Meal, Burra Isle *** N, W, NW, NE, A4, T, CP, (Can be very crowded at times), IP.
Gulberwick S. of Lerwick * W, SW, NW, N, A2.
Sands of Sound, Lerwick ** W, NW, N, A2, (Can be busy during fine weather and holidays), IP.
Sand Garth, Bressay * SW, S, SE, A2.
White Ayre, Bressay ** S, A4.
Cumliewick, S. Mainland ** E, S, SE, NE, A3, IP.
Levenwick, S. Mainland *** S, SE, SW, W, A1, CP, IP.
Maywick, S. Mainland * S, SE, E, W, SW, A2, IP.
St Ninian's Isle, Bigton **** N, S, E, W, A3, IP, (Tombolo beach link to island. Ancient remains).
Quendale **** N, NE, NW, W, A3, IP.
Rerwick ** N, W, NW, NE, E, SE, A4.
Scousburgh *** S, SE, NE, A1 (Sand dunes behind beach. Caravans nearby. Can be crowded).
West Voe of Sumburgh *** E, SE, NE, N, A2, T, CP, IP.
Grutness ** S, SW, W, NW, N, A1, CP, IP.

BEST CLIFF SCENERY

Almost anywhere in Shetland can produce fabulous cliff scenery. Some of the best views anywhere can be had from the inter-island ferries, while crossing from one island to another.

DRAMATIC PHYSICAL FEATURE CHECKLIST

Aesha Head, Papa Stour
Back of Ollaberry Fault
Deepdale, Walls
Drongs Stacks, Hillswick
Eshaness cliffs
Gloup Voe, Yell
Grind of the Navir, Eshaness
Hams of Muckle Roe
Muckle Flugga
St Ninian's Isle tombolo
Sheep Rock, Fair Isle
Sneck O Da Smaalie, Foula
Stanes of Stofast, Lunna Ness
Villians of Hamnavoe, Northmavine
Ronas Hill, Northmavine
Clift Hills
Hermaness
Fitful Head
Foula

APPENDIX

Plant Checklist

This is a shortened list of Shetland's wild plants, which, apart from those listed as rarities, can be found with little difficulty during the spring or summer months. The habitats have been roughly divided into groups, as a number of plants can be found in more than one habitat; for example, dry banks and verges can often support plants commonly found on cliff faces. Underlying limestone or serpentine rock can alter the plant species' range considerably, and certain habitats, such as saltmarsh or fellfield, have very specialised plant communities. Mosses, sedges, rushes and shrubs follow the flowering plants in each habitat group. There are great differences between specimens of the same plant where one is found on grazed, or exposed ground, and another in sheltered, sheep-free areas. Spring squill can flower at ground level in grazed cliff-top pasture, yet just over the sea fence, it can reach eight inches in height.

The common English names of the plants are listed in alphabetical order, followed by the Shetland name in bold and lastly the Latin name in italics. Shetland plant names are gradually dying out, but a number are included here, though some names have been lost through time. Though only one dialect name per plant is used in the checklist, there is considerable variation in local names from place to place in Shetland and you may well come across different ones.

For those with a particular interest in botany, consult David Malcolm's *Shetland's Wild Flowers*, or *The flowering plants and ferns of the Shetland Islands*, by Walter Scott and Richard Palmer.

BANKS, VERGES & DRY GRASSLAND

Autumn hawkbit - *Leontodon autumnalis*

Bird's-foot trefoil (**Caticlews**)- *Lotus corniculatus*

Bush vetch - *Vicia sepium*

Common daisy (**Kokkiloorie**) - *Bellis perennis*

Dandelion (**Bitter aks**) - *Taraxacum officinale*

Fairy flax - *Linum catharticum*

Field gentian (**Deadman's mittens**) - *Gentianella campestris*

Frog orchid - *Coeloglossum viride*

Hogweed (**Keksie**) - *Heracleum sphondylium*

Kidney vetch - *Anthyllis vulnaria*

Lady's bedstraw (**Hunders**) - *Galium verum*

Meadow buttercup (**Kraa's taes**) - *Ranunculus acris*

Meadow vetchling - *Lathyrus pratensis*

Mountain everlasting - *Antennaria dioica*

Pignut (**Swine's murricks**) - *Conopodium majus*

Red clover - *Trifolium pratense*

Self heal - *Prunella vulgaris*

Slender St John's-wort - *Hypericum pulchrum*

Sneezewort (**Pepper girse**) - *Achillea ptarmica*

Spear thistle - *Cirsium vulgare*

Spring squill (**Grice's mooricks**) - *Scilla verna*

Tufted vetch (**Moose peas**) - *Vicia cracca*

White clover (**Smora**) - *Trifolium repens*

Yarrow - *Achillea millefolium*

Yellow rattle (**Fool's pennies**) - *Rhinanthus minor*

False oat-grass (**Ockrabung**) - *Arrhenatherum eliatus*

HILLS AND MOORS

Bell heather - *Erica cinerea*
Bilberry (**Blaeberry**) - *Vaccinium myrtillus*
Common dog violet (**Snori**) - *Viola riviniana*
Cross leaved heath - *Erica tetralix*
Crowberry (**Berry hedder**) - *Empetrum nigrum*
Eyebright (**Lammas flooer**) - *Euphrasia officinalis*
Heather (**Ling**) - *Calluna vulgaris*
Heath bedstraw - *Galium saxatile*
Heath milkwort - *Polygala serpyllifolia*
Heath speedwell - *Veronica officinalis*
Heath spotted-orchid (**Curly dodie**) - *Dactylorhiza maculata*
Lousewort (**Sookie flooer**) - *Pedicularis sylvatica*
Marsh violet - *Viola palustris*
Sheep's sorrel - *Rumex acetosella*
Tormentil (**Bark flooer**) - *Potentilla erecta*
Wild thyme - *Thymus praecox*

Cotton grass (**Luckaminnie's Oo**) - *Eriophorum angustifolium*
Hair moss - *Polytrichum commune*
Heath rush (**Burra**) - *Juncus squarrosus*
Mat grass - *Nardus stricta*
Purple moor grass - *Molinia caerulea*
Splendid moss - *Hylocomium splendens*
Vivaparous fescue - *Festuca vivipara*

MARSHES, BOGS, STREAMSIDES, DITCHES, LOCHS & WET GRASSLAND

Angelica (**Spootie trumps**) - *Angelica sylvestris*
Bog asphodel - *Narthecium ossifragum*
Bog pimpernel - *Anagallis tenellis*
Bogbean (**Jule girse**) - *Menyanthes trifoliata*
Common butterwort - *Pinguicula vulgaris*
Common marsh bedstraw - *Galium palustre*
Creeping forget-me-not - *Myosotis secunda*
Devil's bit scabious - *Succisa pratensis*
Double orange mimulus - *Mimulus x burnetii*
Early marsh orchid - *Dactylorhiza incarnata*
Grass of Parnassus (**White Kaitrins**) - *Parnassia palustris*

Lady's smock (**Moddoo dokkies**) - *Cardamine pratensis*
Lesser celandine - *Ranunculus ficaria*
Lesser spearwort - *Ranunculus flammula*
Marsh cinquefoil - *Potentilla palustris*
Marsh lousewort - *Pedicularis palustris*
Marsh marigold (**Blogga flooer**) - *Caltha palustris*
Marsh pennywort - *Hydrocotyle vulgaris*
Marsh ragwort (**Gowans**) - *Senecio aquaticus*
Marsh thistle - *Cirsium palustre*
Marsh willowherb - *Epilobium palustre*
Meadowsweet - *Filipendula ulmaria*
Monkey flower - *Mimulus guttatus*
Northern marsh-orchid (**Curly dodie**) - *Dactylorhiza majalis subsp. purpurella*
Primrose (**Mayflooer**) - *Primula vulgaris*
Ragged robin - *Lychnis flos-cuculi*
Round leaved sundew - *Drosera rotundifolia*
Water avens - *Geum rivale*
Water forget-me-not - *Myosotis scorpioides*
Water mint - *Mentha aquatica*
Yellow iris (**Seggie**) - *Iris pseudacorus*

Sphagnum moss - *Sphagnum (various)*
Water horsetail - *Equisetum fluviatile*

CLIFF FACES, ROCKY OUTCROPS & GORGES

Alpine meadow rue - *Thalictrum alpinum*
Birdsfoot trefoil (**Caticlews**) - *Lotus corniculatus*
Creeping willow - *Salix repens*
Dwarf juniper - *Juniperus communis*
Glaucous dog rose (**Klingra**) - *Rosa caesa subsp. glauca*
Golden rod - *Solidago virgaurea*
Honeysuckle - *Lonicera periclymenum*
Meadowsweet (**Julegirse**) - *Filipendula ulmaria*
Moss campion - *Silene acaulis*
Red campion (**Sweet willie**) - *Silene dioica*
Roseroot (**Lady's footstool**) - *Rhodiola rosea*
Scot's lovage - *Ligusticum scoticum*

APPENDIX

Sea campion (**Bogiflooer**) - *Silene vulgaris
subsp. maritima*
Sea mayweed (**Witchie flooers**) - *Matricaria
maritima*
Sheepsbit - *Jasione montana*

Broad buckler fern - *Dryopteris dilatata*
Common polypody - *Polypodium vulgare*
Greater woodrush - *Luzula sylvatica*
Hard fern (**Trowie cairds**) - *Blechnum spicant*
Wavy hair grass - *Deschampsia flexuosa*

SEASHORES
Buckshorn plantain - *Plantago coronopus*
Common scurvygrass (**Sailors' hope**) -
Cochlearia officinalis
Curled dock - *Rumex crispus*
Orache - *Atriplex subsp.*
Sea milkwort - *Glaux maritima*
Sea plantain - *Plantago maritima*
Sea rocket - *Cakile maritima*
Sea sandwort - *Honckenya peploides*
Silverweed (**Blue girse**) - *Potentilla anserina*
Thrift or Sea pinks (**Banks flooer**) - *Armeria
maritima*

Lyme grass - *Elymus arenarius*
Marram grass - *Ammophila arenaria*
Yellow-orange lichen - *Xanthoria parietina*

ARABLE LAND
Bugloss - *Anchusa arvensis*
Changing forget-me-not - *Myosotis discolor*
Chickweed - *Stellaria media*
Common hemp nettle - *Galeopsis tetrahit*
Common nettle - *Urtica dioica*
Corn spurrey (**Meldie**) - *Spergula arvensis*
Creeping buttercup - *Ranunculus acris*
Field forget-me-not - *Myosotis arvensis*
Fumitory - *Fumaria officinalis*
Groundsel - *Senecio vulgaris*
Northern dead nettle - *Lamium moluccellifolium*
Northern knot grass - *Polygonum boreale*
Red dead nettle - *Lamium purpureum*
Ribwort plantain (**Johnsmas flooer**) - *Plantago
lanceolata*

GARDEN ESCAPES / INTRODUCTIONS
Bluebell - *Hyacinthoides hispanica x H.
non-scripta*
Double green daffodil - *Narcissus various*
Magellan ragwort (**New Zealand daisy**) -
Senecio smithii
Meadow cranesbill - *Geranium pratense*
Montbretia - *Tritonia x crocosmiflora*
Pheasants eye narcissus (**Grave flooer**) -
Narcissus poeticus
Pink purslane - *Montia sibirica*

Quaking grass - *Briza media*
Tussock grass (**Tussie girse**) - *Poa flabellata*

RARITIES AND PLANTS LESS COMMONLY SEEN
Alpine Lady's mantle - *Alchemilla alpina*
Autumn gentian - *Gentianella amarella*
Birch - *Betula pubescens*
Dwarf cornel - *Cornus suecica*
Edmondston's Chickweed (**Shetland
Mouse-ear**) - *Cerastium nigrescens*
English stonecrop - *Sedum anglicum*
Germander speedwell - *Veronica chamaedrys*
Long-headed poppy - *Papaver dubium*
Northern rock-cress - *Cardaminopsis petraea*
Norwegian sandwort - *Arenaria norvegica
subsp. norvegica*
Oyster plant - *Mertensia maritima*
Purple saxifrage - *Saxifraga oppositifolia*
Rowan - *Sorbus aucuparia*
Sea aster - *Aster tripolium*
Trailing azalea - *Loiseleuria procumbens*
Tway-blade - *Listera cordata*
Water lily - *Nymphaea alba*

Adders tongue - *Ophioglossum azoricum*
Moonwort - *Botrychium lunaria*
Royal fern - *Osmunda regalis*
Wilson's filmy fern - *Hymenophyllum wilsonii*

Bird Checklist

This list is not definitive and more species could easily be seen by an observant visitor. In addition, especially after a spell of south-easterly winds, many other species may turn up. A simplified breeding habitat key is given below. Bear in mind that birds may be seen in very different habitats from time to time. The local Shetland name is given in brackets.

Bird nesting habitats.
1) Coast
2) Sea cliffs
3) Hills and heather moorland
4) Loch and stream sides
5) Gardens and trees
6) Croft and pasture land

4	Red-throated diver (Raingoose) *Gavia stellata*
1,2	Great black-backed gull (Swaabie) *Larus marinus*
1,2,3	Fulmar (Maalie) *Fulmarus glacialis*
3,6	Common gull (Tina maa) *Larua canus*
1,2	Storm petrel (Aalamootie) *Hydrobates pelagicus*
1,2	Lesser black-backed gull (Peerie swaabie) *Larus fuscus*
2	Gannet (Solan) *Sula bassana*
1, 2	Herring gull (Maa) *Larus argentatus*
2	Shag (Scarf) *Phalacrocorax aristotelis*
2	Kittiwake (Rippack maa) *Rissa tridactyla*
2	Cormorant (Muckle scarf) *Phalacrocorax carbo*
1	Common tern (Tirrick) *Sterna hirundo*
4	Mute swan *Cygnus olor*
1,3	Arctic tern (Tirrick) *Sterna paradisœa*
1	Shelduck (Links goose) *Tadorna tadorna*
2	Guillemot (Lungwie) *Uria aalge*
4	Teal *Anas crecca*
2	Razorbill (Sea craa) *Alca torda*
4	Mallard (Stock deuk) *Anas platyrynchos*
2	Black guillemot (Tystie) *Cepphus grylle*
4	Tufted duck *Aythya fuligula*
2	Puffin (Tammie norie) *Fratercula arctica*
1,3	Eider (Dunter) *Somateria mollissima*
2	Rock dove (Wild doo) *Columba livia*
4	Red-breasted merganser *Melanitta serrator*
5	Wood pigeon *Columba palambus*

3	Merlin (Peerie hawk) *Falco columbarius*
6	Collared dove *Streptopelia decaocta*
3	Red grouse *Lagopus lagopus*
3,6	Skylark (Laverock) *Alauda arvensis*
1,3	Oystercatcher (Shalder) *Haematopus ostralegus*
6	Swallow *Hirundo rustica*
1	Ringed plover (Saandy loo) *Charadrius hiaticula*
3,6	Meadow pipit (Teetick) *Anthus pratensis*
3	Golden plover (Plivver) *Pluvialis apricarius*
1	Rock pipit (Banks sparrow) *Anthus petrosus*
6	Lapwing (Tieves nacket) *Vanellus vanellus*
1,5	Wren (Robbie cuddie) *Troglodytes troglodytes*
3	Dunlin (Plivver's page) *Calidris alpina*
3,6	Wheatear (Staneshakker) *Oenanthe oenanthe*
4	Snipe (Snippick) *Gallinago gallinago*
5	Blackbird (Blackie) *Turdus merula*
3	Whimbrel (Peerie whaap) *Numenius phaeopus*
5	Rook (Craa) *Corvus frugilegus*
3,6	Curlew (Whaap) *Numenius arquata*
2,3	Hooded crow (Craa) *Corvus corone*
6	Redshank (Ebb-cock) *Tringa totanus*
2	Raven (Corbie) *Corvus corax*
4	Common sandpiper *Actitis hypoleucus*
2,3,5,6	Starling (Stari) *Sturnus vulgaris*
4	Red-necked phalarope *Phalaropus lobatus*
5,6	House sparrow (Sporrow) *Passer domesticus*
3	Arctic skua (Skootie aalun) *Stercorarius parasiticus*
1,3	Twite (Lintie) *Carduelis flavirostris*
3	Great skua (Bonxie) *Stercorarius skua*
4	Reed bunting *Emberiza schoeniclus*
4,6	Black-headed gull (Heedie maa) *Larus ridibundus*

Try to visit the RSPB reserves of Sumburgh Head, Spiggie and Fetlar if at all possible. For keen birdwatchers, a stay in Fair Isle at the famous bird observatory is strongly recommended.

Bibliography

Airfield Focus Peter Ward, GMS Enterprises 1994.

Ancient Shetland Val Turner, Batsford 1998.

Bobby Tulloch's Shetland
Bobby Tulloch, Shetland Times 1993.

The Bod of Gremista
Bod of Gremista Management Committee 1989.

Bressay
Jonathan Wills, Bressay History Group 1991.

The Collected Poems of Vagaland
Shetland Times 1975.

Court Book of Shetland 1615-1629
Gordon Donaldson, Shetland Library 1991.

Diarist in an Age of Social Change
Ronald Sandison, Shetland Times 1997.

Drifting Alone to Norway
TMY Manson, Shetland Publishing Co 1986.

*An Etymological Dictionary of the Norn Language
in Shetland* Jakob Jakobsen, Shetland Folk
Society 1985 reprint.

Exploring Scotland's Heritage
Anna Ritchie, Royal Commission on Ancient
Monuments 1985.

Fair Isle, an Island Saga
Valerie Thom, Edinburgh 1989.

*The flowering plants and ferns of the Shetland
Islands* Walter Scott and Richard Palmer.

The Geology of Western Shetland W Mykura and
J Phemister, Her Majesty's Stationery Office 1976.

Grammar and Usage of the Shetland Dialect
T A Robertson and J J Graham,
Shetland Times 1991.

A Guide to Prehistoric Shetland
Noel Fojut, Shetland Times 1981 and 1986.

Guide to Dunrossness and Fair Isle
Peter Gray, Shetland Times 1992.

A Guide to Shetland's Birds Bobby Tulloch and
Fred Hunter, Shetland Times 1970.

A Guide to Shetland's Mammals
Bobby Tulloch, Shetland Times 1978.

Innocent Passage J Wills and K Warner,
Mainstream Publishing 1993.

Island Futures Roy Gronneberg and
M Magnuson, Thuleprint 1978.

The Islands of Scotland
Hugh MacDiarmid, Batsford 1939.

Kebister Olwyn Owen and Christopher Lowe,
Sutton Publishing 1999.

Lerwick Harbour
J R Nicolson, Shetland Times 1987.

Link Stanes Rhoda Bulter, Shetland Times 1980.

Love's Laebrack Sang
Lollie Graham, Shetland Library 2000.

Manson's Guide to Shetland T M Y Manson 1932.

The Natural History of Shetland
R J Berry and J L Johnson, Collins 1986.

A Naturalist's Shetland J Laughton and T
Johnston, A D Poyser Natural History 1999.

A New Description of Orkney, Shetland etc, John
Brand, Edinburgh and London 1703.

The Northern Isles
Alexander Fenton, Tuckwell Press 1997.

Northern Lights J J Graham and T A Robertson,
Education Committee 1964.

North Sea Oil and the Environment Ed. WJ
Cairns, Elsevier Science Publishers Ltd. 1992.

Orkney and Shetland Archaeological Guide
Lloyd Laing, David and Charles 1974.

Orkney and Shetland
Eric Linklater, Robert Hale 1965.

Orkney and Schetland 1771 George Lowe,
Melven Press 1978 (reprint).

*Orkneyinga Saga: The History of the Earls
of Orkney* Palsson and Edwards, Hogarth Press
London 1978.

Otters Bobby Tulloch, Colin Baxter 1994.

The Place Names of Shetland Jakob Jakobsen,
David Nutt 1936; reprinted 1993.

The Pictish Trail
Anthony Jackson, Orkney Press 1989.

The Ponies of Shetland
Maurice Cox, Shetland Times 1876.

Ports and Harbours Shetland Islands Council
1998/99.

The Quaternary of Shetland
J Birnie, J Gordon, K Bennett and A Hall 1993.

Rural Life in Shetland
Ian Tait, Shetland Museum 2000.

The Sail Fishermen of Shetland
A Halcrow, Shetland Times 1994.

Scord of Brouster Alasdair Whittle, Oxford University Committee for Archaeology 1986.

Sea Change Reginald Byron, Institute of Social and Economic Research 1986.

The Shaping of Shetland
Val Turner, Shetland Times 1998.

Shetland Val Turner, Batsford 1998.

Shetland. An Illustrated Architectural Guide
Mike Finnie, Mainstream 1990.

Shetland Animal Studies
Rod Thorne, Shetland Times 1983.

A Shetland Anthology J J Graham and L I Graham, Shetland Publishing Company 1998.

Shetland and Oil
J R Nicolson, William Luscombe 1975.

Shetland and the Outside World 1469-1969
Donald Withrington, O.U.P. 1983.

Shetland Archaeology
Brian Smith, Shetland Times 1985.

Shetland Bird Reports, Shetland Bird Club.

The Shetland Book
Zetland Education Committee 1967.

Shetland Cattle Stanley Bowie 1995.

Shetland Coastline
Nature Conservancy Council 1980.

The Shetland Dictionary
John J Graham, Shetland Times 1993.

Shetland Documents 1580-1611 and *Shetland Documents 1195-1579* Ed John H Ballantyne & Brian Smith, Shetland Islands Council and Shetland Times 1994 and 1999.

Shetland Field Studies Group archive, 1981 onwards.

Shetland Fishing Saga
C A Goodlad, Shetland Times 1971.

Shetland Folk Books Shetland Folk Society.

Shetland Folklore J R Nicolson, Robert Hale 1981.

Shetland Geology and Geomorphology
Nature Conservancy Council 1976.

Shetland in Statistics 2001, 1999, 1998, 1972 Shetland Islands Council.

The Shetland Isles Andrew T Cluness, Hale 1951.

Shetland: The Isles of Nightless Summer
William Moffatt, Heath Cranton 1934.

Shetland Interpretive Plan Shetland Islands Council 1999.

Shetland Life magazines.

Shetland Life under Earl Patrick
Gordon Donaldson, Oliver and Boyd 1958

Shetland's Living Landscape
David Spence, Thule Press 1979.

Shetland Place-names John Stewart, Shetland Library and Museum 1987.

Shetland Lace Gladys Amedro, Shetland Times 1993.

Shetland's Northern Links, Language and History
D Waugh, Scottish Society for Northern Studies 1996.

Shetland Proverbs and Sayings
Bertie Deyell, Shetland Folk Society 1993.

The Shetland Report The Nevis Institute 1978.

Shetland Sandy Beach Audit
G Macleod, Shetland Amenity Trust 1999.

The Shetland Sheepdog Mary Davis, Ringpress 1994.

The Shetland Sheepdog Margaret Osborne, Popular Dogs Publishing Co 1970.

The Shetland Story
Liv Schei and Gunnie Moberg, Batsford 1988.

Shetland Traditional Lore Jessie Saxby, London 1932.

The Shetland Way of Oil
John Button, Thule Print 1976.

Shetland's Wild Flowers
D Malcolm, Shetland Times 1992.

Shetland Wool Stanley Bowie 1994.

Studies in the Vegetational History of the Faroe and Shetland Islands Johanes Johansen, Foroya Frodskaparfelag 1985.

The Third Statistical Account of Scotland: Shetland James R Coull, Scottish Academic Press 1985.

Toons and Tenants
Brian Smith, Shetland Times 2000.

Traditional Life in Shetland
James R Nicolson, Hale 1978.

Travellers in a Bygone Shetland
Derek Flinn, Scottish Academic Press 1989.

The True Romance of Busta
Frances Scott, Nelson Smith 1996.

A Vehement Thirst after Knowledge
J J Graham, Shetland Times 1998.

Viking Scotland Anna Ritchie, Batsford 1993.

Walking the Coastline of Shetland
nos.1-6 Peter Guy, Shetland Times.

The Windswept Isles
Elizabeth Balneaves, Butler and Tanner 1977.

With Naught but Kin Behind Them
Norah Kendall, Melbourne 1998.

Wrestlers with the Troubled Sea
Louis Johnson, Nelson Smith 1994.

Glossary

Aets: Shetland oats, a tall, strong-stemmed variety.
Ayre: A bar or spit of sand.
Bairns: Children.
Bannocks: Flat scones
Ben: Bedroom end of a traditional crofthouse
Bere: An old variety of barley
Blaand: drink made from the residue of butter churning
Böd: merchant's trading booth circa 17-1800s
Burn: Stream
But: Living, kitchen end of a traditional crofthouse
Byre: Cowshed
Caain: A driving, or gathering of sheep or whales
Caain whale: Pilot whale
Darkening: Dusk
Dratsie: Otter
Dyke: Wall or boundary barrier
Ebb: Low tide point
Essie cairt: Rubbish lorry
Fael: Turf
Foude: A judge during Norse rule
Fourareen: A four-oared open boat
Gaet: Small path or way
Geo: Steep-sided cleft or inlet in coastal cliffs
Gimmer: 1-2-year-old Shetland ewe (no lamb yet)
Grind: Gate, or gateway
Guizer: Disguised person, vistor to a party
Haaf: The deep sea
Hairst: Autumn
Hentilagets: Fragments of wool caught on the ground
Holm: Very small island off shore or in a loch
Inby land: Ground enclosed by a hill dyke
Jarl: Chief Viking
Kale: Cabbage
Kirn: Churn for butter making
Kirn milk: Whey
Kishie: Basket
Lallies: Toys, traditionally hand made
Lawthing: Norse law court
Lodberry: Store built out into the sea for unloading cargo
Lum: Chimney, or hole in a roof to let smoke out
Merk: Productive unit of land, in Norse times
Merrie Dancers: Northern Lights
Moorit: Natural warm brown shade of wool
Ness: A headland
Njugle: Mythical, wicked creature
Noost: Boat-shaped shelter near sea
Oily Muggie: Nickname for Northmavine folk

Ollick: Ling
Ootby land: Land outside a hill dyke
Orca: Killer whale
Park: Enclosed grassland
Peerie: Small
Peerie corn: A small quantity of food
Peerie scar: A small quantity of liquid, i.e milk or tea
Piltock: A young saithe
Planticrub: Small drystone enclosure, usually circular, built to protect plants.
Pone: A long turf cut to lay on a turf roof
Punt: A small dinghy
Quern: Stone for grinding corn by hand
Ranselman: Norse equivalent of a policeman
Reestit mutton: Cured mutton, very delicious!
Rigga rendal: A shared cultivation strip system
Rivlin: Viking shoes
Rooin: Wool-plucking method
Roost: Very noisy, turbulent tidal stream
Scattald: Common grazing area
Selkie: Wild seal
Shaela: A natural grey shade of wool
Sheep's pearls: Sheep's droppings
Sillock: Slightly younger piltock
Simmer Dim: Midsummer twilight
Sixereen: Six-oared boat for deep-sea fishing
Skat: Norse land tax
Skeo: Openwork store for drying meat and fish.
Skerry: Small rock, or islet in the sea
Spoots: Razor shells
Spootie Ebb: An exceptionally low tide
Stack: Large, free-standing sheer crag offshore
Stane: Stone
Stap and crappin: Traditional fish liver dish
Teind: Tithes
Taing: Seaweed
Ting: Norse parliament
Trow: Troll, or goblin-like person
Tup: Ram
Tushkar: Tool for cutting peats
Udal law: Norse legal system
Up Helly Aa: Victorian 'Viking' fire festival
Voar: Spring
Voe: Long sea inlet
Waar: Seaweed
Ward or Wart: Highest point of a hill
Wick: Beach
Yard: Vegetable plot, as in 'kale yard'
Yoal: A Shetland clinker-built boat
Zulu: Fishing boat

Index

(**Bold** type indicates map)

Jill Slee Blackadder lives in Shetland where she is a school teacher, and founder of the Shetland Field Studies Group. She writes regularly for *Shetland Life* magazine and a weekly column for the *Shetland Times*.